Landing Votes

Landing Votes: Representation and Land Reform in Latin America

Nancy D. Lapp

First published 2004 by
PALGRAVE MACMILLAN™
175 Fifth Avenue, New York, N.Y. 10010 and
Houndmills, Basingstoke, Hampshire, England RG21 6XS
Companies and representatives throughout the world

PALGRAVE MACMILLAN is the global academic imprint of the Palgrave Macmillan division of St. Martin's Press, LLC and of Palgrave Macmillan Ltd. Macmillan® is a registered trademark in the United States, United Kingdom and other countries. Palgrave is a registered trademark in the European Union and other countries.

ISBN 1–4039–6504–8 hardback

Library of Congress Cataloging-in-Publication Data
Lapp, Nancy Diane.
    Landing votes : representation and land reform in Latin America / Nancy D. Lapp.
       p. cm.
    Includes bibliographical references and index.
    ISBN 1–4039–6504–8 (cloth: alk. paper)
    1. Land reform—Latin America—Case studies. 2. Suffrage—Latin America—Case studies. 3. Rural poor—Latin America—Political activity—Case studies. I. Title.

HD1333.L29L37 2003
324.6'2'098—dc22   2003058140

A catalogue record for this book is available from the British Library.

Design by Newgen Imaging Systems (P) Ltd., Chennai, India.

First edition: May 2004
10 9 8 7 6 5 4 3 2 1

Printed in the United States of America.

For my "boys":
Kenny, Nicholas, and Joseph

Contents

Acknowledgments

T oo many people have contributed to making this book possible to name. Most of all, I am indebted to Barbara Geddes and Jeffry Frieden for their insight and guidance. In the early stages Michael Wallerstein offered important support, and David López's skepticism improved the final product. Many of my colleagues offered invaluable input while I was still in graduate school at UCLA; I particularly want to thank Glen Biglaiser, David S. Brown, Anthony Gill, Sandra Joireman, Carlos Juarez, Stephen Kay, Maria Sampanis, Shaun Wade, and Kristen P. Williams for reading and critiquing earlier versions of this work. I presented parts of the book to panels at the Latin American Studies Association and the Western Political Science Association, and thus benefited from the discussion and comments of participants. In the latter stages of revision, Suzana Palaska and Martha Castañeda provided able research assistance. An anonymous reviewer provided excellent suggestions for improvement. All errors that persist despite their help remain my own.

The International Studies and Overseas Program at UCLA and the Tinker Foundation made fieldwork in Brazil financially possible, and the NEH provided generous grants to study Portuguese. The Department of Government at California State University, Sacramento, provided time for additional research and revision.

In São Paulo, Artur Ribeiro provided truly invaluable assistance, Marcos Ribeiro kind hospitability, and Luiz and Nora both aid and fun; all made my time in Brazil immeasurably more enjoyable. I thank Fânia both for her help and for sharing her exuberant love of life and Rio. So many of the staff at the National Congress were extremely helpful that I cannot name them all; without all their help the chapter on Brazil could not have been written.

Finally, this book is dedicated to my "boys": my husband Kenny, and sons Nicholas and Joseph. Kenny has been unfailing in his support throughout the entire process, and always ready to help with anything, including tricky translations. He has especially been a superb father to our boys, who will, I hope, someday understand (and approve) why their mother always had to go to work.

CHAPTER 1

Introduction: Connecting Suffrage and Land Reform

Introduction

The poor typically are among the least represented groups in society. Impoverished, uneducated, and isolated from urban centers, the rural poor are often excluded from political participation by either de jure or de facto means. In the past, indigent citizens lacked the legal right to organize or vote; until the mid-twentieth century in much of Latin America, legal political participation was limited to well-off educated elites. When the poor did vote, their votes were frequently coerced and manipulated under the supervision of traditional rural elites.

The dearth of land reform in Latin American democracies exemplifies the lack of meaningful participation by the rural poor. Land reform constitutes the redistribution of wealth from elites to the poor; given the rural poor's lack of influence, such a policy is unlikely. Instead, legislatures dominated by landowners and their allies effectively became "the graveyards of land reform measures" (Huntington 1968, 389). However, at limited times during the twentieth century, the rural poor did benefit from land reforms implemented by democratic (i.e. elected) governments. Why would elected governments attempt land reform?

The answer is that some parties, seeking political support, both extended the franchise to the rural poor and initiated land reform. In countries such as Bolivia, Chile, Colombia, and Venezuela, land reforms coincided with or followed the removal of property and literacy restrictions on voting, and other measures that legalized and enhanced the voting rights of the poor. Elites both initiated and responded to these changes; politicians and their parties actively courted the votes of rural voters, who in turn wanted land reform.

Furthermore, political parties play a decisive role in the meaningful incorporation of the poor. Where stronger or more "institutionalized" parties competed for the votes of the newly enfranchised rural poor, more of the rural poor tended to benefit. In contrast, countries with weaker or "inchoate" political parties saw little change for the rural poor.

Land Reform in Latin America

Long a controversial issue in Latin America, land reform has generated vehement discussion between advocates and opponents. At the heart of the problem lies the unequal distribution of landownership; in the 1960s only 10 percent of the Latin American population owned 90 percent of the land (Carroll 1961).[1] Unequal land distribution allegedly obstructed overall economic growth and caused widespread rural poverty by encouraging inefficient use of the land (Barraclough 1973; Feder 1971; Smith 1965; Griffin 1976; Deininger 1999). *Latifundia*, or inadequately cultivated expanses, contributed to low agricultural productivity, but also coexisted with the more numerous *minifundia*, parcels of intensively cultivated land too small for subsistence. The result: low agricultural productivity and endemic rural poverty. Therefore, land reform became a solution to dual evils: redistribution of the land would increase agricultural productivity as well as decrease poverty by taking land from those who did not use it and giving it to those who did not have it.[2]

Land reform, defined here as the expropriation and redistribution of land by a government, met the vigorous resistance of owners who typically controlled not only land but also political power.[3] As Thomas Carroll wrote, "Land reform, if it is seriously done, implies a drastic rearrangement of property rights, income and social status" (1961, 162–3). Large landowners and their allies benefited from the status quo; land was held as "livelihood,...as financial security (e.g. as a hedge against inflation), as a transfer of wealth across the generations, and as a resource for consumption purposes (e.g. country estates held by urban elites for leisure purposes)" (Ellis 1992, 196). Landowners risked both financial loss and reduction in status and prestige.[4]

Defining Land Reform: Redistribution and Other Policies

Defining land reform as the expropriation and redistribution of land by the government, as this study does, focuses on the core issue: redistribution of wealth from more powerful to less powerful groups in society. By limiting "land reform" to redistribution, the definition excludes many related policies: better provision of credit, revised tax policies, supply of seeds and fertilizer, research and marketing assistance, irrigation, and mechanization.[5] Carroll (1961) observed that such policies "... represent the focus not of land reform but of agricultural development, and ... are most effective where a healthy land tenure situation exists. To put it in another way, land tenure improvement and agricultural development must go hand in hand" (196). Without land reform, agrarian policies benefit the existing large property owners rather than small owners and workers (Grindle 1986). However, most authors agree that policies that fit under the broader category of agrarian reform are necessary if land redistribution schemes are to be successful (e.g. Warriner 1969; Lipton 1974).

Colonization, the distribution of the vast areas of public land, is another type of agrarian reform (King 1977). Settlement of uninhabited land offers a politically convenient alternative to land redistribution, since powerful landlords will not obstruct the distribution of government land. Colonization expands the amount of land under cultivation, while land reform divides up a fixed amount of land. However, colonization is not a perfect substitute for land reform. Public lands are often uninhabited and unused for good reason: the lands are less fertile, and require greater effort in clearing before cultivation (Barraclough 1973). As Carroll explains:

> Experience of all countries that have settlement programs has shown that it is difficult to move large numbers of people into new areas, and that such an operation is extremely costly. Agricultural economists have repeatedly pointed out that in terms of potential production increases, the already established areas offer a much greater, more immediate and less expensive possibility. Social overhead facilities are already available in these areas which are close to the population and market centers. (1961, 197)

Additionally, rather than solve tenure problems, colonization projects often simply re-create previous tenure patterns (Lipton 1974). Colonization has also met with opposition because the policy contributes to deforestation and the depletion of natural resources.

Colonization often accompanies land reform; as long as colonization is only part of the reform, the distinction will not be important. However, when a land reform consists almost entirely of colonization projects, like the Brazilian military's land reform in the 1960s and 1970s, it will not be considered a land reform as specifically defined here. The key distinction is whether the reforms aim to redistribute agricultural land.

Restricting the definition of land reform to redistribution presents the most controversial policy with which to test the argument of this study. Land redistribution threatens the essence of the traditional landowning elite. As Tai pointed out, "once it is raised as an issue, land redistribution will generate more controversy than any other type of reform program; when implemented, it is likely to effect a more profound alteration of the tenure structure than any other reform measure" (1974, 12). If the argument is correct regarding the most controversial aspect of land reform, then the possibilities are greater that it will also apply to other, less controversial policy issues.

The Significance of Democratic Land Reforms

One question that often arises is whether democratic governments have in fact implemented land reforms of any seriousness. Skepticism stems from disillusionment; in many countries, land reform did not cause a wholesale reorganization of property rights or the massive reduction of poverty. As Thiesenhusen noted, "Disappointment in the consequences of land reform has led social scientists to denigrate its importance" (Thiesenhusen 1984, 33).

For the most part, the land reforms discussed here did not fundamentally alter land tenure arrangements. Nevertheless, serious reform attempts occurred under electoral regimes, and with significant results; the challenge becomes deciding which of the land reforms (nearly every Latin American country passed at least one land reform law) were serious and which were not. Counting the amount of land expropriated and the number of beneficiaries presents an important, but insufficient measure. On the one hand, it helps eliminate as insignificant those reforms begun with no intention of fulfilling them. However, other attempts at reform, while serious, faltered in implementation.

For example, significant land reforms in Bolivia and Venezuela affected over one-third of rural households. However, reforms that benefit a smaller number of recipients may also be significant. Conservative Chilean President Jorge Alessandri's land reform legislation, though minor compared with redistribution during the later presidencies of Christian Democrat Eduardo Frei and Socialist Salvador Allende, made future reform possible by establishing the requirement that land be productively used,[6] and by allowing payment for expropriated land in bonds.

Most governments cannot undertake major land reform if they must provide full payment in cash for land at the time of expropriation. Deferred payment through the use of bonds is the only means of ensuring swift implementation of a reform program. Like Chile, in many countries constitutional provisions prohibited the expropriation of land without immediate compensation in cash. Thus, serious land reform in these cases included an amendment allowing payment in bonds. The otherwise minor land reform passed during Alessandri's conservative government was notable because it included this important constitutional amendment.

Consequently, several factors are considered in determining whether a land reform was significant: if the reform endeavors to expropriate and redistribute private land, plans to benefit a large segment of the rural population, provides partial payment of expropriated property in bonds, and, finally, actually benefits a large number of rural inhabitants.

A land reform considered significant for this study might not alter overall tenure patterns, or change agricultural productivity. While desired outcomes, these goals are not necessarily relevant to the political motives of land reform proponents. For this reason, this study does not evaluate the "success" of the land reforms in terms of increased agricultural productivity or even changes in overall land tenure.[7]

Land Reform and the Search for Political Support

Although often considered a means of attracting political support from the rural poor (Tai 1974; Christodoulou 1990), land reform has not been judged likely to occur under democratic regimes. As Samuel Huntington noted, "Pluralistic politics and parliamentary rule are often incompatible with effective land reforms" (1968, 388). While Huntington concedes that "it is at least conceivable that land reforms may be introduced by the leadership of a political party which has won power through democratic means," he suggests that a single party is necessary for land reform in developing democracies: "... a parliamentary system without a dominant party provides no means by which the modernizing elite can effectively displace the landowning conservatives" (1968, 388). Tai echoes this assessment; he found "the competitive regime ... less efficacious" in implementing land reform (1974, 469). Rather, Tai believed that in "developing countries in need of reform it is evident that in those countries where a multiparty or biparty system reigns, the prospect for prompt, effective, and drastic land reform is generally not bright." Instead, reform is more likely to be successful in one-party systems or with a small group of leaders (Tai 1974, 473).

Tai and Huntington reach these conclusions by examining land reforms undertaken by both democratic and undemocratic governments. By underrating the comparatively less-remarkable democratic reforms, they overlook substantial variation in the democratic cases. In Latin America, significant land reform occurred in some biparty and multiparty systems (e.g. Colombia, Chile), although not in other multiparty systems (e.g. Brazil, Ecuador, and Peru). This study, as explained later, concludes that under some circumstances democratic competition between parties actually improves the prospects for reform; both the expansion of suffrage and land reform were themselves spurred by competition between parties. Ultimately, however, the extent of reform depends on the nature of the parties themselves.

Landowner domination of democratic politics poses a serious hurdle for the implementation of land reform. The expropriation and redistribution of land requires governmental action; however, officials in a democratic government depend upon getting reelected. This study assumes that politicians are rational and self-interested individuals whose main goal is "political survival" (Ames 1987; Geddes 1994). No matter what their other interests, such as implementing preferred policies, representing their constituency, or simply wielding political influence, politicians can achieve nothing without first attaining and remaining in office (Downs 1957; Mayhew 1974).

Given the need to win office through winning elections, politicians search for political support at the polls by making promises and taking positions on issues important to voters. As an "appeal to the peasantry" (Collier and Collier 1991) but anathema to the landowner, land reform faltered on the reality of the Latin American electorate: severe restrictions on the rural poor's right to vote.

Restrictions on Suffrage

Until the mid-twentieth century, politicians in Latin America were elected by only a small percentage of the population. With full citizenship limited to the well off and well educated, the majority of the population, more than two-thirds in some cases, was barred from political participation by restrictions on the right to vote.

One such restriction was the literacy requirement, which barred those who could not read or write from voting. This requirement disenfranchised a significant proportion of the population in many countries. For example, when the literacy requirement was removed in 1952, *illiteracy* in Bolivia was 68 percent. In Brazil, nearly one-third of the population could not read or write when the franchise was extended to illiterates in 1985.[8] This effect was further magnified by the difference between rural and urban literacy rates. Rural inhabitants were more likely to be illiterate than the population at large. For example, only 11 percent of the total Chilean population but 31 percent of the rural population was illiterate in 1960 (ECLAC 1985, 125).

Property requirements (minimum income requirements for voters) also prevented the poor from voting. Rural residents, those most likely to favor land reform, are more likely than their urban counterparts to be poor in Latin America. In one study, about 26 percent of urban households were estimated to live below the poverty line, whereas 62 percent of rural households lived in similar circumstances. Around 10 percent of urban households were estimated to be destitute, compared to 34 percent of rural households (Altimir 1982).

Furthermore, difficult registration procedures discouraged voting by the rural poor. For example, after the literacy requirement was removed in Guatemala in 1945, illiterate citizens had to register six months before voting and had to be "accompanied by two honorable witnesses, citizens and residents of the vicinity, who will guarantee the civic capacity of the one who appears, and his desire to exercise the right of suffrage" (Fitzgibbon 1948, 399). Literate citizens simply had to show up at the polls with their identification.

The absence of secret ballots further limited the rural poor's exercise of the franchise. Without this "device to protect the economically dependent from the sanctions of their superiors" (Rokkan et al. 1970, 153–4), poor voters likely feel constrained in their choices at the polls. One egregious example of this practice is the plebiscite for Guatemalan dictator Carlos Castillo Armas in 1956, in which citizens were asked to state publicly whether they thought Castillo Armas should or should not remain in power.[9]

Less blatant practices also compromised the secrecy of elections. The frequent practice of allowing parties to provide ballots to voters (rather than having one official ballot at the polls) allowed party activists to influence voters. For example, in Brazil the Constitution of 1934 called for a secret vote, but the single official ballot (*cedula unica*) was not used nationally until 1962. Parties could provide voters with already completed ballots or at the very least, when parties' ballots differed in size and color from others, a voter's choice was discernable even while the act of voting itself might have been secret.

Another change in electoral procedures with potential effects for those least likely to vote is mandatory voting. A change to mandatory voting laws is significant because such laws are associated with higher participation rates in countries that have them (G.B. Powell 1980). Voter participation increased in Costa Rica by 10 percent of the population after voting became mandatory in 1958. Voting in Venezuelan elections was made mandatory in 1959 and elections in the 1960s were characterized by high levels of participation. Conversely, voting in Colombia was not mandatory, and participation slowly decreased throughout the 1960s (Rezazadeh and McKenzie 1978).[10] However, without the extension of the suffrage to illiterates and the guaranteed secrecy of their votes, mandatory voting only helps the rural elite. Mandatory voting has, in fact, been used by authoritarian regimes to bolster their legitimacy (Ochoa 1987).

The rural poor also suffered from the lack of information. The scarcity of outside sources of information facilitated manipulation by rural elites. Union organizers were frequently restricted, rural unionization being illegal until as late as 1963 in Brazil and 1967 in Chile.[11] "Outside organizers . . . offer alternative sources of economic assistance and protection to the domination of traditional patrons" (Brockett 1991, 257–8). Rural workers also have had to face illegal obstruction and intimidation by landowners, sometimes to the point of being targeted by death squads (Christodoulou 1990, 50).

Control over votes in the countryside enabled the traditional landowning elite to shape the configuration of government, as described by Cohen:

> In the event of parliamentary or municipal elections the landlords and rich farmers are able to persuade the rural population to vote for landlord candidates. Advice on voting is accepted by the peasant without debating it, reflecting the peasant's high esteem for the property owner. As a result, large property owners tend to be over-represented in party membership, parliament and government . . . Where both society at large and government in particular are dominated by landlord interests, it is more realistic to write land reform off. (1978, 13–14)

Whether their votes reflected "high esteem" or simply the lack of alternatives, the rural poor remained subject to influence by traditional elites.

The Timing of Reforms: Expanding Suffrage to the Rural Poor

Despite the excluded status of the rural poor, some parties have seen them as a potential means of political support. Believing that their parties can attract the support of the poor, party leaders attempted to include the poor in the political process by removing restrictions on their participation. However, these parties themselves often failed to achieve office under the existing electoral rules. Even so, parties that championed the cause of the unenfranchised occasionally gained office through unexpected, though not unanticipated, historical events.

Political parties may wait years for the unpredictable, and even temporary, changes in political fortunes that provide the opportunity to influence government policy and pass critical laws, which alter the political rules in their favor. In this case, the parties then changed laws to remove literacy requirements, ease registration procedures, and make voting secret. Furthermore, they made the exercise of the franchise mandatory, which could significantly increase voting by those least likely to do so.

In the process of incorporating the previously excluded rural poor, parties also implemented land reform to reward potential new supporters. Furthermore, the parties helped to organize and mobilize the rural poor. Parties often accompanied the provision of land reform with rural organization to break the dominance of the rural elite through the provision of outside information, to increase the participation of the rural poor, and in some cases to channel land reform benefits to party supporters.

Two main circumstances provide the most common opportunity or "opening" to change electoral rules: splits in the dominant party and democratization. Openings are likely to occur with unexpected election results or as a result of dissension within the ruling elite. Dissension may take the form of a factional split in a party, which often manifests itself in a disagreement between contenders for succession. Such a split provides the opening for minority parties to win elections and then alter election laws to broaden the electorate.

In an example from Colombia, a split in the ruling party proved fortuitous for the out-of-power party. Two Conservative Party presidential candidates in 1930 divided the Conservative vote and allowed the long-excluded Liberal Party to win the presidency. The Liberal Party subsequently won control of the legislature in 1933, and Liberal President Alfonso López Pumarejo, elected in 1934, declared a land reform and universal male suffrage in 1936 to ensure future support for his party.

In Chile, the center and left parties pushed electoral changes through Congress in 1958 with the help of exiting President Carlos Ibáñez; these parties feared a victory for the conservative parties in the next election (Gil 1966, 103). Having run for office as an antiparty independent, ex-dictator Ibáñez willingly assisted in making changes expected to weaken the conservative parties. The center and left parties (e.g. the Christian Democrats and the Socialists) also advocated land reform and later implemented reform programs when in office.[12]

The opportunity for changing electoral rules may await democratization itself, as occurred in Venezuela. The opposition party Democratic Action

(*Acción Democrática*, AD) came to power in 1945 through the help of a military coup prompted in part by disagreement over succession between the then-president and the previous president (Levine 1973).[13] Pressure had been building for increased democracy in Venezuela; the exact timing and nature of the coup favored AD. The leaders of AD had, by the 1930s, turned to the countryside as a basis of political support (Hillman 1994). Once in power, AD immediately instituted direct elections, universal suffrage, and land reform in order to incorporate and reward the rural supporters it had organized and to ensure success in future elections.

Splits in the elite or pressures for democratization may unleash even greater forces: revolution. In the Bolivian case, a widespread uprising ushered in the Revolutionary National Movement (MNR) revolution when the army sought to prevent the MNR leader, Víctor Paz Estenssoro, from assuming the presidency after winning the 1951 election (McDonald and Ruhl 1989, 227). In turn, the MNR eliminated barriers to participation. Voter participation increased sevenfold after the removal of property and literacy requirements and the implementation of a secret ballot by the MNR. The MNR followed these reforms with a widespread land reform in 1953.

The Mexican Revolution began with Francisco Madero's challenge to dictator Porfirio Díaz's "reelection" in 1910. The subsequent rebellion and, ultimately, revolution engendered the progressive Constitution of 1917, which provided the basis for land reform. Although the 1857 Constitution had instituted universal suffrage, elections until 1917 had been indirect (Nohlen 1993, 445). The bulk of the massive Mexican land redistribution would not occur until the 1930s; however, regional leaders and presidents in the 1920s responded not only to popular pressures for land but also used land reform to attract political support. President Álvaro Obregón in particular sought the political support of the peasantry, which was still weakly organized, to shore up his fragile hold on power and to seek a second presidential term in 1928 (Hansis 1971).

The same politicians and parties usually backed both the expansion of suffrage and land reform, expecting to win over the new voters by providing a much-desired benefit. Party leaders who could push through election reforms could reap the rewards of also implementing a land reform. However, the instigators of expanding suffrage were not the only ones to act upon the changes in election law. Competition for votes led to the promotion of land reform by other parties, including conservative parties, as in Chile. Chilean conservatives passed the first Chilean land reform in response to the increase in political participation that resulted from the 1958 reform.[14] Conservatives feared that the new voters would vote against the right in the coming elections.

In Venezuela, AD's primary opponent, COPEI, increasingly competed with AD for support among the rural poor. After previously making only vague promises of "social justice" in rural areas, COPEI embraced land reform in the platform the party presented for the 1946 constituent assembly elections; COPEI declared itself in favor of the expropriation of idle lands and land that "exceeds just limits" (Suárez Figueroa 1977, 124–5). The party continued to advocate land reform after redemocratization in 1958, and began to organize the rural poor as well.

Demand for Land Reform

The argument thus far has focused on the "supply side" of the timing of reform: the incentives of aspirants to public office that lead to the provision of land reform. However, the "demand side" of the land reform question also merits examination. Land reform's usefulness in gaining political support for politicians depends on the politicians' belief that the newly enfranchised voters desire land reform.

Without question, land reform was in demand throughout Latin America. Unequal land concentration, rural poverty and misery, and peasant unrest underscored the need for land reform (Eckstein 1978, 7). Demand for reform, however, remains insufficient for land reform to occur. Although "[w]ithout . . . the strains and stresses produced by the conscious struggle of under-privileged social groups the system is unlikely to change" (Christodoulou 1977, 23), this struggle does not guarantee reform. Persistent demand for land reform in Latin American countries existed for years without result; protests and land invasions more frequently met with repression or neglect than concession. Peasant rebellions themselves were more often narrow in scope, in that the rebellions often arose over local issues of prices, rents, security of land tenure, and work requirements (Powelson 1984, 104). For example, preliminary demands of peasants in highland Peru focused on "onerous labor obligations, personal services or salary claims, and restitution . . . of some pieces of land which the communities claimed" (AID 1970b, 17). Peasant unrest can lead to specific, isolated responses, such as the 1962 Peruvian land reform that applied only in the La Convención Valley, which mainly constituted recognition of de facto possession of land by peasants in a geographically isolated area (AID 1970b, 19). In this case, minor concessions forestalled peasant rebellion (Lehmann 1971).

Argentina and Uruguay deserve special mention; neither country experienced the same widespread need for land reform that was apparent in other Latin American countries. Unlike the rest of Latin America, both lacked the traditional Latin American peasantry; Argentina and Uruguay historically have had a low ratio of labor to land. Despite a high concentration of landownership in these countries, labor scarcity meant that the redistribution of land was not in demand. Rather than the expropriation and redistribution of land in Argentina and Uruguay, reforms that were more likely were minimum wage legislation, tenant contract regulation, land taxation, and colonization (Barraclough 1973, 77).[15]

A Preliminary Overview of the Reforms

Table 1.1 presents an overview of changes in elections and land reform in democratic countries of Latin America. Land reform attempts coincided with nearly all expansions of suffrage that affected the rural poor. Politicians and their parties simultaneously removed the literacy requirement and initiated land reforms in eight of the 12 countries included in this study: Bolivia, Brazil, Chile, Colombia, Dominican Republic, Ecuador, Guatemala, and Venezuela (1948). In addition, land reform coincided with the implementation of mandatory voting in the two countries where this change occurred after the removal of other restrictions on voting: Costa Rica and Venezuela (the 1960 land reform).[16] Land reforms followed the change to direct elections and subsequent participation of the rural poor in Mexico. In all, land reforms coincided with the expansion of participation in ten of the 12 countries. Elected governments attempted few land reforms in the absence of suffrage expansion, and these reforms tended to be less significant.

The extent of the land reforms varied. Extensive reforms occurred in Bolivia, Chile, Costa Rica, Guatemala, and Venezuela. Subsequent events, however, affected and in some cases reversed land reform in Chile, Dominican Republic, Guatemala, and Venezuela (1947). Attempts at reform in Brazil and Ecuador brought minimal results. The lack of democratic reform in Brazil, as well as in Ecuador and Peru, requires further examination of institutional factors that weaken parties, decrease the representation of the poor, and, consequently, explain the lack of significant reform.

Party Accountability and the Search for Political Support

Thus far, this study has assumed that once a party extends the right to vote to the rural poor and initiates land reform, the rural poor will vote for that party. This assumption provides the incentive for the party to expand suffrage in the first place; the party follows through with land reform so that the new voters continue their support. Presumably, if the rural poor become

Table 1.1 Electoral Changes and Land Reform by Democratic Governments (to 1990)

Country[a]	Electoral Law Changes[b]	Land Reform Initiated by Electoral Regimes	Percent Rural Households Affected[c]
Bolivia	1929 M		
	1952 L, P, S	**1953**	33
Brazil	1932 M		
	1946 P		
	1962 S	**1964**	0
	1985 L	**1985**	.3
Chile	1874 P		
	1925 M		
	1958 S	**1962**	.1
		1967	4
	1970 L	**1970**	13
Colombia	**1936** P, L	**1936**	n/a
		1961	9
		1968	
		1988	
Costa Rica	1913 P, L		
	1925 S		
	1959 M	**1961**	9
Dominican	1865 P		
Republic	**1962** L, S	**1962**	3
	1963 M		
Ecuador	1861 P, S		
	1967 M		
	1979 L	1979	1
Guatemala	**1945** P, L, M	**1945/1952**	13
	1956 S		
Mexico	**1857** P, L		
	1917 M	**1915/1917**	7
Panama	1904 P, L, S		
	1928 M		
		1962	1.7
Peru	1931 P, M		
	1963 S	1964	2.4
	1979 L	None	
Venezuela	**1945** P, L, S	**1948**	10
	1959 M	**1960**	39

Notes to table 1.1

[a] Argentina and Uruguay omitted because of lack of demand for land reform. Cuba, El Salvador, Honduras, and Nicaragua omitted because no reforms initiated by electoral regimes or expansion of suffrage under electoral conditions (see chapter 2 for details).

[b] See table in appendix and country notes below. L, literacy requirement removed; P, property requirement removed; S, effective secret ballot; M, mandatory vote. See table in appendix for sources.

[c] See below for individual country notes and sources. Unless otherwise noted, beneficiary information from Carmen Diana Deere, "Rural Women and State Policy: The Latin American Reform Experience," *World Development* 13, no. 9 (1985, 1039). Figures vary in sources because reporting is not exact and because calculations are made for different time periods (time periods in parentheses below).

Bolivia: (1952–1970) This is a conservative figure; Carrie Meyer (1989, 4) gives a much larger figure for land redistribution (79 percent) for a longer time period (1953–1975).

Brazil: (1985–1989) Beneficiary information from Brazil (1990, 50). Removal of the literacy requirement decreed in 1964 but overturned. Vote not mandatory for illiterates.

Chile: (1963–1964; 1965–1970; 1971–1973) Beneficiary information calculated for time periods respectively from Kaufman (1967, 19); Eckstein (1978, appendix A, 6); King (1977, 171). Deere (1985, 1039) and Meyer (1989, 4), estimate a total of 20 percent for the entire period.

Colombia: (1961–1975) Sufficiently reliable information for 1936 reform unavailable.

Costa Rica: (1961–1975)

Dominican Republic: (1962–1970) Meyer (1989, 4) gives a larger figure for land redistribution (19 percent) for a longer time period (1962–1986).

Ecuador: (1980–1982) Beneficiary figure calculated from estimate of 9,717 families receiving land in Haney and Haney (1989, 73). Vote not mandatory for illiterates.

Guatemala: (1952–1954) Voting was secret in 1945 for literate men and women (Yashar 1997, 122). Vote not mandatory for illiterates. Beneficiaries calculated conservatively with lowest beneficiary estimate of 88,000 by AID and estimated total Guatemalan households based on an average of four persons per household in a total population of 2,791,000.

Mexico: (1915–1927) A conservative estimate calculated from Álvaro Obregón's own estimate of 826,061 individuals receiving both confirmed and provisional land (Bassols Batalla 1967, 184) and Silva Herzog's estimate of 12,000,000 "individuals who depended on a rural salary" (1959, 122). The total amount of subsequent land redistribution, which includes the Cárdenas years and beyond, is much greater: 52.4 percent in the period from 1917 through 1980 (Meyer 1989, 4). Land reforms initiated: 1915 is the date of Carranza's agrarian decree, 1917 the date of the new constitution (with provisions on land reform). Other land reform laws and decrees followed.

Panama: (1962–1969).

Peru: (1963–1969) Beneficiary figure from Wilkie (1974, 3). Susana Lastarria-Cornhiel states less than 2 percent received land (1989, 138).

Venezuela: (1945–1948; 1959–1975) The 1947 reform was largely reversed. The 1947 beneficiaries are calculated from AID, 4. The 1960 reform beneficiaries are from Meyer (1989, 4).

dissatisfied with the performance of the reforming party, disappointed voters can punish the party by choosing another at the polls. In other words, party politicians are accountable to the voters.

Accountability of politicians requires that the electorate reward and punish parties at the polls. Voters cannot know for certain what a particular candidate will do once he or she wins office. The individual voter must make his or her own decision at the polls with a large measure of uncertainty. However, voters can use past performance as a reasonable guide to future behavior (Fiorina 1981). If the chosen candidate fails to live up to campaign promises or past accomplishments, the voters can remove the representative from office in future elections. The threat of future support or retaliation induces political parties to fulfill their promised agenda. In this case, that agenda is land reform.

Rewarding and punishing the right candidates, however, can be difficult. To make effective choices, voters require information about the candidates' past behavior; furthermore, voters must render their choices at the ballot box. These basic requirements, obtaining information and effectively participating in the balloting procedure, are least likely to be achieved by the rural poor, who lack independent sources of information about the political process and the particular choices presented in any given election. They are the least likely to have the skills and ability to process information and make use of it.

As was explained earlier in this chapter, the political parties that seek the support of the rural poor overcome the barriers to their participation. As "a team of men seeking to control the governing apparatus in a duly constituted election" (Downs 1957, 25), parties remove legal suffrage proscriptions, simplify voting procedures to encourage participation, establish secret ballots to eliminate outright manipulation by local elites, and provide outside information through party organizations.

Furthermore, parties serve as a guide for the electorate by reducing the cost of information and candidate selection. Monitoring the activities of an incumbent party is an easier task than tracking the performance of individual candidates. At election time, voters can approve of the incumbent party, or punish it by voting for a challenger. Party affiliation, therefore, serves as an effective rule of thumb for all voters, but especially for the poor and less educated.

Rewarding or punishing a party for its performance in office is fairly uncomplicated in a two-party context; the voter simply chooses the other party. Making the choice between incumbent becomes more difficult, but not impossible, in a multiparty system, where the choice is no longer simply whether one approves or disapproves of the party in power. Particularly in multiparty systems, party strength or "institutionalization" becomes an important variable in facilitating electoral choices; "institutionalized" parties most effectively ease difficulties of accountability.

The Importance of Party Institutionalization

Following on the work of Scott Mainwaring, this study proposes that where what he calls "institutionalized" parties competed for the votes of the newly enfranchised rural poor, the poor were more likely to see land reform results and to participate in politics. In contrast, where parties were not institutionalized and therefore "inchoate" (again, Mainwaring's term), the poor were more likely to remain excluded from meaningful political representation. Institutionalized party systems are, as Mainwaring and Scully (1995) point out, those in which parties have roots in society, stable structures, and are viewed as legitimate vehicles for representation. Institutionalized parties are more likely than inchoate ones to be held accountable because they, in turn, hold their own officials accountable, and present clear choices for the electorate. Institutionalized parties present a coherent party program, continuity in party officials, and the ability to discipline party politicians. Coherence and cohesiveness decrease information costs and increase credibility: all party candidates are expected to follow the party program. A cohesive party's agenda and accomplishments are clearer and facilitate the electorate's ability to reward or punish party politicians. Inchoate parties lack a coherent party program, stable affiliations, and discipline. Under such conditions, voters experience more difficulties in obtaining clear information; they also cannot assume that party officials will follow the party platform.

Certain electoral rules contribute to party institutionalization (Coppedge 1994b; Grofman and Lijphart 1986; Mainwaring 1991; Mainwaring and Scully 1995). These same procedures also facilitate the electorate's ability to reward or punish party politicians. Closed-list proportional representation (PR), for example, tends to increase party strength. It also makes choices at the polls simpler. Closed-list PR encourages party discipline because party leaders choose the order of candidates on the party list; leaders therefore exercise significant discretion over which candidates are likely to win office. Candidates who displease party leaders can be placed low on the party list, thus reducing the probability of their election.

In contrast, open-list PR decreases party control. While the overall votes received by a party determines the seats won by the party as a whole, an individual candidate's position on the party list is determined by how many votes he or she receives. Party leaders cannot punish disobedient candidates by reducing their chances at the polls.

Furthermore, open-list PR encourages fractious behavior among party candidates. Since one's position on the list depends on individual vote totals, party candidates campaign not only against competitors from opposing parties, but also against those of their own party. They must distinguish themselves from fellow party members on issues other than the party platform (Geddes and Ribeiro 1992). Open-list PR thus reduces the coherence of the party agenda.

Open-list PR also contributes to a more complicated ballot than closed-list PR. A simple ballot leads to simpler choices at the polls. For example, voting was easy under the closed-list Venezuelan system. Voters chose between ballots that displayed only party emblem and color.[17] Voters did not choose individual candidates, and no one had to read or write to vote for the party of his or her choice. In contrast, open-list PR involves voting for individual candidates. Where district magnitude is low, as in Chile, this entails a manageable number of candidates that are listed on the ballot. However, high district magnitude (ranging from eight to 70 seats per district [Ames 1995]) and other features of the Brazilian system contribute to a large number of candidates. Since the ballot could not list all the candidates, voters wrote in the name or number of their candidate. While more difficult for all voters, such a system is particularly difficult for poor, less educated voters.

Other electoral practices also influence party institutionalization. Where parties partially or fully fund political campaigns, candidates risk losing all-important campaign resources when they deviate from party requirements. Where parties do not provide campaign funds, individual candidates have more freedom to depart from the party program. Not beholden to the party purse strings, candidates instead must please the individuals who provide campaign contributions.

Electoral laws also influence the ability of candidates to change parties or form new ones. For example, in Brazil, politicians easily change parties. In inchoate party systems, politicians are more likely to find success in creating their own parties to run for office, even for the presidency, as did Alberto Fujimori in Peru and Fernando Collor in Brazil.

Open-list PR, high district magnitude, individual campaign financing, and party switching decrease the coherence of parties, as well as the probability that a party will be able to accomplish its goals once in office, since parties cannot control their own officials. These practices also decrease the ability of the electorate to reward and punish politicians.

In conclusion, institutionalized parties provide a clear guide for voters because the party itself exercises control over politicians through candidate selection and discipline. Politicians exhibit loyalty to their party, and campaign as members of the party rather than as individuals. Institutionalized parties reduce information costs because the parties tend to promote a coherent program (whether ideological or not), which all candidates support. This function becomes particularly important when the newly enfranchised are the rural poor; the poor already face significant challenges in receiving information and expressing their preferences at the polls.

Institutionalized parties benefit from promoting reform. The party is more likely to achieve its reform goals, because party officials adhere to party discipline. A coherent, credible party platform informs voters and provides a guide at election time. Individual politicians benefit when the party as a whole benefits. Moreover, institutionalized parties have an incentive to encourage increased participation by new voters through easier voting procedures and increased mobilization; the more voters overall, the greater the success of the party that they support.

Inchoate parties, on the other hand, do not exercise control over party officials, and party loyalty is generally low. Inchoate parties are unlikely to command the discipline required for the passage of reform laws. Politicians switch parties frequently, and political campaigns are individualistic; candidates campaign under party labels, but primarily promote themselves rather than their party. Party affiliation does not provide a clear guide for voters, and individual politicians cannot assume that they will benefit from supporting the party program. Instead, politicians must rely on personalistic strategies to garner political support and they must provide rewards to wealthy campaign contributors and powerful elites who can deliver necessary political support.

The expansion of suffrage has not affected parties in inchoate party systems in the same fashion as those in institutionalized party systems. Individual politicians in inchoate parties do not have an incentive to encourage the rural poor *per se* to vote. Instead, they have an incentive to cater to specific supporters, rich or poor; the politicians cater to this selective constituency through particularistic provision of pork-barrel goods. Easier voting procedures or increased rural organization are broad policies that conceivably might allow other politicians to attract support among a politician's traditional clientele.

The distinction between inchoate and institutionalized parties corresponds well to the variation in results summarized in table 1.1. The three exceptions to the general coincidence of suffrage expansion and land reform are Brazil, Ecuador, and Peru. In Brazil and Ecuador, land reforms coincided with the extension of suffrage to the rural poor, but the results were meager. In Peru, land reform did not occur at the time of suffrage expansion in 1979.

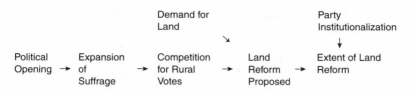

Figure 1.1 The Timing of Land Reform

Political parties in all three countries are inchoate in comparison with those in other Latin American countries. Chapter 2 examines all the cases listed in table 1.1 in more detail. Following that, the case studies of Chile, Venezuela, and Brazil further explore the coincidence of suffrage expansion and land reform as well as the differences in party systems and outcomes. Figure 1.1 depicts the argument.

In the wake of a political "opening" or opportunity, parties remove restrictions on participation by the rural poor. Competition for their votes ensues. If demand for land reform exists, then politicians propose land reform to attract the support of the rural poor. Politicians attempt land reforms whether parties are "institutionalized" or "inchoate," but the institutionalization of parties determines the significance of the reforms. Where parties are institutionalized, significant land reform results as parties promote land reform and encourage the participation of the rural poor. Where parties are inchoate, land reform attempts are similarly undeveloped; in some cases, no serious democratic land reform is attempted.

Examining Land Reform

This study argues that: (1) democratic Latin American land reforms occurred when suffrage was extended to the rural poor; (2) politicians and parties initiated both land reform and the expansion of suffrage to gain political support; and (3) land reforms were more significant when attempted by strong, institutionalized parties. In order to evaluate the argument, this study uses a case study approach.

Key information regarding the process of land reform and expanding suffrage is only available through examination of the actions and statements of the political participants. There is a subjective aspect to the process. When politicians expand suffrage and initiate land reform legislation at the same time, they are working on the *expectation* that the two will work together to ensure greater support. As Rae explains regarding a related issue, the "perceived effect of electoral systems may be just as important as their actual consequences" (1967, 79).

Moreover, in some cases relatively few new voters could effect changes in electoral outcomes. The expectation that election reforms will lead to increased participation can be especially important if elections are close. In Chile, for example, elections were closely contested during the decade of increasing voter participation. Presidential elections in 1958 and 1970 were decided by less than 3 percent and 1.5 percent of the vote, respectively.[18] Many observers feared that the votes of the newly enfranchised (through the secret ballot, easier registration procedures, increased penalties for not voting and, in 1970, illiterate vote) would tip the election outcomes to the left.

Chapter 2 proceeds with an examination of the evidence initially presented in table 1.1. These cases are examined in greater, yet brief, detail. The description fills in vital information about the process and specifically addresses two potential problems: selection on the dependent variable and the impact of international influence during the Alliance for Progress, the most persuasive rival explanation for the timing of reforms.

Three case studies supplement the cursory comparative examination in chapter 2: Chile, Venezuela, and Brazil. An important factor in selecting these countries was the desire to examine expansion of suffrage and land reforms that occurred before, during, and after the Alliance for Progress era. The three countries include cases that span the twentieth century, from the 1940s to the 1980s. The impact of the land reforms and expansions of suffrage varied substantially. One persuasive reason for the variation is the difference in party systems; these three cases encompass both "institutionalized" and "inchoate" parties as well as different electoral rules.

Chapter 3 begins the case studies with Chile, a case of accelerating reforms in a democratic country during the 1960s. The expansion of suffrage began in Chile in 1958 with the use of the secret ballot, mandatory and easier voter registration; the process culminated in the removal of literacy requirements in 1970. Voter participation doubled. Land reforms accompanied the changes in electoral rules: land reform laws by a conservative government in 1962 and 1963; another by a moderate Christian Democratic government in 1967; and finally, an explosion of land redistribution by a Socialist government in 1970.

The Chilean case is an important one in part because it appears at first to be one of the best exemplars of the Alliance for Progress influence. However, the chapter points out that the strategy of extending suffrage and promoting land reform predated renewed U.S. interest in the region. Chilean politics were also characterized by highly competitive party politics and institutionalized, cohesive parties.

It hardly seems necessary to acknowledge that the Chilean land reforms have been studied in great depth. Is yet another study warranted? Inclusion of the Chilean case is necessary in part because of its already-described role in examining the main rival hypothesis. It is also necessary because many of the previous case studies of Chile have advanced the hypothesis that the land reforms and the increasing political participation were linked. This study relies heavily on these previous works; it also endeavors to apply this work more broadly. The same connection between expansion of suffrage and land reform has not been applied to other Latin American countries. Furthermore, the Chilean case is particularly important in comparative perspective, being a country with a multiparty system and an open-list PR system and a recipient of large amounts of international aid.

In contrast to Chile, the Venezuelan case in chapter 4 includes periods of expanding suffrage and land reform that occurred not only at the time of the Alliance for Progress, but also earlier in the century. Universal suffrage was established and a land reform law passed during the *trienio* from 1945–1948; following redemocratization and the institution of compulsory voting in 1958, a new land reform passed in 1960. At both times, participation rates were extremely high. Institutionalized, competitive parties were also present. Leaders of the party that expanded suffrage and promoted land reform, AD, had turned to the rural poor by the 1930s in a strategic attempt to gain political office. Moreover, the parties that formed in opposition also eventually altered their own political strategies. They began to include land reform in their own party platforms, thus attempting to compete effectively with AD.

Chapter 5 examines the relationship between land reform and suffrage in Brazil. Attempts at combining land reform and the expansion of suffrage by President João Goulart in the 1960s were unsuccessful. His inability to pass a land reform bill and remove the literacy requirement through the legislature led him to decree both in 1964. Shortly thereafter he was overthrown by the military. Both issues returned when the military stepped down from rule in the 1980s. Conservative President José Sarney announced a sweeping land reform in the same month that he endorsed the removal of the literacy requirement and a return to direct elections. This move, however, did not lead to a significant land reform in Brazil.

Originally, Brazil was considered as a case study for just this reason; it appeared to contradict the argument of this thesis. Here was a country with high levels of poverty and illiteracy, notoriously maldistributed land, active grassroots movements in favor of reform, and the removal of restrictions on the franchise for illiterates. And yet, despite many attempts, a significant land reform did not occur. However, upon further examination, it became apparent that the Brazilian case did conform to the argument; politicians attempted to use land reform and the extension of suffrage to illiterates in order to gain the support of the rural poor. The question then becomes, why did the expansion of suffrage, the demand for land reform, and the search for political support result in significant land reforms in countries such as Chile and Venezuela, but not in Brazil?

The differences in outcome between Brazil and the other cases reveal important differences in the political systems of Brazil, Venezuela, and Chile. Particular features of the Brazilian system, such as weak or inchoate parties, make personalistic, clientelistic methods of support pervasive and thus reduce the effectiveness of broad-based appeals for support. This in turn reduces the likelihood of effective representation of perpetually underrepresented groups in society. The Brazilian case also points out the limits of international pressure in altering the policy choices of democratic governments; likewise, pressure from the rural poor and its allies has been insufficient in bringing about significant reform.

This study argues that extending and improving the rights of suffrage to the rural poor can lead to important changes in policies. A connection between expansion of suffrage and land reform implies that democratic electoral politics can matter in Latin America. Furthermore, the extent to which the rural poor meaningfully participate in democratic politics depends on electoral practices that increase or decrease the accountability of politicians to the electorate.

CHAPTER 2

Cases of Reform: An Overview

Introduction

N early all expansions of suffrage to the rural poor in Latin America coincided with land reforms. This book argues that politicians seeking to secure political power both extended suffrage and attempted land reform to gain the support of the previously disenfranchised rural poor. This chapter presents a comparative overview of most Latin American countries before exploring the dynamics of these reforms in more depth in case studies on Chile, Venezuela, and Brazil. Information on the removal of restrictions on suffrage details the evolution of the right to vote in Latin America. Necessary preconditions for reform such as illiteracy and the demand for reform help to establish whether politicians and their parties could expect new voters to support parties that implemented land reform.

In addition, this comparative overview addresses the impact of international influence on reform. Such pressure from international organizations and countries, particularly the United States, constitutes a plausible alternative explanation for the timing of reforms in Latin America. However, the evidence suggests that political competition for the votes of the rural poor best explains the timing of land reforms.

Case Selection

This study includes most but not all Latin American countries.[1] The argument rests upon competition within "democratic" countries, and what constitutes a "democracy" is generously defined: countries in which relatively free and fair elections take place and legal opposition allowed. Designating such countries as Costa Rica and pre-1973 Chile as democratic is uncontroversial. And yet, Chile did not have universal suffrage until 1970, when the literacy requirement was dropped. This study examines the evolution of representative democracy; implementing universal suffrage is a major step toward the current standards of liberal democracy. The implementation of universal suffrage and the ensuing political struggles shaped the evolution of democracy in Latin America. Because of the nature of incomplete and evolutionary democratic practices, the study includes countries where politics were still in flux. And yet, some measure of competition must exist in order to include a country in the study. Therefore, countries that did not experience relatively free and fair elections, plus legal opposition, during the relevant time periods have been omitted. In practice, this means that only Cuba, El Salvador, Honduras, Nicaragua, and Paraguay have been excluded.[2]

Finally, the starting point of this study (1900) predates all relevant expansions of suffrage in Latin America.[3] The end point (1990) falls five years after the last major expansion: the extension of the franchise to Brazilian illiterates.[4]

Precursors of Reform

This study focuses on the actions and motivations of elites who seek to gain or retain political office. If the removal of restrictions on voting dramatically changed the makeup of the electorate, then politicians would change the policies that they advocated in hopes of attracting the support of new voters. This section looks at whether a significant proportion of the population would be affected by the expansion of suffrage, and whether land reform would be suitable for attracting the support of new voters. In other words, was there reason for politicians to believe that many more citizens would be enfranchised by the removal of the voting restrictions? Were the newly enfranchised likely to desire land reform?

As table 2.1 indicates, literacy restrictions disenfranchised much of the population in many countries. At the time of expansion of suffrage, three-quarters of the Mexican population and two-thirds of the Bolivian population could not read or write. Over one-half of the population of Venezuela and approximately one-third of the population of Brazil, Colombia, and the Dominican Republic were illiterate.

Also, illiteracy was greater in rural areas than in urban areas. For example, 11 percent of the overall Chilean population of 1960 was illiterate and therefore unable to vote; but in rural areas 31 percent of the population was illiterate (in 1960). In another striking case, that of Brazil, 61 percent of the rural population was illiterate in 1950, compared to only 20 percent of urban

Table 2.1   Illiteracy and Removal of Literacy Requirement[a]

Country	Year Literacy Requirement Eliminated	Illiteracy at Time of Removal (Data) (%)	Male Illiteracy, Rural/Urban[b] (%)
Argentina	1912[c]	35 (1914)[d]	17/5 (1960)
Bolivia	1952	68 (1950)	—
Brazil	1985	32 (1980)	61/20 (1950)
Chile	1970	11 (1970)	31/7 (1960)
Colombia	1936	44 (1938)	38/12 (1964)
Costa Rica	1913[f]	21 (1950)	21/4 (1963)
Dominican Republic	1962	36 (1960)	—
Ecuador	1979	26 (1974)	38/8 (1962)
Guatemala	1945	71 (1950)	70/27 (1964)
Mexico	1857/1917	78 (1910)	43/17 (1960)
Panama	1904	30 (1950)	37/6 (1960)
Peru	1979	17 (1981)	42/31 (1961)[e]
Uruguay	1918	10 (1963)	18/7 (1963)
Venezuela	1945	59 (1941)	—

Notes

[a] Population 15 years or older.

[b] Rural female literacy equal or less than the rate of male literacy except in Uruguay.

[c] No previous literacy requirement, but change in electoral laws (McDonald and Ruhl 1989, 155).

[d] Over age 7, from Rudolph (1985).

[e] Female urban.

[f] Mandatory vote implemented 1959.

Sources: ECLAC (1985, 125); Colombian and Venezuelan literacy from Vanhanen (1975, 242, 255); Mexico literacy from Silva Herzog (1959, 122); Brazil literacy from IBGE (1992, 358); rural/urban illiteracy from Ruddle and Barrows (1974, 159–60).

inhabitants. Therefore, removing the literacy requirement would have a greater effect on suffrage in rural areas than urban areas.

Given the large numbers of newly enfranchised rural inhabitants, the second question is whether land reform was a plausible policy for attracting their votes. Demand is a necessary but insufficient factor; without a perceived need for land reform, no motivation for providing reform would exist. However, need did not in itself lead to land reform. Demand for land reform existed at times when land reforms were not implemented, and the level of demand for land reform varied among Latin American countries that experienced reforms. Land reforms occurred in countries at different levels of modernization, as measured by factors such as urbanization, the share of agriculture in the economy, and agricultural workforce.

Table 2.2 indicates the differences in demand for reform among Latin American countries. As mentioned in chapter 1, landownership in Latin American countries is highly concentrated; the Gini index in the first column of the table is a measure of this concentration. Landownership is more concentrated as the number approaches 1. The estimates for Latin America are high, including .94 for Bolivia in 1950 and Chile in 1936 (compared to .71 for the United States in 1959). Although a good first approximation, the Gini index is an unsatisfactory measure of demand. The index often uses data that does not distinguish between actual ownership of land and rented farms, and therefore may underestimate the concentration of landownership (Prosterman and Riedinger 1987, 25). Furthermore, the concentration of landownership does not indicate the importance of agriculture, how many people reside in rural areas and make their living from agriculture, or whether there is excess pressure for land. For example, although Costa Rica had relatively less concentrated landownership, half of the country's workforce depended upon agriculture.

Table 2.2 gives other indicators for a more complete picture of the state of demand: population density, percentage of the male labor force working in agriculture, importance of agriculture to the economy, and urbanization.

In most countries a large percentage of the pre-reform workforce was employed in agriculture: around 70 percent in Bolivia, Colombia (1938), and Guatemala; 50 percent or more in Costa Rica, the Dominican Republic, and Panama. However, democratic land reforms did occur in Chile and Venezuela, which had a lower proportion of the population working in agriculture (30 percent and 34 percent, respectively).

Argentina and Uruguay stand out as countries in which even at the beginning of the twentieth century relatively few people depended for their livelihood on the land. In both countries, a majority of the population lived in cities long before other Latin American countries. Argentina was more urbanized in 1914 than many Latin American countries were in the 1950s and 1960s. In 1914, 33 percent of the population lived in cities larger than 20,000 residents; 40 percent of the population lived in communities greater than 5,000 (Remmer 1984, 57).

Fewer landholdings were extremely small in Argentina and Uruguay than in other countries. In Argentina, 16 percent of landholdings were under 5 hectares (1960); 30 percent of Uruguayan landholdings were under 10 hectares (1970). In contrast, 29 percent of Bolivian farms and 27 percent of Ecuadorian farms were less than *one* hectare (1950 and 1954); 49 percent of Chilean farms were under *five* hectares; and 51 percent of Brazilian landholdings less than 10 hectares (1970) (Ruddle and Barrows 1974).

Table 2.2   Land Concentration and the Importance of Agriculture

Country	Land Concentration (Gini)	Population Density (Pop/mi²)	Labor Force in Agriculture (%)	Agriculture Share in GDP (%)	Urbanization (%)[a]
Argentina	.86 (1960)	7 (1912)	20 (1914)	17 (1965)	33 (1914)
Bolivia	.94 (1950)	7 (1953)	73 (1950)	23 (1965)	19 (1950)
Brazil	.84 (1960)	24 (1964)	52 (1960)	29 (1964)	28 (1960)
		48 (1994)	31 (1980)	11 (1987)	62 (1990)
Chile	.94 (1936)	26 (1960)	30 (1960)	10 (1965)	51 (1960)
Colombia	.86 (1960)	19 (1936)	71 (1938)[b]		13 (1938)
		33 (1961)	51 (1960)	32 (1965)	37 (1960)
Costa Rica	.78 (1963)	56 (1959)	52 (1960)	31 (1964)	24 (1960)
Dominican Republic	.80 (1960)	169 (1962)	66 (1960)	24 (1964)	19 (1960)
Ecuador	.86 (1954)	44 (1964)	58 (1960)	34 (1965)	28 (1960)
		74 (1978)	39 (1980)	16 (1987)	43 (1980)
Guatemala	.86 (1950)	59 (1946)	69 (1950)	28 (1965)	11 (1950)
Mexico	.69 (1960)	19 (1910)	—	17 (1965)	24 (1950)
Panama	.73 (1961)	13 (1903)	56 (1950)	24 (1965)	33 (1960)
Peru	.93 (1961)	24 (1964)	52 (1960)	20 (1964)	29 (1960)
		34 (1978)	40 (1980)	11 (1987)	50 (1980)
Uruguay	.82 (1961)	20 (1919)	21 (1950)	16 (1964)	24 (1919)
Venezuela	.90 (1956)	12 (1946)	43 (1950)		19 (1946)
		19 (1959)	34 (1960)	28 (1963)	47 (1960)

Notes
[a] Population living in cities greater than 20,000.
[b] Male only.

Sources: Taylor and Hudson (1972) for Land Concentration (267–8) and Agriculture Share in GDP (338–40), except Huntington (1968, 382) for land concentration in Bolivia and Chile; Population density from Banks (1971); Labor Force in Agriculture for 1950 and 1960 from ECLAC (1985, 102, 103), other years from ECLAC (2001, 26); Urbanization for 1950 and 1960 from ECLAC (1985, 80), other years from ECLAC (2001, 15) except Colombia in 1938 from Duff (1968, 108), Uruguay (cities over 25,000) and Venezuela from Banks (1971, 96, 97), and Argentina from Remmer (1984).

The population pressure on the land was low in Argentina and Uruguay. Argentina's population density for 1912 (estimated by Banks 1971) was seven people per square mile; lower than all other Latin American countries for which data were available.[5] Remmer estimated that in 1914 there were 20.6 hectares of agricultural land per Argentine, but only around 4 hectares per Chilean. Solon Barraclough estimated that in 1960 the population density in 1960 for "100 cultivated hectares in farms" (rather than total area) in Argentina was 10.4 compared to much higher figures in other countries: 43.3 in Brazil (1950); 79.4 in Chile; 154.3 in Colombia; 108.5 in Ecuador; 157.9 in Guatemala; 176.3 in Peru (Barraclough 1973, 50). In Uruguay, the country's "small population ... kept land distribution from becoming a major political issue" (Hudson and Meditz 1992, 120).

Argentina and Uruguay did not have the same "peasant problem" as their Latin American neighbors. Instead of a labor surplus, the countries experienced a shortage. To fill the need, massive numbers of immigrants flooded these two countries lured by the prospect of employment. Over a million people immigrated to Argentina between 1901 and 1910 (Germani 1969).[6] During the same time period, 136,000 immigrated to Uruguay; this figure comprised 15 percent of Uruguay's population in 1900 (Sánchez-Albornoz 1989). In 1914, 30 percent of the Argentine population was foreign-born (Germani 1969, 333); approximately 46 percent of the workforce was immigrant (Remmer 1984, 51). In Uruguay, 68 percent of the population was foreign-born in 1868 (Sánchez-Albornoz 1989, 88).

Relatively high wages in Argentina further indicate labor scarcity (and the reason for the influx of immigrants); wages in Argentina were high even in comparison with European rates (Remmer 1984, 46). Furthermore, poverty levels were lower in Argentina than in other Latin American countries. In 1970, 1 percent of rural households lived below the level of "destitution," compared to 42 percent in Brazil, 23 percent in Colombia, 11 percent in Chile, 39 percent in Peru, and 19 percent in Venezuela (Altimir 1982, 82).

Clearly politicians in countries other than Argentina and Uruguay had reason to believe that a sizeable segment of the population would be able to participate for the first time, and more freely, in elections. Given the demand for land, politicians also had reason to believe that they could capture the support of the new participants by implementing reform. The data suggests that the expansion of suffrage was an important factor in the timing of land reforms undertaken by elected governments in Latin America. Another possible reason for the timing of the reforms is international pressure; this will be addressed before discussing the cases of reform in more detail.

International Influence

The influence of international pressure constitutes the most significant rival explanation for the timing of land reforms in Latin America. Most notably, this pressure found expression in the U.S. Alliance for Progress. Aid to Latin America increased in the early 1960s, and both aid and advice stressed the benefits of increased democracy and redistributive social policies. This section therefore primarily focuses on U.S. aid to Latin America, since it is mainly renewed U.S. attention toward the region in the 1960s that offers an alternative explanation for the timing of the reforms.

After a period of inattention in the 1950s, the U.S. attention refocused on Latin America with the unruly reception of Vice President Richard Nixon during his tour of Latin America in 1958, and by the Cuban Revolution in 1959 (Boucher 1979; Hirschman 1961; Loehr, Price, and Raichur, 1976). Angry protestors met Nixon throughout his tour of Latin America in May 1958, and at one point the vice president narrowly escaped a rowdy crowd (Niess 1990).

The Eisenhower administration then signaled its acceptance of Operation Pan America, which had been proposed originally by Brazilian President Juscelino Kubitschek (Niess 1990). The new attention toward Latin America was emphasized by President Eisenhower's own trip to the region in February and March of 1960 (Niess 1990). The Eisenhower administration set up the Inter-American Development Bank (IDB) in October 1960 and promised $500 million for the Social Progress Trust Fund at Bogotá, where the Act of Bogotá was signed on September 13, 1960. This money was not forthcoming during the Eisenhower administration.

It was not until 1961 that the United States appeared serious about beginning a major aid plan for Latin America with the announcement of an Alliance for Progress in 1961. Acknowledging social and economic reasons for implementing land reform, U.S. officials also believed that the poverty and frustration of landless and land-poor peasants could easily erupt into support for another revolution along the lines of the Cuban one in 1959. Land reform, it was argued, could serve as a "substitute" for revolution (Huntington 1968).[7] This concern is evident in Kennedy's speech in March 1961 announcing the Alliance for Progress:

> Throughout Latin America, . . . millions of men and women suffer the daily degradations of poverty and hunger. . . . And each day the problems grow more urgent. Population growth is outpacing economic growth—low living standards are further endangered—and discontent—the discontent of a people who know that abundance and the tools of progress are at last within their reach—that discontent is growing. If we are to meet a problem so staggering in its dimension, our own approach must itself be equally bold . . . I have called upon all people of the hemisphere to join in a new Alliance for Progress—*Alianza para Progreso*—a vast cooperative effort, unparalleled in magnitude and nobility of purpose, to satisfy the basic needs of the American people for homes, work and land, health and schools—*techo, trabajo y tierra, salud y escuela.* (U.S. President 1962, 171–2)

Kennedy also announced his request to Congress for $500 million (the funds promised by the Eisenhower administration) "as a first step in fulfilling the Act of Bogotá." The funds would "be used to combat illiteracy, improve the productivity and use of the land, wipe out disease, attack archaic tax and land-tenure structures, provide educational opportunities, and offer a broad range of projects designed to make the benefits of increasing abundance available to all" (U.S. President 1962, 173).

Kennedy approved the first Latin American aid program in May 1961. His actions were followed by a conference in Punta del Este, Uruguay, where the Charter of Punta del Este was signed on August 17, 1961. As Levinson and de Onís explain, the objectives of the Charter included increasing income and reducing income disparity; diversifying exports and decreasing dependence on primary products and capital imports; accelerating industrialization; increasing agricultural production; eliminating adult illiteracy and ensuring a minimum of six years primary education; increasing life expectancy and improving public health; increasing construction of low-cost housing; maintaining stable price levels; improving integration agreements; and, where applicable, encouraging " . . . programs of comprehensive agrarian reform leading to the effective transformation, where required, of unjust structures and systems of land tenure and use, with a view to replacing latifundia and dwarf holdings by an equitable system of land tenure . . . " (Levinson and de Onís 1970).

Land reform was not the only focus of the endeavor; indeed, the redistribution of land was discouraged by the United States if it involved expropriation. U.S. aid could only be used as an indirect subsidy for the land reform as defined in this study. U.S. aid could not be used for the expropriation of land (Rowles 1985; Powelson 1984, 95). Loans and grants could be used for "land improvement, production credit, machinery and fertilizer, roads, irrigation, and essential services for the peasant families, which the IDB and USAID have financed in limited amounts" (Levinson and de Onís 1970, 229–30).[8] The greater impetus for land reform came from domestic sources. According to Levinson and de Onís, Latin American representatives negotiated stronger language regarding land reform, over the reservations of U.S. representatives (Levinson and de Onís 1970). And Kennedy himself acknowledged the earlier Latin American–sponsored Operation Pan America in his Alliance for Progress Speech when he called for a bold approach "consistent with the majestic concept of Operation Pan America" (U.S. President 1962, 172).

Table 2.3 gives figures on economic assistance from the United States to the Latin American countries that are examined in this chapter. Figures for the years in which democratic land reforms were passed are underlined.

Table 2.3 Economic Assistance from United States (Millions of Dollars)

Year	ARG	BOL	BRZ	CHI	COL	COS	DR	ECU	GUA	PAN	PER	URU	VEN
1951	5	.5	27	2	2	.7	.1	.7	.7	.9	21	3	.2
1952	—	2	59	12	3	2	.2	2	1	3	2	.4	3
1953	—	1	381	1	6	3	.3	1	.2	2	2	.2	.1
1954	—	18	5	1	1	2	.2	7	.2	2	3	.2	.1
1955	62	32	56	6	5	5	.3	4	10	3	110	.4	.2
1956	16	28	96	30	12	21	.3	5	34	10	13	.2	.2
1957	99	27	325	40	18	11	.2	8	19	27	16	.3	4
1958	.1	22	25	43	97	3	.2	6	18	6	19	.2	.2
1959	175	25	133	45	6	8	.2	9	12	2	63	18	.7
1960	.8	15	16	45	54	11	.3	9	12	2	25	23	16
1961	69	31	304	139	90	10	.1	13	32	16	59	3	120
1962	79	37	203	232	76	10	35	37	9	25	78	7	66
1963	133	63	142	84	126	14	50	37	13	9	17	22	47
1964	11	76	345	127	124	16	14	27	14	25	76	7	45
1965	10	13	273	131	33	15	75	26	13	24	36	-.5	41
1966	28	36	379	108	99	14	108	28	4	13	43	7	9
1967	3	28	269	285	144	8	58	5	20	35	32	3	37
1968	32	15	325	103	105	11	65	14	17	20	17	33	70
1969	59	33	34	100	128	18	29	13	79	17	28	4	4
1970	23	5	198	29	127	19	20	29	32	12	14	19	19

Note: Assistance from AID and antecedent agencies (Economic Cooperation Administration, Technical Cooperation Administration, Mutual Security Agency, Foreign Operations Administration, International Cooperation Administration, Development Loan Fund); includes U.S. contributions to multilateral organizations. Data are on an obligation and loan authorization basis, rather than on expenditure.

Source: AID, U.S. Overseas Loans and Grants and Assistance from International Organizations, Washington, DC: Department of State various years.

At first glance, it may seem that land reforms occurred when the United States increased its level of aid but the relationship is not so clear. In Bolivia, an increase in U.S. aid *followed* the land reform. Despite being the recipient of the greatest amount of U.S. aid, an elected Brazilian government did not implement a land reform in the 1960s.[9]

Most of the aid from the United States was in the form of Export-Import Bank long-term loans. For example, $119.4 million of the $119.6 million that Venezuela received in 1961 was in the form of Export-Import Bank long-term loans; the remaining .2 million was a development grant. The only country for which this did not apply was the Dominican Republic. In 1962, most of the aid the country received was in loans; from 1963 until 1966, the bulk of the aid was in grants rather than loans.

Table 2.3 does not include funding for time periods prior to 1951. The one case that occurred before this period for which there are readily available data is Venezuela. In the years 1946–1948, the United States gave Venezuela a total of $3.3 million. Of that total, $2.3 million was in the form of Export-Import Bank long-term loans.

Of course, the United States was not the only source of external aid for Latin American countries. Table 2.4 details aid from international organizations. Except for Uruguay, international organizations gave less aid to Latin American countries than the United States between 1961 and 1965. The relationship between international aid and land reform is less persuasive than that of U.S. aid. Again, land reform was not accomplished by an elected government in Brazil, which received substantial amounts of aid.

Finally, it is not clear that U.S. aid actually went to the promotion of land reform. According to King, 10 percent of U.S. aid to Latin America went to agriculture between 1962 and 1968; of this amount, half went to commercial farmers. Only 15 percent went toward agrarian reform or its beneficiaries (King 1977, 47). Furthermore, some countries that received U.S. aid during the 1960s did not have democratic land reforms. Land reforms in countries like Venezuela and Costa Rica were already passed or in the process of being formulated before the United States demonstrated its commitment to greater aid.

The influence of international pressure on the timing of land reforms is a difficult rival explanation to dismiss. However, as explained here, international pressure is an insufficient explanation for the timing of land reforms. Land reforms occurred at times other than periods of elevated international pressure and assistance, as in Colombia (1936) and Venezuela (1948). In addition, more of the rural poor were affected when reforms coincided with the expansion of suffrage, regardless of the time period. Reforms attempted

Table 2.4 Assistance from International Organizations (Millions of Dollars)

Year	ARG	BOL	BRZ	CHI	COL	COS	DR	ECU	GUA	PAN	PER	URU	VEN
1951	—	—	15	—	23	—	—	—	—	—	—	33	—
1952	—	*	13	1	3	*	—	.1	*	*	3	—	*
1953	—	.3	4	.3	25	.2	.1	.5	.2	.1	2	*	*
1954	—	.3	50	20	15	.1	.1	8	.1	1	2	*	*
1955	—	.3	.4	.4	26	.2	*	.4	.2	.1	26	.1	.1
1956	.1	.4	.4	.4	17	.1	.1	5	19	6	5	6	.2
1957	.1	.5	2	15	.4	3	*	.4	.2	.2	5	26	.3
1958	.4	.6	18	25	.4	.2	*	20	.3	.1	.4	.2	.3
1959	.9	.5	91	3	20	4	.1	14	.5	.1	7	.3	.3
1960	6	1	2	36	45	2	*	2	.3	.1	37	7	2
1961	53	12	17	36	46	9	*	2	1	7	12	.2	12
1962	134	5	31	19	98	20	*	7	6	3	17	12	48
1963	36	9	23	31	89	7	*	8	1	5	18	24	17
1964	6	2	31	44	69	23	7	25	4	.8	31	5	88
1965	55	20	164	12	27	2	8	.9	2	4	37	21	56
1966	30	7	153	72	75	12	.9	8	.6	11	84	.3	66
1967	78	16	253	95	56	4	4	22	32	12	41	2	33
1968	120	29	143	19	86	3	26	6	14	.4	41	12	33
1969	192	18	190	49	203	8	9	15	28	2	2	25	86
1970	179	32	380	76	185	42	26	13	17	53	11	14	77

Note: * Less than $50,000. Does not include U.S. contributions to multilateral organizations (included in table 2.3).

Source: AID, *U.S. Overseas Loans and Grants and Assistance from International Organizations,* Washington, DC: Department of State, various years.

Table 2.5 Electoral Changes and Participation

Country	Major Changes in Election Law[a]	Increase in Voting[b] (%)	Democratic Land Reform Initiated	Rural Households Affected by Land Reform (%)[c]
Bolivia	1952	660	1953	33
Brazil	1985	17	1964	0
		36[d]	1985	.3
Chile	1958	56	1962	.1
	1967	74	1967	4
	1970	53	1970	13
Colombia	1936	28	1936	n/a
	1958[e]	147[d,f]	1961	9
			1968	
Costa Rica	1959	71	1961	9
Dominican Republic	1962	—	1962	3
Ecuador	1979	74	1979	1
Guatemala	1945	38	1945/1952	13
Mexico	1857/1917	—[f]	1915/1917	7
Panama	1904	—	1962	1.7
Peru	1963	49	1964	2.4
	1979	60	—	—
Venezuela	1945	625	1948	10
	1959	10	1960	39

Notes
[a] See table in appendix.
[b] Difference in votes cast in elections before and after change in electoral rules.
[c] See sources and notes for table 1.1.
[d] Participation subsequently decreased.
[e] Redemocratization.
[f] Estimate problematic, since elections resumed after undemocratic period.

by elected governments at other times, such as in Panama and Peru, had little effect.

Finally, international pressure from the United States also entailed opposition to the promoters of reform. The United States supported the removal of leaders who attempted or implemented land reform in such cases as Guatemala, Chile, and Brazil.

Domestic political concerns outweighed the influence of international actors. A further indication that this was the case is that land reforms were more likely to be significant when the expansion of suffrage was likewise significant—especially when voting increased significantly. Table 2.5 gives the increase in voting following the main changes in election law.

Panama is an anomalous case, because its official expansion of suffrage occurred when the country gained independence and yet came under the control of the United States in 1904. The country remained a "virtual protectorate" of the United States until the 1930s (McDonald and Ruhl 1989). Because of the Panama Canal, the United States continued to maintain a substantial presence in the country. A land reform law was passed in Panama in 1962 in the absence of any legal expansion of suffrage; voter participation had increased slightly, with a 6 percent increase between 1956 and 1964. However, this reform had relatively few beneficiaries: 2,594 families received land (Wilkie 1974).

The Timing of Land Reform: Cases of Significant Reform

In most of the countries examined in this study, land reform attempts accompanied the extension of suffrage to the rural poor. The resulting effects varied from paltry to significant. These results correspond closely to whether the party systems in these countries were institutionalized or inchoate. Countries with strong or institutionalized parties experienced significant land reform, while countries with weak or inchoate parties did not.

In the following countries, land reforms coincided with the extension of effective suffrage to the rural poor, although in some cases these reforms were reversed by subsequent military regimes. One similarity among these cases is the ability of the rural poor to identify the party that would most likely champion their cause, either because of the institutionalized parties in multiparty systems in Chile and Venezuela, or because of the clarity of choices in one- or two-party systems.

Bolivia

Credit for land reform is most easily claimed in a single-party system, as (at the time) in Bolivia and Guatemala. Suffrage expanded dramatically in Bolivia when a widespread uprising ushered in the Revolutionary National Movement (*Movimiento Nacionalista Revolucionario*, MNR) revolution in 1953. Until this period, Bolivian political participation was low because the population was disenfranchised by literacy and property requirements: only 4 percent of the population voted in the 1951 presidential elections. As already mentioned earlier, the rate of illiteracy was high in Bolivia: 68 percent of the total population was illiterate at the time of expansion of suffrage.

Most of the population lived in rural areas. The unequal distribution of land contributed to Bolivian poverty: whereas 1 percent of all farms occupied 82 percent of the land (Eckstein 1978), 78 percent of farms occupied only 1 percent of the land (Carroll 1961, 177).[10] A majority of all Bolivian families (53 percent) were landless (Prosterman and Riedinger 1987).

The catalyst for reform occurred when Víctor Paz Estenssoro, leader of the MNR, won the 1951 election but was prevented from assuming the presidency (McDonald and Ruhl 1989, 227).[11] A widespread uprising supported the MNR "revolution"—in turn, the MNR eliminated barriers to participation. Voter participation increased over sevenfold after the removal of property and literacy requirements and the implementation of a secret ballot by the MNR in 1952.

The MNR followed these reforms with a widespread land reform in 1953 (Decree Law No. 4364). The MNR responded to takeovers and uprisings on the part of peasants in the countryside. However, the MNR already considered the peasantry as a possible source of support, and had begun to campaign and seek support in the countryside by at least 1949 (Patch 1960). In conjunction with the land reform, the MNR sought to organize the peasant movement "with the objective of obtaining an electoral clientele and at the same time avoid the radicalization of the peasants" (Fioravanti 1976, 3).

Rural unions were guaranteed a part in the distribution of lands (Carroll 1961). Three of the nine positions on the Agrarian Reform Board, which oversaw the reform, were reserved for labor and rural representatives (Jemio 1973). In addition, the first Minister of Peasant Affairs, also included on the board, had developed links with the rural unions (Patch 1960). The minister, Ñuflo Chávez, hoped to build his political career on rural support; he later became vice president under President Hernán Siles.[12]

The Bolivian land reform law was sweeping in scope, and much of the redistribution of land occurred between 1953 and 1955. "In two or three years, one-half of Bolivia's rural families had become farm operators and presumptive landowners; as of 1970 about 78 percent of landholdings with 30 percent of reported land area were operated by land reform beneficiaries" (Eckstein 1978, 23). The actual granting of titles to land occurred more slowly, which is not surprising given the procedure for reviewing petitions: after consulting with the landowners and potential beneficiaries, the appropriate land judge would rule upon the petition for land made originally through the local agrarian union. His decision then had to be reviewed by the Agrarian Reform Board, the National Congress, and the President. By 1960, there were 59,000 official beneficiaries of the reform (Carroll 1961, 176). However, the law stated that peasants who were subjected to feudal conditions were to be considered owners of the property that they worked. Thus, "after August 2, 1953, there were no longer any peasants without their own land in Bolivia" (Jemio 1973, 42–3). By 1970, 217,000 families had officially benefited from the reform. Bolivian politicians assumed that these beneficiaries would support the MNR, the party that had promoted the redistribution of the land.

Mexico

One usually associates land reform in Mexico with the presidency of Lázaro Cárdenas (1934–1940) and the long-term single-party rule of the PRI (*Partido Revolucionario Institucional*, Institutional Revolutionary Party). However, land reform figured prominently in the competitive but fluctuating political struggles that followed the Mexican Revolution of 1910. Although the PRI was yet to be created, the fluid electoral system at this time most resembles a single-party system.

Land issues became increasingly salient in Mexico during the latter half of the nineteenth century. Landownership became enormously concentrated during the rule of Porfirio Díaz (1876–1910); an estimated 97 percent of the rural population did not own land by 1910 (Silva Herzog 1959, 123). Tannenbaum notes, "nearly one half of the total rural population resided within haciendas" and that according to the 1910 census, there were "only 834 *hacendados* in all of Mexico" (Tannenbaum 1950, 141, 137). In addition, rural revolts clearly signaled discontent with the status quo.

Despite the social pressures underlying the revolutionary struggles, the revolution itself began with competition among elites and an emerging middle class. After dictator Porfirio Díaz reneged on his promise of stepping down from office, Francisco Madero challenged him in a bid for the presidency in 1910. Díaz's repression of the opposition, including the arrest of Madero, sparked a rebellion and ultimately unleashed the revolution. Disorder and disintegration followed Díaz's exile. After Madero's assassination in 1913, forces under leaders as diverse as Pancho Villa, Emiliano Zapata, and Álvaro Obregón united to unseat the man who had had Madero killed: Victoriano Huerta. Unity quickly crumbled under Huerta's successor to the presidency, Venustiano Carranza. General Obregón became crucial in defeating Pancho Villa and assisting in the consolidation of Carranza's tenuous control of the country. However, Carranza attempted to impose his own successor in the 1920 presidential election to thwart the candidacy of the popular Obregón. Ultimately Carranza moved to arrest Obregón and repress his supporters, again sparking a rebellion (and costing Carranza his life during his attempted flight).

In the meantime, pressure for land reform exploded. Emiliano Zapata's movement famously rebelled against Madero's rule in the quest for land justice. In the *Plan de Ayala* of 1911 Zapata proclaimed, "...the immense majority of Mexico's villages and citizens own only the ground on which they stand...For this reason, through prior compensation, one-third of such monopolies will be expropriated from their powerful owners in order that the villages and citizens of Mexico may obtain *ejidos*, colonies, town sites, and rural properties for sowing or tilling, and in order that the welfare and prosperity of the Mexican people will be promoted in every way" (Wilkie 1969, 46). Pancho Villa expropriated property in the north of Mexico, and other regional leaders such as future president, Plutarco Elías Calles, began their own land reforms in the areas that they controlled (Hall 1981).

Carranza had decreed his own land reform in 1915 in response to these pressures. Provisions for land reform were enshrined in the progressive 1917 Constitution, which Carranza opposed but Álvaro Obregón generally supported (Hall 1981). Obregón built up political support among labor and peasant groups and handily won the election of 1920 (Hall 1981). Though relatively moderate himself, Obregón was sympathetic to the social goals of the Constitution and thought Carranza to be too conservative and reactionary; despite his own reform decree, Carranza had opposed land redistribution from 1916 to 1920 (Hansis 1971, 303).[13] Obregón made contacts within the Zapatista movement (and he fled to the Zapatistas when Carranza attempted to have him arrested).[14]

Obregón's land reform program, according to Hansis, was "one of the most advanced for its time and easily the most radical in Latin America" (Hansis 1971, 303). Obregón issued "an agrarian decree on April 10, 1922, which recognized peasant demand for land as a 'national exigency, powerful and irresistible,' and created the *ejidal* system" (Hansis 1971, 306). Ultimately, Obregón distributed more than 1.5 million hectares of land (Silva Herzog 1959, 280). When he ran for a second presidential term in 1928, Obregón indicated that he would more vigorously address the land question. Although he won the election handily, he never took office; Obregón was assassinated in July 1928.

Land reform after the revolution but before the consolidation of the PRI (roughly from 1915 to 1930) occurred in a relatively open and competitive political environment. Leaders such as Carranza, Obregón, and Calles sought support to shore up their rule, fend off rebellions, and build political support for future electoral campaigns. They used land reform as one strategy to achieve these goals. They sought the support of the landless, the overwhelming majority of the rural population. Although the 1857 Constitution mandated universal suffrage, the free exercise of this right was restricted until the revolution and the direct presidential election held in 1917. After all,

Madero launched his challenge against Porfirio Díaz with a call for "no reelection, electoral reform (effective suffrage), and revision of the Constitution of 1857 (Camp 2003, 41). In addition, the 1917 Constitution declared, "citizens of the Republic are obliged to . . . vote in popular elections."[15] At this time, the majority of the population (78 percent) was illiterate.

Obregón's land reform policies were pale in comparison with the land redistribution that eventually followed. Lázaro Cárdenas, in a much more authoritarian and thus uncompetitive political system distributed far more land and affected the lives of far more Mexicans. By the late 1960s, at least half of the rural population had received land. However, as Hansis states, "despite his imperfect response to agrarian problems, Obregón offered peasants the greatest hope for the future. When his administration was challenged, the agrarians cast their lot with Obregón and loyally defended his regime" (Hansis 1971, 292).

Guatemala

A single party dominated Guatemalan politics after the overthrow of dictator Jorge Ubico in 1944. Disaffection for Ubico among Guatemala's "growing body of schoolteachers, shopkeepers, skilled workers and students" led to protests; ultimately a military rebellion unseated the dictator (Schlesinger and Kinzer 1999, 25–35). In the wake of this opening, illiterates were given the right to vote (in 1945). At the same time, President Juan José Arévalo began a mild land reform (Levinson and de Onís 1970, 83). Unequal land distribution and illiteracy were high in Guatemala at mid-century. Illiterates comprised 71 percent of the population in 1950. Land tenure was egregiously maldistributed: about 2 percent of the holdings occupied over 70 percent of the land, and 1.35 percent of the irrigated holdings occupied 87 percent of the land (Barraclough 1973, 234).

Arévalo's land reform mostly entailed colonization schemes, but a comprehensive land survey was undertaken in 1947 to assess the state of agricultural holdings in the country; the results became available in 1950 (Melville and Melville 1971). This provided the basis for the next land reform. In addition, union organization was legalized and encouraged, and the National Peasant Federation of Guatemala formed in 1950.

The next President, Jacobo Arbenz Guzmán, began a major land reform plan in 1952 (Decree 900). The reform entailed the expropriation and redistribution of idle lands over 672 acres (Gleijeses 1992, 351).[16] Productively used lands were not targeted. Also, a National Agrarian Credit Bank was created in 1953 in order to promote the redistribution and use of land (Carroll 1961). This was important because a World Bank study concluded that in

1951, "agrarian credit practically does not exist for the indigenous people" (Gleijeses 1992, 356).

The government expropriated 160,000 hectares of United Fruit Company lands (of the 220,000 hectares the company owned) and compensated the company based on the value of the property as declared for tax purposes, an amount the company found grossly insufficient (Carroll 1961; Nyrop 1983b). This and the perceived communist nature of the Arbenz government led to the U.S.-supported coup that overthrew Arbenz in 1954 and established Carlos Castillo Armas in power. During Arbenz's 17 months in office, 1,002 farms totaling 603,615 hectares were expropriated (Prosterman et al. 1990, 164). Estimates of beneficiaries of the Arbenz reform vary from 89,000 to 138,000 families, the former figure given by the Castillo Armas administration itself; the land reform thus benefited at least 13 percent of the rural population.[17] The subsequent dictatorship repealed the land reform decree.

The Guatemalan reform occurred without significant international pressure: the reform occurred prior to the Alliance for Progress, with little probability that the United States would provide funds for the Arbenz regime (Gleijeses 1992). In fact, the United States helped orchestrate Arbenz's ouster. The impetus for reform came from reformist politicians in Guatemala; these politicians also expected the rural poor to support them at the polls after receiving redistributed land.

Colombia

The dynamics of land reform differed slightly in the context of a two-party system, of which Colombia is the main example. In a two-party system, punishing incumbents is relatively easy: when dissatisfied, one votes for the other party. The distinction between parties is clear and whether institutionalized or not, incumbent parties have to compete with the opposition knowing that voters can choose the other party if dissatisfied.

Two parties, the Conservative and Liberal, traditionally dominated politics in Colombia, and two major instances of expanding suffrage and the passage of land reform laws occurred. The first occurred in 1936, when Liberal President Alfonso López Pumarejo decreed both universal suffrage and a land reform. Following redemocratization in 1958, another land reform law was passed in 1961. More minor reform laws were passed in 1968 and 1988.

The potential impact of extending the franchise to illiterates was great: in 1938, only 56 percent of the population over 10 was *literate* (Vanhanen 1975, 242). Furthermore, the country was primarily rural. In 1938, 71 percent of Colombians lived in communities of less than 1,500 inhabitants

(Duff 1968). In addition, the rural landless and land-poor had already expressed their preference for more land of their own through recent protests and land invasions.

As mentioned in chapter 1, the Liberal Party won control of the Colombian presidency after a long period of Conservative Party dominance because of a split in the Conservative Party in 1930. The Liberal Party won control of the legislature in 1933, and in 1936 Liberal President López Pumarejo decreed both universal suffrage and a land reform, which was passed by a Congress "dominated by large landowners" (Sanders 1980, 3). López also moved to institute "clean elections" through the use of an identification card. This was perceived as a disadvantage to the Conservative Party, which was thought to be a minority party elected only through manipulation of elections (Stoller 1995). López Pumarejo had been the instigator of the Liberal Party's ascension to power, spent the years during his Liberal predecessor's term (1930–1934) canvassing the countryside, and was himself elected president in 1934 (Stoller 1995).

López's reforms were a bid to achieve Liberal dominance of the electorate, and they succeeded until *la violencia*, a civil war that began in 1948. The land reform's potential benefit to the Liberal Party was heightened by the president's ability to appoint governors, who in turn appointed mayors, who were able to increase votes for their own parties through their influence over local elections (McDonald and Ruhl 1989, 79). The mayors also handled the applications made by rural workers for title to land (AID 1970a, 14), and headed the local police force. The party could influence who voted and who received land, and thus reward its rural supporters.

The immediate electoral effect of the change in suffrage is difficult to determine since the Conservative Party abstained in the 1934 and 1938 presidential elections, and in the 1935 and 1937 congressional elections. However, the 5 percent increase in voter participation during a period of Conservative boycott suggests that the newly registered voters were supporters of the Liberal López. Peasants were encouraged to vote "in substantial numbers" (Wilde 1978, 31). The Liberal Party's vote share increased from 45 percent in 1930 to 59 percent in the 1942 presidential election. The Liberal Party maintained the presidency until 1946 when the Liberal Party itself split and a Conservative Party candidate won the election.

The long-standing conflict between Liberals and Conservatives that broke down into *la violencia* claimed more than 200,000 lives and led to authoritarian rule under General Gustavo Rojas Pinilla until 1958. The return to democracy was arranged through pacts between the Conservative and Liberal

Parties, which established the *Frente Nacional* or National Front (Hartlyn 1988; Wilde 1978). The second major land reform occurred after redemocratization.

Electoral considerations were tempered by the National Front political pact arranged during the transition to democracy. The National Front agreement aimed at *reducing* political participation in the wake of the bloody decade of violence that preceded it. The pact instituted a rotation of presidents and the division of all legislative and bureaucratic posts evenly between the Liberal and Conservative Parties regardless of the actual vote tally. The land reform law of 1961 was carefully negotiated in this spirit of bipartisan cooperation, notwithstanding opposition that had derailed previous attempts in 1960 (Hirschman 1963).

Though the 1961 reform occurred in the absence of a formal expansion of suffrage, the reform did take place in a period of competition for new votes. Redemocratization presented a new generation of voters not restricted by literacy and property requirements who had turned 21 after 1948 and had never before voted in free and fair elections. Furthermore, the numbers of poor and illiterate citizens remained high; while the literacy rate had increased, over 25 percent of the total population over 15 years old was still illiterate (Vanhanen 1975, 242).

Even with largely predetermined electoral outcomes between parties, electoral competition continued. Despite the National Front agreement, rivals in intraparty conflict still cared about vote totals because party factions were able to present their own candidates for the legislature. The total votes received by a faction's candidate determined whether or not that candidate received a legislative post (ICSPS 1965). Almost all factions supported land reform, although some factions within the Liberal Party pressed for a more radical reform, and some Conservative factions opposed the 1961 law (Bagley 1979).

Subsequent land reform activities corresponded to other electoral developments. In 1968, a new land reform law accompanied President Carlos Lleras Restrepo's attempt to organize a peasant support group (Osterling 1989). The ANUC (National Association of Peasant Users) was to organize those who received government services (Zamosc 1990). By 1975, approximately 10 percent of rural households had benefited from the reforms (Deere 1985).

In the Colombian case, choices were clear for new voters: the Liberal Party in 1936 was the party that instituted universal male suffrage and implemented land reform. Initially the Liberal Party benefited politically. However, after redemocratization, the Conservative Party competed with the

Liberal Party by promoting land reform to obtain the support of new voters. In this two-party system, the choice between parties was clear.

Chile

Multiparty systems present the most difficult case for accountability. Voters must distinguish between multiple candidates for office and face greater obstacles in obtaining adequate information with which to reward or punish incumbents. Even in these circumstances, competing parties proposed and implemented land reform. However, where parties were more institutionalized, parties were more likely to vigorously pursue reforms both of election rules and land distribution. Parties in these circumstances could wager that voters would identify their party platform and recognize the accomplishments achieved by the party, rather than individual politicians. In Chile, several parties proposed and implemented reforms to garner the support of the newly participating poor.

Despite Chile's long democratic tradition, rural votes were still subject to manipulation through the lack of secret ballots, bribes, and other forms of pressure during the first half of the twentieth century. Changes in Chile's electoral rules clearly threatened the ability of landowners to control the votes of rural workers (Loveman 1979).

Participation increased substantially following electoral reforms that began in 1958. Ballots became secret in 1958, voter registration mandatory and the overall procedures easier. The percentage of the population voting in presidential elections increased from almost 18 percent in 1958 to nearly 32 percent in 1964 (Gil and Parrish 1965). Participation further increased to 37 percent in the congressional election of 1973, after the extension of suffrage to illiterates in 1970 (Nohlen 1993).

Fearing that the newly participating voters were likely to support leftist parties in upcoming elections, the conservative parties joined forces with the more center-oriented Radical Party. As part of this coalition, the conservatives agreed to a moderate land reform and their congressional coalition passed the first democratic Chilean land reform in 1962, as well as an important constitutional amendment in 1963 which allowed for the payment of expropriated land with bonds. While the numbers affected by this reform were low, it was still important. Payment in bonds allows meaningful redistribution of land by the state; the previous requirement of prior compensation in cash curtailed the government's actions because of financial limits.

The 1962 land reform law passed during Conservative President Jorge Alessandri's term occurred not only after the changes in electoral laws, but also after the announcement of the Alliance for Progress. Chile benefited enormously from financial support from the United States at this time. However, electoral concerns were paramount. The fear of a victory by Socialist Salvador Allende in the 1964 presidential race led the conservative parties to abandon their own coalitional candidate for president and instead back Christian Democrat Eduardo Frei.

The Christian Democrats, who had played an instrumental part in the 1958 electoral changes, had also advocated land reform. After winning the presidency, Frei immediately began making more thorough use of the Alessandri reform law while passing another, more comprehensive land reform law in 1967. In addition, the Christian Democratic government legalized rural unionization and used government agencies in its aggressive efforts to create rural unions aligned with the party (Valenzuela 1978). Their actions spurred frantic attempts by all parties to organize rural workers.

Salvador Allende narrowly won the 1970 presidential race with a platform which, among other sweeping changes, promised more extensive land reform. Unable to pass any new legislation, the Allende administration still oversaw a large expansion of expropriations and redistribution of land. Illiterate participation was also enhanced when the ballot was changed to one in which voters could choose between party icons rather than having to read the names of candidates. Both political participation and land reform ended with the coup of 1973.

The Chilean case will be explored more thoroughly in chapter 3.

Costa Rica

Another example of multiparty politics, Costa Rica also has been considered an exemplar of democratic government in Latin America. The franchise has been practically universal since 1949, with no property requirement and a secret ballot.[18] However, another change was made in 1959, which increased participation significantly: voting was made mandatory.[19] Voter registration increased from 65 to 81 percent of the eligible population, and actual voters increased from 22 to 32 percent of the total population between 1958 and 1962. Most of the new voters resided in the rural areas (Blutstein 1970, 203).[20] At this time (1963), 16 percent of the population was illiterate.

While not as highly concentrated as in other Latin American countries, landownership was unequally distributed in Costa Rica. In 1955, 51 percent of all farms occupied 5 percent of the land, while only 6 percent of the farms controlled 61 percent of the land (Brockett 1988, 73). Many rural families did not have any land; as late as 1970 (after the land reform had been initiated), about 22 percent were landless (Brockett 1988, 74; Nelson 1983,

106).[21] Land reform became a more serious issue during the 1950s. Many rural poor had taken over land as squatters, and land disputes increased (Brockett 1988, 124). Land reform legislation was discussed during the 1950s; prior attempts, which included attempts at creating a special institute for land reform, as well as passage of a land reform law, were unsuccessful in 1955 and 1958, respectively (Rowles 1985). The successful land reform coincided with the start of compulsory voting.[22]

The process of Costa Rican land reform preceded the Alliance for Progress. A law of economic encouragement, which was passed on November 9, 1959, included a deadline for a general law on land reform by June 30, 1960. The land reform law was proposed in 1960 and finally passed in October 1961 (Law 2825). The Institute of Lands and Land Settlement was formed in 1962 in order to carry out the reform.[23] By 1975, over 18,000 Costa Ricans, or 9 percent of rural households, had benefited from the reforms (Deere 1985).

The main party that backed the reform was the National Liberation Party (*Partido Liberación Nacional*, PLN), whose traditional base of support was in the rural part of the country (Martz 1967). The PLN retained a plurality in the Legislative Assembly, but had lost the presidency in 1958 because of a split in its own ranks.[24] Passage of land reform legislation may have helped the party improve its political support; the PLN and its allies increased their representation in the legislature from 44.4 percent (20 out of 45 seats) to 50.8 percent (29 out of 57 seats) in 1962 (Nohlen 1993, 197). The PLN also recaptured the presidency in the 1962 election.

Venezuela

Venezuela may at first not appear to fit into the category of a multiparty system. From about 1978 until the 1990s, two major parties overwhelmingly dominated Venezuelan politics: AD and COPEI. However, at the time of democratization this dominance was not as clear. Even when AD won the overwhelming majority of votes in elections in the 1940s (at least 70 percent), three other parties won seats in the legislature. Eventually AD's main opposition, COPEI, overcame AD dominance and won the presidency in the 1960s.

Venezuela's political system was not democratic before the AD party took power via a military coup in 1945. National elections had been indirect and noncompetitive. The opportunity for opening the system appeared with a breach in the ruling establishment. Disagreement arose between the existing president, Isaías Medina Angarita (1941–1945), and the former president, Eleazar López Contreras (1935–1941), over presidential succession in 1945.

The leaders of AD had spent years seeking a democratic Venezuela and preparing for the time when such a system of government would exist.[25] Many of the leaders of AD (and other parties) had been involved in the student protests of 1928 and a later uprising after the death of dictator Juan Vicente Gómez in 1935. Both in exile and back in Venezuela, AD's future leaders turned to a strategy of organizing supporters in the countryside. As early as 1931, leaders such as Rómulo Betancourt recognized that the working and middle classes would be insufficient sources of political support. By 1936, the manifesto of AD's predecessor party called for universal suffrage and a "radical struggle against illiteracy." Furthermore, the party program called for land reform (Suárez Figueroa 1977, 182–90).

Once in power via the military coup, AD initiated universal suffrage and direct elections for president and the legislature. Voting was made easy; voters simply chose between colored cards, which they placed in an envelope in the secrecy of the polling booth. The party also legalized rural unionization, formed new unions, and increased membership in rural unions. AD also launched the promised land reform. According to Powell (1971), AD proceeded to use land reform as a means of building up its political support by using land distribution to recruit and reward party loyalists.

AD reaped the benefits of its policies. The party won 78 percent of the vote in elections for a constituent assembly in 1946, and over 70 percent in all other elections held during the *trienio*, the three-year period of democratic government from 1945 to 1948 (Nohlen 1993, 667–5). However, after alienating most of its opponents and important segments of society, AD was in turn overthrown by a military coup in 1948 (Martz and Baloyra 1976).

After redemocratization in 1958, the right to vote again became universal. In addition, voting was made mandatory and highly encouraged. As during the *trienio*, ballots displayed only distinctive party colors and emblems, making the act of voting easy for illiterates, which were still 37 percent of the population in 1961. Participation increased and over 90 percent of the population went to the polls in 1963 (Martz 1966). Rural unions were again legalized and encouraged by AD as well. Unions affiliated with AD played an important role in designating beneficiaries of the 1960 land reform. The party easily won the majority of rural votes in 1958 and 1963 (ICSPS 1968).

Parties competed for the support of the rural poor. However, this competition was tempered by the desire to avoid a repeat of the events of the *trienio*. Guaranteeing the success of the new democratic endeavor in Venezuela was the primary concern of the regime. New AD President Rómulo Betancourt kept a preelection promise to include both of the main opposition parties, COPEI and URD, in his government.

The cooperation among parties benefited AD's competitors. AD's main rival, COPEI, used its position in the government to compete for the support of peasants. A stalwart *copeyano*, Víctor Giménez Landínez, was named Minister of Agriculture; from this position he pushed for land reform and also criticized AD's efforts as inadequate. COPEI also created its own peasant organization to compete with AD-controlled organizations and a National Secretary for Agriculture in 1960 to coordinate its agrarian activities (Combellas Lares 1985). At first, COPEI incorporated its outreach to peasants through its worker organization, the FTC (*Frente de Trabajadores Copeyanos*, Front of Copeyano Workers); the party later created a separate organization, the MASC (*Movimiento Agrario Socialcristiano*, Social Christian Agrarian Movement), in 1965 (Herman 1980; Combellas Lares 1985).

International pressure fails to explain the timing of reform in Venezuela. The 1948 land reform occurred prior to the Alliance for Progress and in the absence of significant international pressure for reform. The later law of 1960 was passed in February and signed into law the following month—before the announcement of the Alliance for Progress and the increased role of the United States in Latin America. In fact, land reform had been pursued by President Betancourt's government since it had taken office in January 1959. Furthermore, Venezuela received relatively little in foreign aid in comparison to other Latin American recipients, yet the Venezuelan land reform affected far more of the rural poor than other reforms. By 1982, 31 percent of rural families benefited from the reform (Wilkie et al. 1990). Finally, opposition parties would not be in the position to benefit from foreign aid; the possibility of foreign aid does not explain the increasing support of COPEI for reform, or the attempts on the part of COPEI to organize the rural poor.

The Venezuelan case is dealt with in detail in the subsequent case studies.

Dominican Republic

One country not yet mentioned is the Dominican Republic. The Dominican case is problematic because the elected regime was so short-lived, yet an opposition party did initiate universal suffrage and an ambitious land reform. As with Panama, the United States has played a substantial role in the Dominican Republic, including occupying the island nation between 1916 and 1924, and again sending troops in 1965. Dominican politics were greatly influenced by the long, U.S.-supported, dictatorship of Rafael Trujillo, which ended with his assassination in 1961.[26] McDonald and Ruhl called Trujillo's rule "one of the most brutal, repressive, self-serving, and authoritarian in recent Latin American history" (1989, 321). Trujillo's death led to a short democratic regime that extended suffrage and attempted land reform.

Juan Bosch, who had founded the opposition Dominican Revolutionary Party (*Partido Revolucionario Dominicano*, PRD) in 1939, easily won the presidency in the free and fair election of December 1962. In 1962, the literacy requirement for voting was removed and the ballot made secret; voting was made mandatory in the 1963 Constitution (Nohlen 1993). Voting was made easy, with colored ballots to help illiterates choose parties. Presumably, participation should have increased in the wake of electoral changes, since 36 percent of the population was illiterate in 1960. However, participation levels dropped between 1957 and 1962 (from 46 percent to 29 percent); this indicates a high level of electoral fraud under the Trujillo dictatorship (McDonald and Ruhl 1989, 329–31).[27]

Upon taking office, the Bosch government began a land reform. Landownership was highly concentrated in the Dominican Republic. Trujillo, his relatives, and allies, had controlled as much as 60 percent of the arable land (Haggerty 1991). In 1960, 46 percent of landholdings were under 5 hectares, while a third of the land was occupied by landholdings larger than 200 hectares (Ruddle and Barrows 1974). Nearly two-thirds of the workforce was employed in agriculture, and 80 percent of the population lived in rural areas. As late as the early 1980s, 16 percent of all families were landless (Prosterman and Riedinger 1987, 27).

The new government began its reform by confiscating Trujillo's land for redistribution and by creating the Dominican Agrarian Institute (*Instituto Agrario Dominicano*, IAD) to oversee land reform (Haggerty 1991). Little progress was made on reform, however, since a military coup overthrew Bosch's government in September 1963. Supporters of Bosch staged a revolution in 1965, which led to civil war and intervention by the United States. Land reform continued sporadically, with 9,717 families benefiting by 1969 (Wilkie 1974). The IAD continued redistribution; 59,411 families benefited from its activity in a 20-year period (Wilkie et al. 1990).

The Timing of Land Reform: Cases of Failed Reform

In some cases, even though land reform attempts coincided with the expansion of suffrage elected regimes did not pursue significant redistribution. These countries, including primarily Brazil, Ecuador, and Peru, share a similar characteristic: weak or inchoate political parties in a multiparty system. A weak party organization and rampant personalism reduce the benefits of offering a programmatic policy such as land reform; instead, politicians rely on personalistic appeals. It is therefore unsurprising that the only substantial reforms, when they have occurred, have been undertaken by military regimes in these countries.

Another telling similarity among these cases is the late date at which suffrage was extended to illiterates: in Ecuador and Peru in 1979 and in Brazil in 1985. In Ecuador and Brazil, voting remains voluntary for those who cannot read or write. Parties and politicians did not see the rural poor as an effective source of political support.

Brazil

Brazilian politicians made two main attempts at land reform. Both attempts coincided with efforts to extend the franchise to the rural poor. The first attempt occurred in the 1960s, during a period of rapidly increasing political participation. The second attempt occurred after redemocratization in the 1960s.

Vice President João Goulart became president in 1961 following the unexpected resignation of President Jânio Quadros. Goulart's presidency was tenuous from the start and was further hindered by his party's minority status in Congress. Following the adoption of a secret ballot in 1962 and the legalization of rural unions in 1963, Goulart proposed both land reform and the expansion of suffrage to illiterates. At this time, an estimated 90 percent of rural inhabitants in Brazil were illiterate (Cehelsky 1979). Unable to get his proposed legislation passed by Congress, Goulart decreed both a land reform and the extension of suffrage in March 1964. Within weeks, Goulart was ousted by the military. The new military regime passed a land reform months after Goulart's fall; while the law as written envisioned a comprehensive land reform, no significant redistribution of land resulted. The military's efforts focused instead on colonization of the Amazon region.

Following redemocratization in 1985, another Brazilian vice president unexpectedly became president. José Sarney succeeded president-elect Tancredo Neves when the latter died just before taking office. Sarney was a conservative landowning Northeasterner who had been leader of the pro-military PDS (*Partido Democrático Social*, Democratic Social Party) from 1979 to 1984. Lacking political support, Sarney proposed both the extension of the right to vote to illiterates and the beginning of an ambitious land reform plan in May 1985. However, the plan (the PNRA) was only minimally implemented.

The next battle for land reform in Brazil took place during the Constituent Assembly, which met in 1987 and 1988. Major progress on land reform was anticipated, but the resulting land reform provisions in the Constitution of 1988 were less far-reaching than proponents had sought. A key proposal for land reform proponents, the expropriation of productive land, was defeated. Further delays in implementing reform occurred with the drafting of the enabling legislation.

The participation of the rural poor was not encouraged. While obligatory for most Brazilians, the 1988 Constitution made voting voluntary for illiterates. The difficult voting procedures that prevailed in Brazil after 1986 (described in chapter 5) compare unfavorably with the extremely easy voting procedure in Venezuela. And while not as easy as the Venezuelan method, the Chilean procedure involved simply drawing a line next to a candidate's name. The parties with apparently the most to gain in facilitating the voting of the newly enfranchised Brazilians did not do so. Nor was land reform implemented in more than an ad hoc manner. Chapter 5 discusses the Brazilian case in detail.

Ecuador

Voter participation increased dramatically after the literacy requirement was removed in 1979 in Ecuador. At the same time, landownership was highly unequal. In the highlands, 90 percent of all farms were confined to 16 percent of the land, while .3 percent of farms occupied nearly half of the land. Rural disturbances also highlighted the importance of the land issue (Zamosc 1990). A new land reform plan, calling for the distribution of land to 77,000 peasants, was announced by newly elected President Jaime Roldós (Handelman 1980). However, the Agricultural Development Law of 1979 actually weakened the land reform effort by reducing the ability of the government to expropriate inefficiently utilized lands and by banning participants in land invasions from benefiting from redistribution of the land (Haney 1989, 72). Korovkin argued that the law "put an end to the policy of land reform and emphasized the need to create a stable political climate in rural areas as a precondition for increasing agricultural production" (1997). In addition, President Roldós died in an airplane crash in May 1981, and his successor had to deal with the debt crisis of 1982. The government has not implemented any land reform since redemocratization (Zamosc 1994).[28]

Most of Ecuador's land reform history occurred under military regimes. Land reform had been promised in 1959 by successful presidential candidate José María Velasco Ibarra, and subsequently land reform proposals were debated in the Ecuadorian legislature (Barraclough 1973; Carroll 1961; Handelman 1980; Zamosc 1990). While illiterates could not vote in the 1960s (which kept almost two-thirds of the population from voting), other changes occurred. In 1964, a single identity card was established that reduced multiple or "phantom voting." In 1967, voter registration procedures were made easier and voting was made mandatory. However, periods of democratic rule during this period were few.

The most significant land reform occurred in 1964, when a military junta promulgated Decree 1480 (July 1964), which called for expropriation of land and eliminated the *huasipingo* (a system of virtual serfdom in which peasants received a plot of land in exchange for labor performed on an estate). President Velasco, once again in office in 1970, passed the only "democratic" law of this period, Decree 1001 (December 1970); yet this short (months long) interregnum between military governments does raise the question of how "democratic" it could be. This law banned sharecropping in the coastal areas of rice production; the decree was followed by expropriation of the rice plantations. By 1976, almost all had been expropriated (Handelman 1980). The mostly military reforms had a significant effect on the rural poor. About 16 percent of Ecuador's farmland was affected (Handelman 1980); an estimated 20 percent of rural families benefited by the 1970s (Hanratty 1991).

Peru

Land reform has been a major issue in Peru since at least the mid-1950s (Eckstein 1978, 27). Land was unequally distributed: before 1960, 80.7 percent of properties were classified as *minifundios* and occupied only 6.6 percent of the land, while .4 percent of all farms took up 55.7 percent of the land (Colque Huayllaro 1966, 54). Furthermore, 1.3 percent of farms took up 83.8 percent of agricultural land (Kay 1983, 193). Land invasions and peasant uprisings in the early 1960s led to repression by the government, as well as a minor local reform by the military in the La Convención Valley (Handelman 1975).[29]

An official commission on land reform had been appointed in 1956 and presented a proposed land reform bill in 1960 (AID 1970b). Land reform became a campaign issue in the early 1960s. Fernando Belaúnde Terry promised a land reform that would divide up *latifundios*, increase assistance to peasants, and give land to those who worked it (*Corrêio da Manhã*, August 1, 1963). A minor democratic land reform was passed through the recalcitrant Congress in 1964 (Law No. 15037). This coincided with the change to a secret ballot and the legalization of rural organization in 1963. Voter participation had increased by 49 percent since 1956. Kay argued that "Belaúnde's 1964 agrarian reform was clearly designed for political purposes and was confined to only those areas where rural conflicts were most intense. By distributing land to the insurrectionary peasants the government hoped to buy social peace as well as to have a free hand in repressing the incipient guerrilla struggle" (Kay 2001, 748).

Moreover, illiterates were still excluded from voting. McClintock (1981) points out that the traditional landed elite were able to resist changes and to manipulate votes. The one "institutionalized" party in Peru, the APRA

(American Popular Revolutionary Alliance, *Alianza Popular Revolucionaria Americana*) might have extended suffrage and implemented reform; APRA leader Víctor Haya de la Torre won a plurality in the 1962 presidential election, but was prevented from taking office by a short-lived military coup that held new elections.[30] While the military made some election changes (e.g. proportional representation), it did not wish to extend suffrage to illiterates (Cotler 1978).

Estimates of beneficiaries of the 1964 reform vary. As noted in table 1.1, James Wilkie estimated that 2.4 percent of rural households received land. Susana Lastarria-Cornhiel estimate that the figure is less than 2 percent. According to Eckstein, about 1 percent of rural families (10,000 families) received 4 percent of the agricultural land (Eckstein 1978). Clearly, the reform was not far-reaching. A much more extensive redistribution of land occurred under the military, which took power in 1968 (McClintock 1981). In comparison to the former reform, 375,246 rural families benefited from the military land reform between 1969 and 1979; about 35 percent of rural families received land (Kay 1983).

No significant effort at land reform followed the extension of the franchise to illiterates in 1979. It is not entirely clear that the expropriation and redistribution of land would be a reasonable policy to offer for political support in the 1980s. After all, in the previous decade, 15,826 farms, constituting approximately 41 percent of Peru's agricultural land, had been expropriated, and over one-third of rural families had received land. However, many Peruvians were left out of the reform—65 percent did not benefit. In fact, many peasants in the southern highlands were worse off as a result of the reform (McClintock 1984). Discontent from the results of the land reform contributed to support for the guerrilla group Sendero Luminoso in the highlands of Peru (Seligmann 1995; Kay 2001).

Conclusion

This general examination of the relationship between the expansion of suffrage to the rural poor and the initiation of land reform provides persuasive evidence that land reform has been associated with the extension of suffrage to the rural poor. However, such a broad overview lacks the rich detail that more in-depth case studies can bring to the understanding of political processes. The following chapters present case studies of three countries that have already been discussed briefly: Chile, Venezuela, and Brazil. All had long histories of demand for land reform, and all experienced the expansion of suffrage; however, they did not have similar outcomes. As the case studies illustrate, the primary explanation for the different outcomes is the difference in party institutionalization.

CHAPTER 3

Chile: Accelerating Reforms from Alessandri to Allende

Introduction

D
espite a long democratic tradition, political participation in Chile remained limited until the mid-twentieth century. At that time a series of electoral reforms increased political participation and decreased the ability of elites, particularly rural elites, to influence the voting behavior of lower socioeconomic groups. At the same time, progressively more extensive land reforms took place.

This chapter argues that the Chilean land reforms coincided with the electoral reforms because party politicians sought to attract the political support of new rural voters by sponsoring land reform. Parties of the left and center instigated the electoral reforms, which increased the number of voters and reduced the traditional rural elite's ability to manipulate the electorate. In turn, promises of land reform attracted the support of these predominantly poor rural voters.

The chapter first presents the argument and its relation to previous literature on the Chilean land reforms. The rest of the chapter describes the process of electoral expansion and land reform in Chile from 1958 to 1973. The process of accelerating electoral and land reform is divided into three stages. The stages pertain to the three different presidential regimes of the period: from the modest beginnings of the Alessandri administration to the socialist revolution attempted by the Allende administration.

Land Reform in Chile

Explanations of the land reforms in Chile can be grouped into four major categories: demand for reform; class; international pressure; and domestic political competition. These categories are not mutually exclusive, and many analysts of the Chilean reforms subscribe to more than one explanation. For example, Loveman explained the motivation for the 1962 land reform as a combination of international and domestic political concerns (1976a).

The first explanatory categories emphasize the economic and social transformation in Chile in the twentieth century. Industrialization and the spread of capitalism to rural areas led to the decline of the landed oligarchy (Kay 1981). Federico Gil described these changes (1966, 7):

> As a result of the Chilean *hacienda* system a strong paternalistic relationship between peasants and owners developed and is a major factor in the politics of the Chilean valley. The region is also the stage upon which the transition that Chile is presently undergoing stands out more vividly: the change from an agricultural, traditional society dominated by a landowning oligarchy with a semi-servile class at its service, into an industrial, complex, modern society. The re-structuration of society seems more evident here as a result of the appearance of new groups which demand participation in the whole realm of public affairs.

These new groups included an urban-based bourgeoisie that sought to eliminate the quasi-feudal traditional economic system in the countryside, in part because the countryside was unable to provide food for the rest of the industrializing country. Attacks on the land tenure system focused on the inefficiency of production as well as the maldistribution of the land. Part of the attack on the rural system was instigated by low agricultural productivity, which was believed to have caused Chile to import a substantial portion of its foodstuffs. Swift (1971) considered the Chilean farmers' inability to produce enough food for the population "the most striking feature of Chilean agriculture" (9). Thus, rectifying low agricultural productivity was one motivation for land reform (King 1977; Swift 1971).

Highly concentrated landownership combined with landlessness provided other reasons for reform. Prior to land reform, 43 percent of the active agricultural population owned no land in 1955 (Kay and Silva 1992, 134). Fifty-five percent of farmed area was held in *latifundia* of over 5,000 hectares; this accounted for only .5 percent of the total number of farms. Sixty-three percent of all landholdings were less than 20 hectares and accounted for less than 2 percent of the agricultural area (King 1977, 161). Even in 1965, 81.4 percent of all holdings were less than 5 hectares in size and took up 9.7 percent of the land. Fifty-five percent were over 80 hectares and took up 55.4 percent of the land (Castillo and Lehmann 1983).

Social and economic changes also increased the political participation of the working class, and thus increased the demand for land reform. Borón (1971) pointed to "social and economic conditions [which] substantially transformed the economic and social structure of Chile, around 1960, thus unleashing a self-sustaining process of increase in political participation accompanied by a strengthening of the union and organizational structures of the working class" (68). The capitalist transformation created a "proletariat" which, in turn, led to organization of workers and eventual militancy (Kay 1981).

Broad social and economic factors explain the demand for land reform, but by themselves do not explain why land reform occurred. A Chilean observer and political participant, Jacques Chonchol, noted that the Chilean land reforms did not occur because of demand from below by the rural poor, but because of the competition between political parties (Silva 1992, 217). While demand existed, significant unrest did not occur in the early stages of the reform. In particular, social and economic factors do not explain the timing of land reform.

International pressure is the main rival hypothesis addressed in this study. This explanation highlights the influence of the Alliance for Progress and the foreign policy of the United States in particular, in the passage of land reform laws in Latin America. Many analysts note the exertion of international pressure and its influence (e.g. King 1977; Loveman 1976a). Muñoz (1991) emphasizes the attention that the United States focused on Chile during the 1960s. During first the Alessandri government and later the Christian Democratic (*Partido Demócrata Cristiano*, PDC) government, Chile received substantial amounts of aid. Muñoz argues that the main motivation for this aid was concern by the U.S. government over the rise of the left in the country. Eduardo Frei and his party, the Christian Democratic party, with U.S. backing, would therefore make Chile a "showcase" for democracy and reformism in the region.

Attributing land reform in Chile to international pressure implies that governments in Chile would have been unable or unwilling to carry out land reform without the aid of the United States and the Alliance for Progress; this is unlikely. In addition, the timing does not match events, for the process of electoral reforms that led to increased participation (and eventual land reform) began prior to the Alliance for Progress. Although the United States extended aid and support to Chile during the 1960s, this aid did not directly target land reform as a goal.

Domestic political competition best explains the timing of land reforms in Chile, rather than the influence of international pressure. Politicians wanted to attain office and believed that land reform policies would help them achieve their goal. Domestic electoral concerns explain why opposition parties pushed through changes in electoral rules and supported land reform in 1958, before the beginning of the Alliance for Progress. In addition, opposition parties were in no position to benefit from international aid, since they themselves did not occupy the government at the time. Election concerns also explain why the Alessandri government, supported by conservative members of his coalition, passed a land reform in 1962 in the absence of a crisis atmosphere with no obvious threat from revolutionary rural peasants (Kaufman 1967).

Political Competition: Expansion of Suffrage and the Search for Political Support

At mid-century most of the Chilean population technically could vote, with the exception of a sizeable portion of the population (primarily rural) kept from the polls by the literacy requirement. However, not until 1958 could the literate population vote secretly. At the same time, penalties for voter fraud were increased and campaigns further regulated. In addition, the penalties for not voting increased, and registration became easier. Finally, the literacy requirement was dropped in 1970. In addition to the outright changes in election laws, laws governing legal union organization were changed. The specific election changes will be described in detail in the ensuing section.

Others have noted the rapidly increasing political participation and expansion of the Chilean electorate after 1958 (e.g. Cruz-Coke 1984; Gil 1966; Valenzuela and Valenzuela 1986). At the time, changes in electoral rules were widely expected to increase the numbers of voters participating in elections. The reforms led to the rising belief that more people would be voting, and would be voting outside of the control of the traditional conservative oligarchy. Lehmann (1974) expressed the opinion of many when he wrote, "Until about 1958 the agrarian structure was crucial to the preservation of political power since landowners could use their power and patronage to control the votes of their workers. It is since 1958, with a combination of changes in electoral legislation and agricultural organization that the stability of this order has been threatened" (71–2). This is because of the hold that conservative parties had over the rural electorate: "in the rural areas the United Conservative and Liberal Parties [*Partido Conservador*, PCU, and the *Partido Liberal*, PL] exercised a virtual dictatorship over the electorate, that was completely controlled through registration and voting" (Cruz-Coke 1984, 29).[1] Gil (1966) thought that the "new independent voting behavior of the farm worker . . . has had a profoundly damaging effect on the electoral fortunes of the Conservative Party in recent years" (248).

Disciplined and Competitive Parties

The election law changes took place in a period of intense competition between the strong, competitive Chilean political parties (see Valenzuela 1978). Despite differences within the parties on ideology and strategy, the Chilean parties maintained their cohesiveness. While factional splits occurred, party members usually respected party discipline until actual breaks occurred.

Recent election results before the changes had been close, and the new voters promised, or threatened, to tip the balance in favor of one party over the other. The candidate backed by the conservative United Conservative and Liberal Parties had beaten Socialist Salvador Allende by less than 3 percent of the vote in 1958. Therefore, the changes in electoral rules beginning in 1958 had the potential to significantly alter the outcome of subsequent elections. The expectation was that more of the rural population would vote. Moreover, with the secret ballot, they would be able to do so without their choices being monitored. This in turn fed fears that the rural poor would tend to vote for the Chilean left, and thus threaten the survival of the conservative parties and the privileges of the landed elite. This prediction seemed to come true in 1970 when a three-way presidential race made possible the election of Socialist Salvador Allende. As a result, parties that had resisted the expansion of suffrage backed the adoption of land reform.

Karen Remmer found that in an earlier period of Chile's history, political competition between parties did not endow disadvantaged groups with greater political leverage. Between 1890 and 1930, government policy, including agricultural policy, reflected the interests of the privileged classes. However, Remmer emphasizes that this occurred at a time in which lower socioeconomic groups were effectively disenfranchised through difficult registration and voting procedures, the literacy requirement, and manipulation by rural elites (Remmer 1984). But in the late 1950s, the situation differed in that competitive parties had extended the franchise by eliminating barriers to participation. Politicians of the left and center instigated the incorporation of the rural poor in the first place to create a new group of potential supporters and to capture its support by implementing a desired benefit. The same parties that encouraged increasing electoral participation also made serious attempts at land reform.

Expansion of Suffrage in Chile, 1958–1973

As noted, Chile had an extensive history of democracy. From 1891 on, elections were free, fair, and orderly.[2] However, Chile did not have universal suffrage until late in the twentieth century.[3] Changes in election rules at mid-century, including the implementation of a secret ballot, stronger penalties for non-voting, and the removal of the literacy requirement, promised to significantly increase the numbers of people who went to the polls, and who they voted for at those polls.

Changes in Elections

Prior to 1958, although elections were legally secret parties supplied their own ballots. This increased the ability of parties to unduly influence voters' choices. Vote buying (*el cohecho*, or bribe) was common, as was sabotaging an opponent by removing his ballots from the official polling station, or by substituting ballots that had his name misspelled. Party members would also pay voters to use ballots that had already been filled out by party activists.[4]

Beginning in 1958, several reforms in electoral laws were made. The changes were pushed through the legislature with the help of exiting President Carlos Ibáñez by the center and left parties, who were concerned over the prospects of a conservative win in the next election. As Gil (1966, 103) states, "...the Center and Left parties, alarmed by the unexpected strength shown by the forces of the Right in a by-election,[5] organized a parliamentary bloc to sponsor certain electoral reforms and other legislative measures designed to improve their chances in the coming presidential election." The members of this bloc, the FRAP (*Frente de Acción Popular*),[6] Radical party, Christian Democrats, Agrarian Labor (*Partido Agrario Laborista*, PAL) and National Party (*Partido Nacional*),[7] were able to get the help of ex-dictator Ibáñez (*El Mercurio*, April 16, 1958, 19). Ibáñez "had run as an independent, denouncing the party system" (Stallings 1978, 32), and was willing to aid in making changes that would be damaging to the conservative parties.

In April 1958, Ibáñez submitted proposals to reform the existing laws on electoral registration and elections. He also submitted proposals to abrogate the Law in Defense of Democracy (*Ley de Defensa de la Democracia*), which had banned the Communist Party (*Partido Comunista de Chile*, PCCh) in 1948.[8] He submitted these under "urgency" in order to get them passed as soon as possible—in time for the presidential election that would take place in the fall.[9] The bloc wanted to abrogate the *Ley de Defensa* and to institute an election reform that would "combat *el cohecho*" with such measures as a single ballot and severe punishment for those caught trying to bribe voters (*El Mercurio*, April 18, 1958, 19). As *El Mercurio* editorialized, the changes occurred because of "the anxiety of the parties that are going to the presidential fight"; these parties wanted to improve their chances with the electorate (April 28, 1958).

The proposals passed in June over the objections of the Conservative and Liberal Parties, whose members abstained or walked out during votes and attempted to get the electoral changes postponed until after the presidential election (*El Mercurio*, April 28, 1958, 3). The members viewed the changes as an attempt to thwart the anticipated victory of Jorge Alessandri, the presidential candidate backed by conservatives, in the fall election. As one Conservative member stated in explaining why they were trying to block the rapid reforms: "... we think a reform of the electoral registration law and also of the general law of elections is necessary. But we think that the modifications that have been proposed ... should be the fruit of prudent examination, in a manner that does not favor one political sector to the detriment of another" (*El Mercurio*, April 24, 1958, 23). As Conservative Party Deputy Sergio Diez argued, the left–center parliamentary bloc "in which were united the partisans of the candidates Allende, Frei, and Bossay [the FRAP, PDC, and independent candidates, respectively] ... maneuvered ... to impede the triumph of don Jorge Alessandri." He went on to say, "The United Conservative and Liberal Parties had never opposed the electoral reform, ... but they do oppose expediting an electoral reform on the eve of a presidential election that appears sponsored by a group that has no other purpose than to cause damage to ... Mr. Alessandri" (*El Mercurio*, April 27, 1958, 31).

Nevertheless, the legislature passed the major electoral change (Law 12.918) in June 1958, over the objections of the PCU and PL.[10] Law 12.918 mandated that a single ballot be provided (*cédula única*), thus ensuring the secrecy of the act of voting (Gil 1966, 206–21). Prior to this, the vote was not effectively secret because the political parties provided their own ballots. Voters had to get their ballots from the party of their choice. The nonuniform ballots were easily identified at the polls and, as described earlier, had made fraud, such as directly buying off voters, easier to commit.

The left–center bloc had wanted to eliminate the practice of vote-buying, and the new law stipulated that anyone who tried to bribe, or accepted a bribe, to alter his or her vote would be sent to prison. A measure of the seriousness of the effort was that, unlike other offenses, no fines in lieu of the prison term were allowed. The official ballot would also help reduce voting fraud or manipulation by controlling access to ballots. Another change was compulsory voter registration. While voting had been mandatory in Chile since 1925 (Torres Dujisin 1989), registration had not been. Those who failed to register were now threatened with prison time.

The Communist Party was legalized in time for the election with the repeal of the *Ley de Defensa*. While the formerly banned members could participate in the election, the party was not able to present its own candidates until the 1960 municipal elections (Cruz-Coke 1984, 69).

The reforms were expected to lead to an increase in political participation (i.e. voting) and to a reduction in the influence of rural elites, which would tip the electoral balance away from the right and toward the center and left in subsequent elections because rural elites would lose their traditional control over how their employees and other associated rural groups voted. However, contrary to expectations, the reforms did not prevent a conservative victory in 1958. One Alessandri supporter remarked, "the electoral reform that they had hurriedly made in order to frustrate the victory of Senator Alessandri would confirm a smashing triumph" (*El Mercurio,* September 2, 1958). While Alessandri's victory in reality was far from "smashing," he did win: with 31.2 percent of the vote he edged out the Socialist Allende, who won 28.5 percent of the vote.

Another major revision of election laws occurred in May 1962. Both the law governing registration (*Ley general de inscripciones electorales,* Law 14.853, May 14, 1962) and the law governing elections (*Ley general de elecciones,* Law 14.852, May 16, 1962) were revised. The penalties for not registering to vote were increased, and proof of registration was required to use banks, obtain credit or government services, to leave the country, and apply for jobs (Torres Dujisin 1989). In addition, registration became easier. Before 1962, registration locations were only open a few days a month, and hours were restricted (Gil 1966, 207–8). But with the changes came increased hours of operation to facilitate registration. Finally, voter registration lists were made permanent, ending the necessity of reregistering every few years.[11]

Yet another measure that affected the participation of rural voters was the 1967 legalization of rural unions, which had been severely restricted until then (Loveman 1976b). Urban labor organizations such as industrial and craft unions had been legal since 1924, but rural unions were not (J. Samuel Valenzuela 1976). While legalizing rural organization did not increase the number of eligible voters, it did increase the likelihood of electoral participation by increasing legal political activity in rural areas. Unions provided an alternative source of information as well as possible outside resources for the rural poor. Chilean parties sponsored rural unions and provided various means of support, such as advice and supplies during strikes; parties expected support from the unions in return (J. Samuel Valenzuela 1976, 159). Intense competition in unionization followed this change (Petras 1976; Loveman 1976a,b).

The last major reform was the extension of the franchise to illiterates in 1970. Removal of the literacy requirement had long been advocated by the

Socialist and Communist parties, and was first officially proposed by Frei in 1965. Passage of legislation giving the right to vote to illiterates had to wait until January 1969, when it joined a package of reforms proposed by President Frei (Law 17.284, *Diario Oficial de la República de Chile*, January 23, 1970, 1–3).[12] Besides approving the extension of the right to vote to illiterates,[13] the reform package included the reduction of the voting age from 21 to 18, the creation of a Constitutional Tribunal, the ability to call for a plebiscite when the executive and legislature deadlocked over a constitutional reform question, and other institutional changes that gave more control and discretion to the presidency. All of the provisions of the 1970 reforms took effect on November 4, 1970, after the presidential elections (Evans de la Cuadra 1970, 5).

Results of Electoral Changes: Increasing Voters

The removal of voting restrictions for illiterates increased the actual number of citizens who could vote. While 90 percent of the Chilean population over 15 were literate in 1970 (Vanhanen 1975, 241), literacy was much lower in the countryside. Only 7 percent of urban males were illiterate in Chile in 1960, compared to 31 percent of rural males. Therefore, even in highly literate Chile the literacy restriction blocked many from voting, particularly in rural areas. At the time the law was signed, it was estimated that the electorate would grow by 37 percent (*El Mercurio*, January 22, 1970).

The law did not specify how illiterates would vote: this was left for a subsequent law that would establish the procedures by which illiterates would register and vote (*El Mercurio*, January 22, 1970; Evans de la Cuadra 1970, 17). The same laws (revised in May 1962) regarding registration and voting procedures applied to illiterates (Evans de la Cuadra, 18). However, after 1970 special measures were taken so that those who did not read or write could take part in elections. One such change was creation of a ballot with icons, which those who could not read and write could use.

A significant increase in registered voters and voter participation followed the changes in electoral laws. The percentage of the population that *registered* to vote in 1958 was 20.5 percent, while the percentage that registered in 1964 was 35 percent, and that percentage increased to 37.8 percent in 1970. The percentage that actually *voted* showed a greater increase, from 17.1 percent in 1958 to 30.4 percent and 31.5 percent in 1964 and 1970, respectively. These figures increase further for the 1973 congressional contest to 45.7 percent of the population registered and 37.4 percent having voted (Nohlen 1993, 239). (See table 3.1.)

Table 3.1   The Chilean Electorate, 1952–1973

Year	Type	Pop'n (1,000)	Number Registered	% Pop'n	Number Voted	% Reg.	% Pop'n
1952	P	6,300	1,105,029	17.5	957,102	86.6	15.2
1953	C	6,460	1,100,027	17	779,621	70.9	12.1
1957	C	7,140	1,284,159	17.9	878,229	68.5	12.3
1958	P	7,320	1,497,493	20.5	1,250,350	83.5	17.1
1961	C	7,760	1,858,980	24	1,385,676	74.5	17.9
1964	P	8,330	2,915,121	35	2,530,697	86.8	30.4
1965	C	8,510	2,920,615	34.3	2,353,123	80.6	27.7
1969	C	9,566	3,244,892	35.3	2,406,129	74.2	26.2
1970	P	9,370	3,539,747	37.8	2,954,799	83.5	31.5
1973	C	9,860	4,510,060	45.7	3,687,105	81.8	37.4

Type of election: P, Presidential; C, Congressional.

Sources: Nohlen (1993, 239); Cruz-Coke (1984, 38); Torres Dujisin (1989, 25, 30); El Mercurio.

Land Reform During the Alessandri Regime

Accounts of land reform in Chile tend to leave out the land reform passed by the conservative Alessandri government in 1962. However, as we shall see, this law was an important first step in land reform. Attempting to forestall an anticipated erosion of electoral support for the conservative parties following the 1958 and 1962 electoral reforms, the Alessandri coalition passed this first land reform law.[14] Paramount among their concerns was the possible victory of the left; these fears eventually led conservative parties to join forces with the centrist Radical party, and eventually to abandon their own chosen candidate for the 1964 presidential race in favor of the Christian Democratic candidate, Eduardo Frei.

Electoral Competition

While no presidential candidate had received an absolute majority of votes since 1942, the 1958 presidential election was closer than usual.[15] As expected, Jorge Alessandri, the independent conservative candidate backed by the Liberal and conservative parties beat Socialist Salvador Allende; however, he did so by less than 3 percent of the vote. Allende might well have won if the leftist Antonio Zamorano had not entered the race and drained off a small but significant number of votes that most likely would have gone to Allende. In this context, a relatively small change in who voted, or how they voted, could be expected to alter future election outcomes. The forecast appeared most promising for the political left; the voters who were expected to be most affected by the electoral changes and most likely to begin to vote were the poor. The poor, in turn, were considered likely supporters of the Socialists and Communists. In addition, the Communist Party had recently been legalized, which meant not only that the Communist Party could compete in elections, but also that the previously banned party members could themselves once again participate in elections.

The congressional elections of 1961 substantiated this view of the predominant electoral trends and contributed to conservative fears: compared to the 1957 congressional elections, conservative parties lost votes, while the leftist parties gained. These gains are shown in tables 3.2 and 3.3. The newly re-legalized Communist Party won 16 seats in the Chamber of Deputies and four seats in the Senate and received about 11 percent of the vote. The Christian Democratic Party increased its share of the vote from 9 percent in the 1957 congressional elections to 16 percent in the election of 1961.[16] The Radical Party (*Partido Radical*, PR) maintained its share of votes but gained seats (from 36 to 39 in the Chamber and 9 to 13 in the Senate). All these parties advocated land reform as part of their campaign platforms.

Meanwhile, the Conservative Party and Liberal Party lost support, declining from a combined 33 percent of the vote to 30 percent. More importantly, the parties fell from a combined 54 seats to 45 seats in the Chamber of Deputies, and from 15 to 13 seats in the Senate. The result of the congressional election was that these conservative parties for "the first time in their history" lost "joint control of one-third of the votes in the congress" (Kaufman 1967, 10). This was the all-important "*tercio constitucional*" according to Cruz-Coke (1984). The importance of the *tercio* lay in the ability to block legislation—revisions of a bill that had already been passed by a majority of both houses could be enforced by a simple majority in the initiating house and a one-third vote in favor by the second house (Kaufman 1967, 10).[17]

The dismal results of the 1961 congressional elections and the apparent shift of the electorate to the left led the Conservative and Liberal Parties to support moderate land reform as a means of attracting support and votes in future elections, especially the 1964 presidential elections. The Liberal and Conservative Parties turned to the Radical Party as a coalition partner in order to prevent deterioration in support (Kaufman 1967). The Radical Party, in turn, insisted on the adoption of land reform as a condition of its participation in the governing coalition and cabinet (Stallings 1978, 85–94). In August 1961 the Radical Party joined the Conservatives and Liberals in an alliance that became formally known as the Democratic Front (*Frente*

Table 3.2 Evolution of Party Share of Votes, 1949–1973

Year	Type	PCU	PL	PDC	PAL	PR	PCCh	PS
1949	C	23	19	4[a]	8	28	—[b]	9
1952	P	{	28}		47	20	—	5
1953	C	14	11	3[a]	15	14		14
1957	C	18	15	9	8	22	—	11
1958	P	{	32}	21		15	{	29}
1960	M	14	15	14		21	9	10
1961	C	14	16	16	11	22	11	
1963	M	11	13	23		22	13	12
1964	P	{[c]		56}	↺	5	{	39}
1965	C	5	7	42		13	12	10
1967	M		14[d]	36		16	15	14
1969	C		20	30		13	16	12
1970	P		35	28			{	37}
1971	M		18	26		8	17	22
1973	C	{	21	29	DR 2} PIR 2 IC 2	{ 4	16	19} API 1 MAPU 3

Type of election: P, Presidential; C, Congressional; M, Municipal.
Percentages rounded off, smallest parties not included. The appendix lists major parties.
Brackets indicate parties within a coalition. DR, *Democracia Radical*; PIR, *Partido Izquierda Radical*; IC, *Izquierda Cristiana*.

Notes
[a] The PDC as such was formed in 1957; prior to this it was the Falange Nacional.
[b] PCCh illegal from 1948 to 1958.
[c] PCU and PL supported Frei in 1964.
[d] PCU and PL joined to form National Party.

Sources: Ruddle and Gillette (1972, 75); SALA (1969, 166); *Keesing's Contemporary Archives* (January 1, 1971–December 31, 1972, 24872); Cruz-Coke (1984, 53–89); Gil (1966); Urzúa Valenzuela (1992, 378, 621–39, 671).

Democrático) in October 1962 (Gil 1966, 81). The concern driving the Liberal and Conservative Parties' support for land reform was electoral. As one party leader noted later:

> Many conservatives already thought that the party could never again exercise any influence in the national destiny, and the weakest were already beginning... to abandon a ship that they believed condemned to sink. The only way out of this problem was to form a combination with the PR [Radical Party].[18]

Table 3.3   Distribution of Seats in the Chilean Congress

Distribution of Seats in the Chamber of Deputies, 1957–1973

Year	PCU	PL	PR	PDC	PS	PCCh	Other
1957	22	32	36	14	13	—	24[a]
1961	17	28	39	23	12	16	12[b]
1965	3	6	20	82	15	18	3[b]
1969	34		24	55	15	22	
1973	34*		5	50*	28	25	8[c]

Notes

* CODE members. The appendix lists major parties.

[a] Agrarian Labor 13, National Party 6 seats, PADENA 5. (Not the same National Party as the one formed by PL and PCU.).

[b] PADENA.

[c] CODE members DR 2, *Izquierda Radical* 1; UP members API 2, MAPU 2, *Izquierda Cristiana* 1.

Sources: 1961 and 1965, Parrish et al. (1967, 38–9); 1957, 1969, and 1973, *Keesing's Contemporary Archives* (1957–1958, 15672; 1969–1970, 24215 and 1973, 25826); Cruz-Coke (1984, 53–89); *El Mercurio*.

Distribution of Seats in Senate, 1957–1973

Year	PCU	PL	PR	PDC	PS	PCCh	Other
1957	6	9	9		8	—	13[a]
1961	4	9	13	4	7	4	4
1965	2	5	9	13	7	5	4
1969	5		6	23	5	9	2
1973	8		2	20	7	9	4

Notes

[a] Includes Agrarian Labor 4, National Party 4. (Not the same National Party as the one formed by PL and PCU.)

Sources: 1961 and 1965, Parrish et al. (1967, 38–9); 1957, 1969, and 1973, *Keesing's Contemporary Archives* (1957–1958, 15672; 1969–1970, 24215; 1973, 25826); Cruz-Coke (1984, 53–89); *El Mercurio*.

The Land Reform Law

The Alessandri government quickly fulfilled its promise of a land reform law by forming a committee that included representatives from all three governing parties (the Conservative, Liberal, and Radical Parties). After four months of deliberations, the committee proposed a constitutional amendment allowing for the payment of land in bonds, after which Alessandri sent a land reform law proposal to the Chamber of Deputies (*Hispanic American Report* [hereafter HAR], 15, no. 1). Alessandri introduced the bill in May 1962, at the same time as the new revision of the election law was taking place. The land reform bill was signed in November 1962 (Law 15.020) in a short ceremony amid little fanfare (*El Mercurio*, November 16, 1962, 1). Reaction to the reform law was generally favorable.

The law allowed the expropriation of unproductive land by the government, a change from the previous focus on modest colonization efforts. The law also, for the first time, acknowledged the "social responsibility" of the ownership of land, which was a step toward future justification for government expropriation of land. As Loveman pointed out, the law was significant because it "based proprietorship on the conditions of productive efficiency, compliance with social legislation, and compatibility with national agrarian planning" (1976a, 239). Moreover, the law provided the basis for more significant action on land reform during the Frei regime while its own land reform proposals moved through the legislature. The Alessandri government had originally intended to settle about 10,000 beneficiaries of the land reform from November 1962 to November 1964 (5,000 families per year), but in the end only 1,200 were affected.[19] However, the law was still significant: parts of the conservative coalition that passed the law had denied that there was an agricultural problem, or at least not one that needed any action on the part of the state.

The 1962 land reform was an important first land reform law, although the law was criticized by land reform advocates as being too weak because "[t]he bill would allow the expropriation of only those privately- and government-owned lands which were not being sufficiently utilized" (*HAR*, 15, no. 8, 741). The purpose of the land reform, according to Article 3 of the law, was to "give access to property rights to those who worked the land, improve the standard of living of the *campesino* population," and increase agricultural productivity. However, the law established the need to fulfill a social obligation in owning land.[20] This opened the door for expropriation. As Swift (1971, 33) noted, in the 1925 Constitution the only limit on property rights was that it was "subject to the limitation imposed by the need to maintain and improve the social order."

The land reform law also created new institutions: the Corporation for Agrarian Reform (*Corporación de Reforma Agrícola*, CORA), to administer land acquisition and distribution; the Agricultural Development Institute (*Instituto de Desarrollo Agropecuario*, INDAP) to administer credit and technical support to small farmers; and CONSFA (*Consejo Superior de Fomento Agropecuario*) to increase production (King 1977, 164; Loveman 1976, 225).[21] These institutions became more important during subsequent land reform periods.

A more significant step in land reform law followed with the passage of a constitutional amendment regarding compensation. The amendment became law (Law 15.295) on October 8, 1963 (Evans de la Cuadra 1970, 5; Kaufman 1967). More controversial than Alessandri's land reform law, the constitutional amendment allowed bonds to be used for compensation. Under the 1925 Constitution, any expropriated property had to be paid for in cash; the constitutional amendment, which eventually both the Chamber of Deputies and Senate approved unanimously, allowed compensation for poorly farmed or abandoned properties to be paid with 10 percent cash and 15-year bonds.[22] Without the amendment, the land reform law would have been useless, since the cash resources necessary for expropriation did not exist. *El Mercurio* editorialized, "Without this article, the expropriation of the poorly worked and abandoned lands is practically unworkable, since a rapid mechanism for expropriating them is lacking" (September 27, 1963, 3).

The Alessandri reforms occurred in the absence of a crisis atmosphere. The right voluntarily agreed to the reforms to improve support at the polls, not as part of an emergency effort to placate an angry peasantry. As Kaufman (1967) pointed out, the right "began to make concessions during a period in which it still retained considerable influence within the political system," and still had "the political resources to obstruct the legislative process" (6). For example, unrest in countryside had not reached intolerable levels; in 1963, only 13 strikes were reported, and no farms were seized by workers (Kay 1992, 140). This was not a period of social and economic crisis in which the landed elite had to grant concessions to save themselves; rather, it was a time in which conservative parties made small concessions to slow the erosion of electoral support.

It is possible to conclude that the Alessandri land reforms came in response to outside pressure. Indeed, the 1962 reform and 1963 constitutional amendment coincided with the beginnings of the U.S. Alliance for Progress. In March of 1962, Teodoro Moscoso, U.S. coordinator for the Alliance, and U.S. Deputy Assistant Secretary of State for Latin American Affairs Richard Goodwin led a group of officials to Chile and pledged aid money (*HAR*, 15, no. 3). The group discussed various reforms, including agrarian reform.[23] However, as shown earlier, the timing of the reforms also suggests a reaction to the expansion of suffrage, not just external pressure. Conservative and Liberal Parties' discussion of the reforms reflected concern over both electoral changes and international pressure. As one party leader told Robert Kaufman,

> The PL and PCU congressmen were not only farmers or industrialists. We had to take into account the political and electoral problems, as well as the technical ones. [The opponents] were concerned only with their occupations, and they didn't see the implications of the problem of an expanded electorate or of external pressures for change. (Kaufman 1967, 17)

Concern over electoral pressures would become more prominent during the 1964 election.

The 1964 Presidential Election

The extent to which the right reacted to electoral incentives is illustrated by their decision finally to abandon their Democratic Front presidential candidate, Julio Durán, in the 1964 election and to back Christian Democrat Eduardo Frei. The impetus for this change was the victory by Socialist Oscar Naranjo in a by-election for a vacant senatorial seat in the predominantly rural province of Curicó on March 15, 1964. Durán, of the Radical party, "staked his candidacy on" victory in this election (Francis 1973, 13). With the triumph of Naranjo over both the conservative and Christian Democratic candidates, Curicó, formerly considered the "most powerful oligarchic heart of reactionary Chile" became the "death certificate of the Democratic Front."[24]

The "political earthquake in Curicó"[25] given that it was traditionally a conservative seat, stunned the parties of the right, confident of victory in the election. Their initial shock soon gave way to fears that the leftist FRAP coalition's candidate, Salvador Allende, might actually win the presidency. Indeed, upon hearing the results of the Curicó election, Allende claimed he would "win the elections, giving Chile a leftist government, freely elected by the people"; Julio Durán claimed that it was "not a disaster, but it could become one if we do not fight with all our might to keep Chile on the democratic path" (*Corrêio da Manhã*, March 17, 1964).

Durán temporarily withdrew from the presidential race. The Democratic Front broke up, and the Liberal and Conservative Parties lent their reluctant support to Christian Democrat Eduardo Frei "because he represent[ed] the maintenance of the democratic regime and ha[d] the best chance of defeating the Marxist candidate."[26] As a result of the reshuffled coalition, Frei won an absolute majority of the vote, 56 percent, and handily beat Allende.[27] As Prothro and Chaparro suggest, the Socialists' victory in the by-election of Curicó led to their loss in the presidential election (1976).

Land Reform and the Search for Political Support During the Frei Regime

Given its victory in the presidential election of 1964, the Christian Democratic Party (PDC) aspired to consolidate its position and to become the largest party in Chile with further electoral successes in the congressional elections of 1965. The PDC did achieve overwhelming victory in the 1965 congressional elections, and gained a majority in the Chamber of Deputies (see table 3.3). The Conservative, Liberal, and Radical Parties lost 14, 22, and 19 seats, respectively, while the PDC gained 59 seats in the Chamber of Deputies, giving the PDC 82 seats out of the total of 147. But the PDC did not achieve a majority in the Senate, where only part of the 45 seats were up for election (although the PDC won 12 of these open seats).[28] The PS and PCCh won 3 and 2 of these seats, respectively; the PCU and PL did not win any (Parrish et al. 1967, 21).

Frei's government sought to sustain its electoral advantage by fulfilling its campaign promises. During the presidential election, both of the candidates (Frei and Allende) had focused their attention on women and rural workers, "convinced that [such voters were] the two keys to victory in the 1964 presidential contest..." (Gil 1966, 214). The key to increasing support among rural workers was to increase their political participation and to reward their participation with land reform. The PDC government proceeded on both issues.

Within a month of becoming president on November 3, 1964, Frei proposed a major constitutional reform. These institutional reforms, which included the use of plebiscites and administrative decentralization, were similar to reforms that had been proposed by Alessandri in 1963.[29] A major difference between the proposals was that the PDC reform included reforms aimed at the lower classes. Frei's goal was "constitutionally affirming the recognition of the fundamental social rights of the Chilean working classes" (*El Mercurio*, December 1, 1964). This included the right to work, the right to a living wage, the right to organize and strike, and the right to education; the PDC stopped enforcing the prohibition on rural unionization. The constitutional reforms also included a revision of property rights in order to facilitate expropriation; the goal was to "extend" the right to property (*El Mercurio*, December 1, 1964, 20).[30]

Furthermore, the PDC proposed that the constitution be changed to allow illiterates and Chileans 18 to 20 years old the right to vote; the proposal was made by PDC deputies Patricio Hurtado and Alberto Jerez (*El Mercurio*, December 11, 1964, 33). The Liberal Party voiced its disfavor of the extension of suffrage to illiterates through Deputy Fernando Maturana:

> We believe...that a country that is making the effort like ours to teach its population to read and write and elevate their cultural level, should not lift this voting requirement for suffrage that is one of the most powerful incentives toward Chilean literacy. It is in our interest to be judged by the most competent electorate. (*El Mercurio*, December 15, 1964, 29)

The bulk of these reforms were approved by the Chamber of Deputies in 1965 (in which the PDC had a majority) but stalled in the Senate (in which the PDC did not have a majority). The property rights reform was detached from the rest of the proposals and did pass. Frei later sought to resurrect the unsuccessful reforms and proposed a package in 1969. In the meantime, Frei's administration aggressively pursued land reform and the organization of potential supporters in the countryside.

Land Reform

Land reform played a major role in the PDC's program.[31] Members of what became the PDC had advocated land reform as early as the 1940s, and the Christian Democratic Party itself advocated land reform in the 1950s and early 1960s (Loveman 1976, 199). For example, the PDC proposed its own land reform measure in 1962 (Feder 1971, 199). The Frei government proposed the new land reform law in November 1965, but moved quickly to implement reform even before the passage of any new legislation. Using the laws already passed during the Alessandri regime, the government expropriated large estates (*fundos*) and distributed the land to families prior to its own, more extensive land reform bill. By the 1967 election, the PDC claimed to have expropriated 347 *fundos* and established 4,827 peasant families on *asentamientos* (cooperative settlements, which are explained below).[32] In addition, they claimed that food production had increased and food imports decreased (*El Mercurio*, April 1, 1967). This was all accomplished before the passage of the PDC's reform law.

Frei proposed his own government's land reform law in November 1965.[33] Among the reasons given for the legislation were concerns over agricultural production and the lack of progress under the Alessandri reform. However, Frei clearly had in mind the rural poor who would potentially benefit from reform. In his speech presenting the bill to Congress, Frei noted the importance of "incorporating into national participation the great masses of peasants who, because of their illiteracy and isolation, have had difficulty in the free exercise of their rights" (12). The PDC planned to give land to 100,000 beneficiaries.

The PDC was in a strong position, since it had an absolute majority of seats in the Chamber of Deputies. However, the PDC did not control a *tercio* in the Senate, controlling only 13 seats, or 29 percent of the total. The value of the *tercio*, as noted earlier, is that a party with a majority in one house and control one-third of the second can essentially ensure passage of its desired legislation.

In all, two years elapsed between the proposal of the land reform in November 1965 and the passage of the PDC land reform law.[34] The PDC itself had delayed the bill's progress in an attempt to avoid mixing the land reform with the copper issue, which was also under consideration, while conservatives hoped to achieve compromises on the copper bill in exchange for support of the land reform bill (Kaufman 1972). Furthermore, many provisions of the bill were opposed by the Conservative and Liberal Parties, as well as important interest groups such as the National Society of Agriculture (*Sociedad Nacional de Agricultura*, SNA), a powerful landowner organization.[35] These groups were careful to express support for land reform in general.

Disagreements within the PDC itself over the extent and goals of the reform also delayed the reform (Loveman 1976b). Internal disagreements did not lead to open displays of opposition in Congress, however, and PDC members of Congress supported the reform measure. The new land reform law (Law 16.640) was passed and signed on July 16, 1967.[36]

The law allowed the expropriation of any land over 80 standardized or "basic" hectares (BIH).[37] This was a change, in that in the past expropriation was based on usage, rather than size. Abandoned or poorly cultivated properties were also subject to expropriation, as were lands that were indirectly farmed (e.g. by tenant farmers) or that were owned by more than one person (Chile 1967). Rather than allowing a waiting period, expropriated lands could be immediately appropriated. Improvements to the land such as buildings, machinery, and animals were to be compensated in cash, but the land itself would be paid for with 10 percent cash and the rest in bonds.[38] This meant that even efficiently cultivated property would be paid for in bonds that would not completely keep up with inflation (Kaufman 1967; Swift 1971). The law would also allow the expropriation and consolidation of *minifundios* to make subsistence farming feasible. One concession to conservatives was the creation of special agrarian tribunals to preside over disputes stemming from expropriations under the law, rather than using the regular court system. One item of particular contention was a retroactive clause, which made territories that had been subdivided among relatives after November 4, 1964 (the date of Frei's election) subject to expropriation.

The Frei reform took into account concerns that agricultural production could drop during a reform.[39] To reduce this threat, a transitional period was created in which workers would manage expropriated properties collectively for three to five years (Castillo and Lehmann 1983, 250; Kaufman 1972; King 1977, 165). These were known as *asentamientos*. These were "the transitory initial stage of the social and economic organization of the *campesinos*, in which they [would] work the expropriated lands through [CORA, the land reform agency]" (Article 66 of the law). The workers who had lived on the land became *asentados* and farmed their new possessions collectively under the supervision of a government official. After about three years (the exact time period was left unclear) the land was to be divided and workers given title to their own plot of land. Conservative opponents of the PDC opposed the collectivist nature of the *asentamientos* (the PDC was slow in granting individual titles), but also feared that the settlements would provide a "massive electoral machine that would guarantee [the PDC] a permanent base of votes, much as the old latifundia system had done for the right itself" (Kaufman 1967, 34–5).

During the Frei regime, 21,000 families received approximately 2.6 million hectares of land.[40] This was far less than the 100,000 beneficiaries that Frei had promised, but still a significant number of beneficiaries. Eighteen percent of Chile's irrigated land was expropriated under Frei's administration (King 1977, 168). Not surprisingly, Frei claimed even greater success; in his final state of the nation address in May 1970 Frei claimed that 1,224 farms, comprising an area of 3.2 million hectares, had been expropriated, and that 150,000 people had benefited (*Facts on File*, June 25–July 1, 1970).

Rural Unionization

If land reform were to increase support, organization was necessary to ensure that potential political support was properly channeled. In 1967, rural unionization was legalized (Law 16.625, *Diario Oficial*, April 29, 1967). The organization of rural unions led to a doubling of organized workers during the Frei administration (Francis 1973, 25).[41] In 1966, before the 1967 legislation, there were just 201 agricultural unions with 10,417 members. In 1970, this number had risen to 476 unions, with 136,984 members (Valenzuela 1978, 30). Membership increased to 253,000 in 1972 (King 1977, 171). Valenzuela states that rural unionization in the 1960s in Chile was highly controlled and fostered by the government and several competing parties (1978, 30).

Once in office, the PDC used INDAP, the credit and support agency, to organize these rural unions (Kaufman 1972; Loveman 1976b); it also set up its own union confederation, *Triunfo Campesino*. During the Frei government, a majority of organized rural workers were affiliated with this confederation, or with one of the other two official confederations (Silva 1992, 218). The unions pushed for higher wages and "helped workers to exert pressure upon the Agrarian Reform Corporation (CORA) to expropriate the farms on which they were working" (Lehmann 1974, 72). It was rare for unions to actually take over farms (Lehmann 1974); however, strikes and unrest on properties could trigger the appointment of an *interventor*, a government official who would oversee the farm and who often would make use of his position to prepare for expropriation (Loveman 1976b). The Frei administration was more likely to respond favorably to actions taken by unions that favored the government than other unions. "The government rarely sent in police against the non-Marxist rural unions . . . and the Catholic, government-oriented unions received clear preference in expropriation of farms and establishment of *asentamientos*" (Loveman 1976b, 250–1). Government officials often gave advice to pro-PDC rural workers and helped them with necessary paperwork.

This was seen as a blatant attempt to garner political support. The Liberal Party not only "denounced . . . the Marxist character" of the PDC reform, but also claimed that it had "only one political end . . . [:] to control the vote of the peasantry through the use of the institution of the *asentamiento*" (*El Mercurio*, December 4, 1965, 37). Opposition parties began to mobilize support in reaction to the PDC's attempts to become the "*partido único*" or "sole party" and to decrease traditional patronage in the Chilean political system. "Their [the PDC] efforts at mobilization and their disdain for some of the traditional clientelistic mechanisms encouraged as never before a frantic race among all sectors to prevent the centrist party from obtaining majority support" (Valenzuela 1978, 37). The leftist FRAP came relatively late into the competition over organization in the countryside, considering that Christian Democrat–oriented organizations got their start (illegally) in the 1950s. The FRAP's main union, the Federation of Peasant and Indians (FCI) had been formed in 1961 (Kaufman 1972).

Julio Durán called PDC behavior "Nazi-like" (*El Mercurio*, April 25, 1967). A PN leader complained "[t]here is fear because the people have seen that the *partido único* has busied itself more than anything with establishing itself throughout the public administration and using all the instruments of the state to perpetuate itself in power" (*El Mercurio*, April 2, 1967). As Francis (1973, 27) put it, parties organized the rural (and urban) poor "not only because they represent[ed] voters but also to exclude other parties from mobilizing them and because these new organizations [were] good vehicles for communication to the masses." Thus, not only were the rural poor an emerging new participant, but also parties feared this group would be co-opted by other parties in the highly competitive environment of party politics.

The unions further broke down the control that the rural employers had over their employees. Unions furnished alternative sources of information and protection for rural inhabitants. The rural unionization law authorized the new unions to engage in collective bargaining, represent individual workers in disputes, and monitor compliance with labor laws (Article 2). The law also removed the large landowners' ability to restrict the access of organizers to workers on their property: "Anyone may visit workers in their dwellings or their union quarters without asking permission of the estate's patron or employer" (Article 12). This increased the information, advice, and resources that workers received beyond those of the rural boss. Strikes and petitions to the government helped to speed up the expropriation process (Loveman 1976b).[42] Side effects of the reform also included programs of credit, technical assistance, and stricter enforcement of the minimum agricultural wage. Real farm wages doubled between 1964 and 1970 (King 1977). In all, rural workers' position improved.

Although successful in its encouragement of rural unionization, the PDC was not able to fully control the organization of rural unions. Rather, unions that supported the PDC were of two kinds: "independent" unions dating from the 1950s (which merged to become the National Confederation of Peasants, or the CNC), and those set up with the help of INDAP after the election of 1964 (Kaufman 1972). These two groups competed with each other.

The agencies that administered the PDC land reform attempted to limit the role of "independent" unions in the reform process. The CNC and the FRAP-supporting FCI (Federation of Peasant and Indians) both sought to have representatives from their groups on the governing boards of INDAP and CORA. Neither got their wish. Instead, *asentados* favoring the PDC were picked as representatives of peasants (Kaufman 1972).

To what extent did the PDC's tactics lead to an increase in support? At first, the PDC achieved remarkable electoral victories, not only in the 1964 presidential race but also in the following congressional elections of 1965. However, the PDC suffered a setback in the April 1967 municipal elections; its share of the vote decreased from 42 to 36 percent of the total vote (see table 3.2). This was seen as a major setback (*New York Times*, April 3, 1967), and *El Mercurio* editorialized that this cast doubt on the idea that the "agrarian reform would bring votes to the parties that brandished it as a banner" (April 8, 1967, 3). However, the PDC maintained support in the countryside more than in urban areas, where it experienced its greatest losses (Kaufman 1972, 124–6). In the immediate aftermath, Jacques Chonchol (the PDC head of INDAP) pointed out the PDC's sustained position in the rural areas vis-à-vis urban areas, and he noted out that over 400,000 rural workers still could not vote because of the literacy requirement, implying that removal of the requirement would help the PDC—if it kept its promises to institute reforms (*El Mercurio*, April 17, 1967, 31). The PDC's official response to the election fell in line with Chonchol's ideas; the party declared passage of the agrarian reform law and acceleration of expropriations as its top priorities.

The party alienated more conservative supporters with many of its policies, but disappointed its more liberal supporters who had expected more significant strides toward such PDC goals as land redistribution. As the 1970 presidential election approached, Jorge Alessandri, once again the conservative-backed candidate, campaigned against the cost of the reform, the alleged reductions in productivity, the political nature of the reform, and the collective approach (Francis 1973, 36–7). The PN called for the distribution of the collectivist *asentamientos* into individually owned parcels (*El Mercurio*, April 1, 1967, 61). Further criticisms included expropriation based on size and the lack of real interest on bonds used for payment.[43]

On the other hand, the left criticized the land reform for being too slow, for being difficult to understand, for not consulting peasants on important matters, and for showing favoritism in selecting recipients (King 1977). Debate over the pace and scope of reforms such as land reform led to splits within the PDC; an important split occurred in May 1969 when the Action Movement for Popular Unity (*Movimiento de Acción Popular Unitaria*, MAPU) split from the PDC and joined with the leftist Popular Unity (*Unidad Popular*, UP) coalition in the 1970 election. One of MAPU's leaders was Jacques Chonchol (*Facts on File*, June 5–11, 1969, 364).

Disagreements over policy, including land reform, also led to splits in the Radical Party; the party split in 1969 into the Radical Party and the Radical Democratic Party (*Partido Democracia Radical*) (Ayres 1976). *Democracia Radical* was made up of the more conservative members of the Radical Party and included former presidential candidate Julio Durán (Alexander 1973, 101–2). In 1970 the Radical Party supported Salvador Allende's presidential coalition; the Radical Democrats supported Jorge Alessandri.

Removal of the Literacy Requirement

The final restriction on suffrage was eliminated in 1970. As already mentioned, the right to vote was extended to illiterates as part of the constitutional reform package approved in January 1970, which went into effect after the presidential elections of that year. Citizens between 18 and 21 years old were given the right to vote and did so for the first time in the April 1971 elections. However, the law neglected to change Article 104 of the constitution, which specified that one had to be 21 years old and able to read and write in order to vote in municipal elections (Cruz-Coke 1984;

Torres Dujisin 1989). Law 17.420 (*Diario Oficial*, March 31, 1971) removed this proscription, although illiterates did not get to vote in the April 1971 municipal elections (*El Mercurio*, April 4, 1971).[44] Illiterates voted for the first time in the congressional elections of March 1973 (*El Mercurio*, March 5, 1973, 9).[45] The estimated 641,000 Chilean illiterates were finally able to go to the polls (Cruz-Coke 1984, 37). As President Frei remarked, "The decade of the seventies opens... under the sign of full electoral participation [;]... through this reform... the Chilean people have the full capacity to govern themselves democratically [;]... the peasants and illiterate workers that day to day labor in the fields and cities will all be able, from now on, to decide the destiny of Chile" (*El Mercurio*, January 22, 1970).

All the details of how illiterates would register to vote, and how they would actually vote (such as the type of ballot they could use) were left to be defined in regular legislation (Evans de la Cuadra 1970). Part of the reason for the delay was slowness in devising a ballot for illiterates (*El Mercurio*, April 4, 1971, 29). For the April 1971 elections, voters still had to either be able to read party and candidate names, or they had to be able to find the number in front of their particular candidate. Law 17.628 of February 24, 1971 mandated that symbols be used on ballots by parties and independent candidates. This enabled voters who could not read to differentiate effectively the choices on the ballot. With these reforms, voting became truly universal and accessible to all.

The new ballots were put in place for the election of March 1973. The symbols of the parties were printed at the top of the list, and voters could make their selection by simply drawing a small vertical line through the horizontal line to the left of their chosen candidate or party (*El Mercurio*, March 3, 1973).[46] A candidate's number also appeared next to his or her name, so that voters did not have to be able to read the name itself. Instead of using a signature for identification at the polling station, illiterates used a thumb print.

Furthermore, the 1973 ballot introduced the party list. Voters had the choice of either picking an individual candidate or a party. It was presumed that illiterates would choose a party emblem rather than an individual candidate (*El Mercurio*, March 4, 1973, 36), thus strengthening the position of parties. Not only illiterates, but also other voters, would be able to choose a party over individuals, which would give the parties more control over elected officials. Illiterates could, however, also memorize the number of an individual candidate and find that candidate on the ballot. In the end, most voters continued to choose individual candidates rather than use the list vote. Only approximately 60,000 votes were made using the list vote, out of over one-and-a-half million votes (Cruz-Coke 1984, 89).

An increase in the numbers of voters, however, was readily apparent. For the March 1973 elections, 4,510,060 people were registered to vote, 717,378 more than two years before. "A large percentage of these are young people between 18 and 21 years old, illiterates, and also women, who have increased extraordinarily their registration in these last two years" (*El Mercurio*, March 3, 1973).

The 1970 Presidential Election

As the 1970 presidential campaign approached, the Liberal and Conservative Parties, which in April 1966 had joined together to form the National Party (PN), resolved not to drop out of the race as they had in 1964. Instead, they believed they had a chance to win with their own candidate, former president Jorge Alessandri. They nearly succeeded. Salvador Allende's *Unidad Popular* (UP) coalition only narrowly defeated Alessandri with 36.5 percent of the vote to Alessandri's 35.2 percent.

The conservative PN had eventually supported the extension of the right to vote to illiterates. The party believed "the motions presented by the Christian Democrats and Marxists to give the vote to illiterates and those over 18 years old are political maneuvers originating in the erroneous belief that this new contingent of citizens will favor their electoral positions" (*El Mercurio*, April 21, 1969, 35). Even so, the PN declared its support for the proposal, expressing its belief that the other parties were wrong, and that the PN would benefit as well. This reflected a rebound in the PN's electoral fortunes.

Allende's bid for the presidency was supported in 1970 by the Socialist, Communist, Radical, *Social Demócrata* Parties, and by MAPU and the Popular Independent Alliance (API, *Acción Popular Independiente*). Ex-president Jorge Alessandri was supported by the National Party, *Democracia Radical* and independents. The Christian Democrats and what was left of PADENA (National Democratic Party, *Partido Democrático Nacional*) supported a third candidate, Radomiro Tomic.

The parties of the UP coalition clearly supported land reform. On December 21, 1969, the coalition's parties "adopted a common program in preparation for a unified stand in the 1970 presidential elections." The Socialist, Communist, Radical Parties, API and MAPU, "pledged to fight imperialism, the bourgeoisie, and large landowners. [They] also stressed the importance of nationalization of large mining firms and acceleration of agrarian reform policies and expropriation of large monopolistic firms" (*Facts on File*, December 25–31, 1969).

Salvador Allende won the most votes on September 4, 1970, but since no candidate received an absolute majority, the winner was decided in Congress between the two candidates who had received the highest number. The UP coalition had insufficient votes in the legislature, but gained the support of the PDC after agreeing to "the maintenance of the party system, the right of free expression of opinion, free and secret voting, and guarantees that the executive, legislative and judicial branches of government would remain independent of each other and that education would continue to be non-ideological" (*Keesing's*, October 3–10, 1970, 24215). Allende's election was confirmed in a joint session of Congress on October 24, and he was sworn in as president on November 3, 1970.

Land Reform During the Allende Regime

Salvador Allende's challenge was to carry out his promised agenda, a democratic transition to socialism, with minority party support in the legislature. Land reform was an important part of the UP's immediate goals and served the dual functions of maintaining the support of coalition members and attracting the vote of the rural poor.

Allende had campaigned throughout most of his four tries for the presidency for more democracy and a change in the Chilean land tenure. Both the Socialist and the Communist Parties (the main parties of the leftist bloc) had for years advocated the reduction of the voting age, universal suffrage, and land reform. Back in 1958, Allende's Socialist Party had urged President Ibáñez to implement a land reform in addition to his repeal of the Law in Defense of Democracy (*El Mercurio*, April 28, 1958). Previous to that, the Socialists had presented a land reform bill in Congress in 1954 (Kaufman 1972, 196). In his 1958 bid for the presidency Allende declared: "We are here to end the preponderance of the *latifundio*" and to bring "more democracy, greater economic development, greater national independence" (*El Mercurio*, September 1, 1958, 25). The Socialists had also advocated the "establishment of an automatic system of voting registration," as well as the guarantee of free education, the right to unionize and strike, and welfare benefits (Gil 1966, 299–300). By the time of Allende's election, rural workers had won the right to unionize. Also, illiterates had won the right to vote; however, they had not yet been able to exercise that vote. The effects of this increase in the franchise would be seen in future elections, and the UP coalition, as well as its opponents, sought to capitalize on the new voters.

Allende promised faster land reform results in the context of a socialist revolution through the ballot box. Knowing that support did not exist in

Congress for another, more radical land reform law, the UP government nevertheless used existing law to oversee a much more dramatic redistribution of land than its predecessors. Despite ideological differences between the PDC and UP land reform goals and methods, the UP did not deviate much from the *asentamiento* program of the Frei administration (Castillo and Lehmann 1983, 255). As permitted under the Frei-era law, the UP called for "expropriation of all rural properties larger than 80 hectares (BIH) ['basic' hectares] by the end of 1972," which it accomplished. During the first year in office the UP government expropriated nearly as much land as the PDC had done during its entire term (Loveman 1976a, 280). Approximately 54,000 beneficiaries received nearly 10 million hectares of land (Eckstein 1978, 34).[47] *Latifundia* were virtually eliminated by the middle of 1972 (King 1977).

Attempts at land expropriation and redistribution were aided by land invasions and takeovers by the rural poor, who were encouraged by parts of the Allende government. In particular, the Movement of the Revolutionary Left (*Movimiento de Izquierda Revolucionario*, MIR) and its rural counterpart, the Revolutionary Peasant Movement (*Movimiento Campesino Revolucionario*, MCR) instigated invasions. They were also joined by radical Socialists and members of MAPU (Loveman 1976, 280–1). Invasions of land took place soon after Allende's confirmation by Congress in October 1970. In an article it titled "La ebullición campesina" (The peasant turmoil) *El Mercurio* (February 7, 1971, 1) gave an extended listing of the *haciendas* and *fundos* that had been invaded between November 1970 and January 1971, some of which were encouraged by the MCR.[48] Not surprisingly, the invasions and the government's complicity were denounced by the SNA and opposition parties such as the PDC. On the other hand, the MIR complained that the UP government was too conciliatory toward large landowners.[49]

In the past, the PDC made "a massive effort to organize what were referred to as 'marginal' segments of society" (Valenzuela 1978, 3) but had left out the smallest, poorest, and least educated of *minifundistas* and itinerant rural workers. These included migratory workers who were the least organized and did not qualify as land recipients in an *asentamiento* because "preference was given to those who had worked for three years on a permanent basis" on the farm (Thiesenhusen 1984, 43). Allende's government increased the scope of the land reform to include those who had been excluded (Castillo and Lehmann 1983). Presumably, these were the people most likely to comprise the 31 percent of the rural population in Chile that was illiterate in 1970. As illiterates gained the right to vote, they represented a potential group of supporters who could counteract the dominance of the

PDC in rural organizations. The coalition partners worked to organize these same groups, and the number of rural workers in unions rose from 140,293 in 1970 to 253,531 in 1972 (Loveman 1976a, 330). Still, even the Allende administration did not successfully reach the most impoverished segments of the Chilean population (Thiesenhusen 1984).

The rural poor were a source of political support in the effort to restructure the Chilean economy and society. As already mentioned, the participation of voters continued to increase after the literacy requirement was removed in 1970. The percentage of registered voters increased from 37.8 in 1970 to 45.7 percent in 1973. The actual percentage of the population voting increased from 31.5 to 37.4 percent (Nohlen 1993, 239). The congressional elections of March 1973 showed that the Socialists and Communists maintained their electoral support and increased their representation in the Chamber of Deputies and Senate; however, the left did not gain as much as expected from increasing participation.

One of the ironies of the increasing participation in Chile is that while it was believed that the left would be the primary beneficiary of the increase, this was not the case. Rather, the immediate beneficiaries of the expansion of suffrage were the Christian Democrats. The belief that the rise in electoral participation in Chile would be correlated with the rise of the left was a misconception (Valenzuela and Valenzuela 1986, 193–7). As seen in table 3.2, the share of the right's vote actually increased: the centrist Radical Party declined most. The abandonment of the Democratic Front candidate in favor of Frei in 1964 obscures the actual gain that the Christian Democratic Party made, since it is not known what proportion voted *for* Frei, rather than *against* Allende once the conservative parties abandoned their own candidate. However, Frei's presidential victory was followed by a large increase in the PDC's vote share in the 1965 congressional elections (from 23 to 42 percent of the vote). In 1970, Allende won the presidential election with a smaller percentage of votes than he had received in his losing bid in 1964. Despite their fears in the middle to late 1960s, the right-wing parties were not threatened with immediate extinction. Cruz-Coke (1984) blames the temporary decline on the divisions within the conservative parties, the rise of the Christian Democratic Party, and tactical errors made in both 1964 and 1970.[50]

In addition, after all the changes in election laws, including the extension of suffrage to illiterates and the change to easier ballots, the Socialist and Communist Parties each won a smaller percentage of the votes cast in 1973 than the National Party or the Christian Democratic Party. To ensure their greatest possible tactical advantage, the National Party, PDC, a fragment of the Radical Party and other small parties banded together to form CODE (*Confederación de la Democracia*) in opposition to the UP coalition (Cruz-Coke 1984, 88). Therefore, only two main parties, representing these coalitions, appeared on the 1973 ballot: CODE and the UP.[51]

In the increasingly heated political competition in Chile, the March 1973 election proved important. Eduardo Frei considered the March 1973 elections the most important of the century for Chile (*El Mercurio*, March 4, 1973, 21). Both the left and CODE considered critical that everyone possible vote. For example, Renan Fuentealba, national president of the PDC claimed that "he who does not [vote] . . . is stabbing Chile in the back" (*El Mercurio*, March 4, 1973). The opposition coalition CODE hoped to achieve a two-thirds majority in the Congress, and thus deny the UP that important *tercio*. The opposition (CODE) considered the election a victory, because the combined parties received 50 percent of the votes. But while *El Mercurio* stated that "The opposition is the indisputable victor of this plebiscite" (March 5, 1973, 3), *Unidad Popular* won enough seats to control a *tercio*, thereby keeping the opposition from a two-thirds majority.

The Military and Land Reform

The long-term effect of the land reform and the continuing increase in illiterate votes cannot be known, since Allende's presidential term and life were cut short by the military coup of 1973. Union organizations were shut down, and rural workers and farmers were arrested and killed. Kay notes that "Peasant activists, trade union leaders, beneficiaries of the agrarian reform and indigenous people were the principal victims of the repression unleashed by the authoritarian state" and that "the once influential peasant trade unions . . . became a shadow of their former selves" (Kay 2001, 746–7).

Cut short as well was the land reform: by April 1979, 30 percent of the expropriated land had been returned to the former owners (Foxley 1986, 33). Another third of the expropriated land was given to rural workers, while the rest was auctioned off (Cruz 1992, 252). Thus, a relatively small number of rural workers benefited by receiving their own lands, and not all of the expropriated properties were returned to their previous owners. But "almost half the former agrarian reform beneficiaries did not receive any" (Kay 2001, 747). In the end, the large properties were forced to become more productive, and although land has become more concentrated, "the agrarian system is today less unequal and more flexible compared with the pre-agrarian reform period" (Kay 2001, 747).

Conclusion

The Chilean land reforms of the 1960s and early 1970s took place in an atmosphere of strongly competing parties. Clearly, the conservatives were not going to receive increased support from leftists, and pursuing too radical a land reform would have alienated conservatives' core supporters. Thus, the restrained Alessandri reform reflected the conservative nature of the government coalition. Support from the rural poor, however, was not unthinkable, and to get that support the Alessandri administration made an important attempt at land reform, walking the line between alienating major supporters (landowners) while attracting new support from the previously secure, and now dangerously uncertain, peasant vote.

The restrained nature of the Alessandri government's land reform makes sense when considering that even in the best circumstances, conservative parties such as those supporting Alessandri could not expect to capture voters' loyalties that were too far to the left; more importantly, they could not risk alienating too much of their own support among large landowners, since land reform is a significant policy with a widespread negative impact for large landowners. In fact, conservatives soon realized that they could not go too far, nor did they need to. After initially moving toward acceptance of land reform and suffering stunning electoral defeats at the hands of the Christian Democratic, Socialist, and Communist Parties, the right rallied for a comeback and aimed for the support of the "neglected" middle class. As one party leader told Robert Kaufman, "If we are successful in gaining their support, we will have captured one-third of the votes and we will be able to play a powerful role. The FRAP and PDC can fight it out for the lower class vote if they want..." (Kaufman 1972, 168).

Michael Francis stated, "Alessandri's much-publicized land reform measures of 1962 and 1963 were only electoral tactics designed to help the rightist coalition to win the 1964 election" (1973, 34). Precisely the point. It is this very motive that makes land reform more likely. Most land reforms *are* electoral tactics; lack of "proper" motive does not make the reforms any less important. Instead, the reform reflects a newfound power, or at least the expected power for groups that previously did not have real representation or voice in governmental policy. The more land reform was seen as a viable electoral "tactic," the more likely it was to be implemented. Land reform is a viable tactic when land reform itself is a viable and desired policy.

The PDC's reform program reflected its more reformist nature and its ability to capture the center; it aggressively sought to increase its support through expanding political participation and implementing land reform.

Finally, the strident UP's endeavor to eliminate capitalist relations in the countryside reflected its Marxist ideology. However, the timing of each reform shows that land reform was a means used by all parties from right to left to attract much-needed support in a closely competitive and expanding electoral arena. Originally, no class crisis forced the right to concede to the demands for changes in the countryside. Rather than obstinately obstruct land reform the right promoted it in order to preserve and improve the right's electoral chances.

The Chilean land reform occurred not long after the Cuban Revolution, and coincided with the initiation of the Alliance for Progress and U.S. support of reforms. However, parties such as the PDC and Socialists had advocated land reform prior to the Cuban Revolution and subsequent U.S. interest in reform. These same parties worked to expand suffrage to decrease the electoral strength of the conservative parties, and later to increase rural organization and extend the franchise to illiterates in order to build up the parties' own electoral strength. The PDC in particular benefited from U.S. support of its reformist government, but judging by its previous actions, it would not have acted differently in the absence of this support.

Distinguishing between the competing hypotheses regarding the timing of land reform is difficult, particularly in Chile, where land reforms and the Alliance for Progress occurred nearly simultaneously. However, several facts can only be explained by the importance of electoral competition. The same parties that had advocated land reform pushed the initial election law changes through the legislature prior to either the Cuban Revolution or the advent of the Alliance for Progress. Although the Frei government became an important "showcase" for Alliance for Progress funds, the Christian Democratic Party was supported because of its position on reform. The Frei government did not suddenly adopt reformist positions because of U.S. pressure and aid. The Alessandri government's change in position, although timed closely with U.S. aid, was accompanied by rapprochement with the Radical Party in a strategy aimed at maintaining the conservative parties' electoral advantage.

The Chilean experience offers insight as to when and why suffrage is expanded. Electoral reforms began when out-of-power groups were able to make use of a propitious moment, in this case an independent and antipartisan president, to alter the rules of the game. In addition, the Chilean experience illustrates the links between the expansion of suffrage and the provision of policies that may benefit newly incorporated groups. Not only the parties that had instigated the electoral changes, but also parties who opposed them, used land reform as a means to gain much-needed support in a highly competitive electoral situation.

CHAPTER 4

Venezuela: Democratization and Reforms

Introduction

U nlike Chile, Venezuela was not democratic for much of the twentieth century. Rather, a series of traditional *caudillos*, or military leaders, governed until 1945. For a three-year period, the so-called *trienio* of 1945–1948, the AD party oversaw a newly democratic regime. AD's rule ended with a coup and military control until 1958, when General Pérez Jiménez was ousted and democratic rule reinstated. These two democratic periods both saw the initiation of land reforms.

As in Chile, Venezuelan political parties were cohesive and disciplined. Competition was intense, notwithstanding AD's position as the majority party. AD was the party that sought to extend the right of suffrage to the rural poor and had the most to gain from offering land reform as a reward to new voters. However, opposition parties also responded to the expansion of suffrage by attempting to attract new support.

This chapter will delve into the changes in suffrage, increasing political participation and land reform in Venezuela during the two periods, the 1940s and 1960s. In both instances AD encouraged political participation on the part of the rural poor and used land reform to attract their political support.

Land Reform in Venezuela

Explanations of the timing of land reform in Venezuela can be grouped into the same four main categories addressed in previous chapters: demand for reform; class; international influence; and domestic political competition. First, it is clear that land reform was in demand, and that peasant participation was important. Land was unequally distributed and underutilized. In 1937, 4 percent of the rural landowners held 78 percent of the agricultural land (Venezuela 1964, 28), and during the 1940s, the main peasant federation, the Venezuelan Peasant Federation (*Federación Campesina de Venezuela*, FCV), publicized this statistic (Martz 1966, 275). This situation did not improve in the 1950s: in 1956, about 2 percent of the farms averaged over 1,000 hectares and occupied 74 percent of the land, while 88 percent of the farms measured less than 20 hectares and occupied 5.4 percent of the land. Furthermore, less than 10 percent of all agricultural land and only about 4 percent of farms over 1,000 hectares was cultivated (Carroll 1961). Ramón Quijada, AD peasant leader, pointed out in 1960 that 80 percent of farmers did not own the lands that they worked, and that much of the arable land remained idle while the majority of these workers had small plots averaging 3 hectares each (*El Nacional*, February 19, 1960).[1] An estimated 400,000 peasants needed land of their own.

Furthermore, peasant unions were important political participants in the reform process, particularly in the second period of land reform. Powell (1969, 87–9) points out the influence of peasant unions after 1958 and argues that peasant unions were not simply the product of reforms, but themselves had an independent influence on these reforms. At the time, Ramón Quijada predicted that the *campesinos* would "not be defrauded this time" because "the peasant mass for the first time in its history possesses an organization that is structured on a national scale with a program and theory for action" (*El Nacional*, February 19, 1960). In addition, it has been suggested that peasant demand led to land reform because of fears of guerrilla war and a Cuban-style revolution (Coppedge 1994b, 156).

Without demand, there would have been no reason for politicians to believe land reform (coupled with universal suffrage) would have given politicians any significant political support. However, the rural unions were for the most part created and controlled by political parties in Venezuela, rather than the other way around. AD was able to control radical leaders who pushed for further and faster land reform than the party was willing to advocate at the time (Levine 1978). The main role an "independent" peasantry played was during the first months of the new regime, when peasants highlighted demands for land reform by spontaneously taking over lands after the ouster of the dictator Pérez Jiménez.

The new director of the National Agrarian Institute (*Instituto Agrario Nacional*, IAN), Ildegar Pérez Segnini, characterized the situation of

February 1959 as follows: (1) the landowners had begun to expel or "clean" their land of peasants immediately after the overthrow of the Pérez Jiménez government;[2] (2) the "rural mass" exerted pressure for land reform because they had been incited by the land reform promises of all of the parties in the 1958 elections; (3) the planting season was fast approaching. Landless peasants "knew that if this month passed them by without their planting, they would undergo another year of misery" (*El Nacional*, February 17, 1960, 29). The CDN (*Comité Directivo Nacional*) of AD urged that immediate attention be given to areas where there was local friction between *campesinos* and landowners, and that the conflicts should be resolved even before the acceptance of a land reform law (*El Nacional*, February 4, 1960, 29). In 1960, 55,000 petitions for land were made (Eckstein 1978, 87), and Segnini estimated that 8,017 families received 525,482 hectares of land in the first year of AD's government (*El Nacional*, February 17, 1960).[3]

The class explanation for land reform conforms with early analyses put forth by opposition politicians themselves: that Venezuela was held under the thrall of a class, rather than one politician (Betancourt in Gómez 1982, 401). Socioeconomic changes within Venezuela set the scene for subsequent events; emerging middle-class groups chafed against the repressive regime of dictator Juan Vicente Gómez (1908–1935). Middle-class opposition also provides the basis for understanding the goals of the politicians who actively opposed the regime, and who sought to protect their own material interests and promote their political aspirations. Both aspirations and material interests were threatened by a regime that limited access to positions within the government. However, the class explanation does not explain the actual timing of the land reforms, nor why the land reforms occurred simultaneously with the expansion of suffrage (an expansion that included all adult Venezuelans).

The Venezuelan case clarifies the possible influence of international pressure, the most persuasive rival to this study's explanation of the timing of land reforms. There are two cases of land reform in Venezuela: during the 1940s *trienio* and in 1960. The *trienio* land reform occurred well before U.S. attention toward reform in Latin America. Furthermore, the nationalistic AD was hostile to the role of foreign companies in Venezuela, particularly oil companies. The second land reform, which occurred upon redemocratization in 1958, is a more likely candidate for international influence. Venezuela's government was considered the kind of reformist government that the United States wanted to support. Despite AD's connection to communism in the past, its leaders were careful to avoid such associations in the 1960s. However, Venezuelan democracy had been reestablished and the new land reform of 1960 passed well before the announcement of the Alliance for Progress by President Kennedy in March of 1961. In addition, Venezuela received relatively small amounts of international aid, compared to other Latin American countries.

Would international attention have caused Venezuelans to do something that they resisted? Or did international attention coincide with what Venezuelans had already planned to do? Venezuelan politicians themselves put pressure on the United States. In the late 1950s, Venezuelans joined other Latin American countries in calling for aid from the United States to assist in reforms that Latin American nations were pursuing. At the same time that Venezuelans were creating a new land reform law and constitution, they were also considering the formation of the Inter-American Development Bank. This was viewed as a concession by the United States to pressures by Latin American countries. As Gonzalo Barrios (AD) said, "The United States...resisted the Latin American initiative. It resisted it, distorted it, delayed it numerous times...and in the end the United States finally ceded to the pressure" (*El Nacional*, February 7, 1960, 30).[4] The United States was perceived as having demonstrated little interest in Latin American economic problems (Rómulo Betancourt, *El Nacional*, February 9, 1960, 25).

Venezuelan leaders were obviously aware of the impact that the United States could have, and welcomed the change in apparent attitude on the part of the U.S. government toward supporting democracy over dictatorship, but also remained skeptical of U.S. motives and commitment. President Betancourt believed that relations with the United States had worsened, principally because the United States had "maintained inconceivably friendly relations with heads of state who were nothing more than despots..." (*El Nacional*, February 9, 1960, 25). After all, the United States had warmly supported the Pérez Jiménez dictatorship (Hellinger 1991).

Political Competition: Expansion of Suffrage and the Search for Political Support

Venezuela's undemocratic government excluded the majority of the Venezuelan population until 1945, from the emerging middle classes to the lower classes. Aspiring leaders, excluded from the government and prohibited from political participation, labored to break into the system by attracting support from other groups outside the system. The long-sought opportunity for getting into political office arose through a fortuitous split in the ruling establishment, a split that in turn prompted a military coup that placed the opposition AD party in power. AD jumped at the chance of finally achieving control of the government.

Once in power, AD instituted universal suffrage and direct elections. AD then turned to the rural poor, its long-term main support, and aggressively organized rural unions and began to initiate a land reform. The party expected to reap a harvest of votes from its long-tended fields.

AD members had sought a new, more open political regime for nearly two decades. At first, the leaders showed a propensity for quick action: they organized student uprisings and, upon exile, attempted an invasion from abroad. However, in the face of setbacks, they soon settled upon a two-pronged strategy of (1) campaigning for direct elections with universal suffrage while (2) simultaneously organizing urban and rural workers. When AD actually got into the government, the party fulfilled this plan by extending suffrage and beginning a land reform to reward the previously organized workers. The rural poor were an important part of AD's electoral support, and AD was able to use the rural unions to implement the reform and to reward and recruit supporters.

Political support was necessary not only to shore up the new regime, but also because of competition from other parties. Opposition to the military government had not been united, and after its fall the disparate and evolving opposition groups competed with each other. AD faced competition from two main opposition parties: COPEI (*Comité de Organización Política Electoral Independiente*, Independent Electoral Political Organizing Committee or Social Christian Party) and URD (*Unión Republicana Demócrata*, Democratic Republican Union). The communist party, the PCV (*Partido Comunista de Venezuela*, Communist Party of Venezuela) also opposed AD.

AD's original competition in organizing urban and rural workers came from the Communist Party, the only other party that seriously attempted to organize urban and rural workers early in the twentieth century. By the time of the *trienio*, AD had displaced the PCV as the leader in union organization. Committed to a democratic regime, AD overwhelmingly won the *trienio* elections, with much of its support coming from the peasant vote it had cultivated. The opposition parties ferociously attacked AD's policies. In the end, rather than risk further losses through the electoral process, the other parties at least tacitly supported the coup that removed AD from power in 1948.

The second opening of the political system in Venezuela occurred in 1958. The unpopular military regime that had replaced AD was ousted and the main parties, including AD, came together in collaboration through a series of pacts (Levine 1978 and 1989; Karl 1986). This assured the democratic government of its continued existence. As had occurred during the *trienio*, universal suffrage was (re)established with the additional change to compulsory voting.

The Venezuelan parties were quick to take advantage of the long sought-after opening of the political system. After ten years of exile, AD could not be sure of retaining the hegemonic position it had enjoyed during the 1945–1948 period. This time other parties competed with AD on its own ground. For example, while not neglecting the predominantly urban basis of its support, COPEI attempted to diminish AD's control in the rural areas through its own organization of peasants and promotion of land reform.

However, the competition between AD and other parties was, by necessity, muted. AD's leaders had learned what an unbridled grab for power could do: the possibility of yet another military coup was quite real. It was not clear at the time that the new democratic regime would survive.

Disciplined and Competitive Parties

Venezuelan parties were highly cohesive groups with a hierarchical structure and strict discipline (Combellas Lares 1985; Coppedge 1994b; Hellinger 1991). The parties maintained this cohesion in part because of the voting system. The use of closed-list PR gave the party leaders power over the rank-and-file because leaders decided where individual politicians fell on the list and thus what their chance of being elected was. Party members who fell into disfavor could be moved down the list in order to make their election impossible, or they could be removed from the list entirely (Myers 1973, 73–4). Furthermore, party members in the legislature who voted against the party line were expelled (Coppedge 1994b). For example, AD expelled 16 AD leaders in April 1960, in part because of newspaper articles that the dissidents had written and criticisms they had made of the National Executive Committee (*Comité Ejecutivo Nacional*, CEN) (*El Nacional*, April 13, 1960).

At the same time, the voting system limited voter choices, since they could not change the lists or choose a particular candidate (Levine 1988).[5] Since voters only chose between parties, the choice at the polls was relatively simple. The system decreased the role of individuality in election campaigns and placed the focus on the party and the party platform. As Molina Vega (1987) pointed out, the list vote "stimulates the electorate to make its decision based on the platform or ideological orientation of the formulas that they present, instead of doing it by giving priority to the personal conditions of the candidates" (81). The party message will then be more consistent and credible. Politicians will have an incentive to campaign for the party as a whole, not his or her own campaign, and the party will be in a better position to implement a promised policy once in office. Furthermore, the simple voting system allowed voters both to easily assess a political party's record and to reward or punish that party. While the system originally benefited AD because it increased the ability of its illiterate supporters to effectively exercise their right to vote, the system also facilitated COPEI's quest to present itself as a credible alternative to AD.

A high level of participation also characterized Venezuelan politics. Institutional features such as the proportional representation system and the mandatory vote encouraged high levels of participation, as did competitive elections and party activity (Molina 1989, 28). As will be discussed later, participation reached high levels in Venezuela after democratization. At the same time, the political parties sought to capture the loyalty of new (presumably rural poor) voters by providing land reform. They were able to do this in part because of strong Venezuelan parties; party discipline facilitated the passage of land reform legislation, and party organization allowed benefits (land) to be channeled to supporters that the party had organized in the countryside.

Oil and the Venezuelan Reforms

Any case study of Venezuela requires a caveat on the subject of oil. Venezuela's good fortune in possessing petroleum reserves sets it apart. The main effect that oil could have had have on reform in Venezuela pertains to the existence of extra funds with which a land reform could be financed. Notwithstanding this windfall, Venezuelan oil does not explain the timing of land reform. Nor does the oil bonanza explain why the land reforms were timed as they were: at the same time as the expansion of suffrage.

Oil revenues may have helped smooth the way for the success of the Venezuelan land reform because of the extra resources that the Venezuelan government had at its disposal. The ability to compensate landowners may have reduced domestic controversy over land reform because there was money for sufficient compensation; oil may have also offered other attractive avenues for investment other than land for large landowners. However, oil does not explain why leaders decided to implement a land reform in the first place, rather than spend the money in other ways or on other policies. After all, oil revenues had not eradicated poverty despite the wealth. As President Betancourt pointed out in his 1960 speech at the signing of the new land reform law, "Today, in this Venezuela where, according to the cold calculations of the economists, there exists the largest income per capita in Latin America, 350,000 families, almost one-third of the total population of the country, have...a subhuman standard of living" (Venezuela 1964, 40).

Expansion of Suffrage During the Trienio

Prior to the *trienio* of 1945–1948, national elections in Venezuela were indirect and noncompetitive.[6] Furthermore, suffrage was limited by property and literacy restrictions.[7] Efforts had been made by excluded groups to open up the political system; protests and uprisings had occurred in 1928 and 1936, and the predecessors of AD and those who would eventually become COPEI and URD attempted to elect alternative candidates to office.

Political Openings: From Death of a Dictator to Military Coup

Disagreements within the ruling elite itself provided the opportunity for opening the political system. The first crack in the system came in 1935 with the death of dictator Juan Vicente Gómez.[8] His successor as president, General Eleazar López Contreras (1935–1941), was relatively more lenient than the dictatorial Gómez. In his "February Program" of 1936 he called for a campaign against illiteracy and for the improvement of agriculture, which included a policy of selling and distributing land. He issued a call for the "study of the problems related to *latifundios* and their parceling" (Suárez Figueroa 1977, 130) and instituted direct elections for municipal councils and state legislative assemblies, which elected the national Chamber of Deputies and Senate, respectively. The president would in turn be chosen by the Chamber of Deputies (ICSPS 1968; Fuenmayor 1981, 236).[9] López Contreras thus proposed reform while also suppressing the protests that arose after Gómez's death (Ewell 1984, 75).

Despite these reforms, López Contreras restricted participation and suppressed popular movements that occurred after Gómez's demise. A precursor of AD, the PDN (*Partido Democrático Nacional*, Democratic Nationalist Party), was able to elect a few candidates to office in 1937 and 1939 in Caracas, but the elections were annulled (Serxner 1959). While novelist Rómulo Gallegos was presented as an opposition candidate for the presidency in 1941, he had no chance of winning under the system controlled by López Contreras.[10]

López Contreras's successor, General Isaías Medina Angarita (1941–1945), presided over a still more tolerant regime. Whereas López Contreras "did everything possible to prevent democratic opposition forces from even registering . . . so that they could not vote" (Fuenmayor 1981, 94), Medina allowed limited but legal party activity, as well as other reforms. As a result, AD was legalized in September 1941. In 1945, Medina extended the franchise to women (only in municipal elections) and instituted direct elections to the Chamber of Deputies (Fuenmayor 1981, 235). He still maintained indirect presidential elections.

Daniel Levine (1973) suggests that Medina may have begun liberalizing in an attempt to gain more support in his impending power struggle with López Contreras, who had made clear his intention to seek another term in office after Medina Angarita's term expired. The disagreement over succession between the current and former presidents caused a split in the ruling establishment that, in turn, provided an opportunity for outsiders. As Betancourt stated, "Through the interstice of that open breach [between Medina Angarita and López Contreras] in the until-then solid front... we audaciously inserted our political movement" (Betancourt 1982, 327).[11] Ewell (1984) noted that the split between the two presidents left their supporters in confusion, and it left the presidents themselves seeking further support.

Medina's liberalizing reforms placated much of the opposition. Promises of future direct elections satisfied opposition leaders who, for the most part, would eventually form COPEI (in opposition to AD). Medina also negotiated with the more strident AD leaders in the selection of his successor while AD pressed for immediate direct elections. As an apparent compromise, Medina chose Diogenes Escalante, for many years the ambassador to Britain and then to the United States. Escalante was considered "neutral" and AD agreed to support his candidacy.[12]

Medina also organized his own political party, the PDV (*Partido Democrático Venezolano*) in 1943 (Ewell 1984, 76). The Communist Party was one of his tacit supporters (Hellinger 1991), and in return for their support, Medina removed the constitutional provision that prohibited the Communists from organizing (Martz 1966).[13] The PCV voiced its support for a widespread land reform and strongly supported a land reform law passed in September 1945 (Fuenmayor 1979). However, the Medina land reform was weak compared to later standards.[14] One problem was that the law called for payment for expropriated land in cash (Venezuela 1964, 67).

Medina's immediate plans fell through with the illness of his planned successor. Escalante was an elderly man and "his state of health left much to be desired." He suffered a stroke after his return to Venezuela, cutting short his candidacy (Fuenmayor 1979, 115–18, 123).[15] In his place, Medina picked Angel Biaggini. The selection angered AD leaders; Betancourt referred to him as a "straw man" that Medina would use to remain the real power behind the office (Betancourt 1982, 331). This encouraged AD to seek other means of achieving office.

AD collaborated with members of the Patriotic Military Union (*Unión Patriótica Militar*, UPM), a group of young military officers unhappy with the regime.[16] Levine (1973) states that the UPM members were uncertain of their own support in the military and needed AD's participation, it being the only national party at the time. This is supported by the declaration made by members of the military itself: "On the 18th of October, 1945, the national army acted against an order of things that the Nation thought corrupt, and the National Armed Forces then became an example of disinterest that was applauded by the people of Venezuela, when, not wanting power for itself, it relinquished it into the hands of the only party that at that time had opposed the regime."[17] That party was AD.

The extent of AD's involvement in the coup is unclear. What is apparent is that the AD at some point welcomed the invitation to attain power. As Betancourt said, "without our proposing it and without looking for it, our political action and the discontent over new military promotions flowed together toward meeting and pact" (Betancourt 1982). The leaders were impatient. It could be that they were frustrated with the slow process of concessions and did not believe that Medina would open up the system to free and fair popular elections. A similar promise to institute direct elections after the selection of López Contreras in 1936 had not been kept.

Another possibility is that AD leaders worried that Medina and Biaggini would expand suffrage on their own terms, while implementing land reform and thus exclude AD and cut into its support in the countryside. Medina had possibly been positioning for a more democratic regime; Biaggini had been Medina's Minister of Agriculture, had supported the land reform law and promised to pursue further land reform (Fuenmayor 1979, 209–15). Furthermore, upon accepting the nomination for president, Biaggini promised to reform the constitution in order to make election of the president direct and secret (in 1951). As it turned out, Medina was unable to attract sufficient support to create a moderate ruling coalition, while at the same time he caused division among the conservative backers of his regime (Myers 1973, 44).

The military coup of October 18, 1945 allowed AD to come to power. Although from their earliest days as political activists the AD founders apparently believed in the need for democratic government, AD leaders saw little hope of coming to power democratically unless the system was opened up. As it was, ironically, it was only through the help of dissatisfied members of the military that AD took control of the government. Rómulo Betancourt became interim president of Venezuela.

Acción Democrática: Outside the System

The leaders of AD had spent years seeking a more democratic Venezuela. Many of the future leaders of AD (as well as other parties) had been involved in the student protests of 1928 and the uprising after Gómez's death in 1935. Their experience was put to good use in building a base of future support. By the time of the *trienio*, AD was viewed as the only truly national party in Venezuela.

Opposition to the Gómez regime included more than just those who would eventually form the AD party. Gómez's heavy-handed rule "... denied status, wealth and power" to such groups as "lower middle class professionals, workers and peasants" (Myers 1973, 43). An example is Gómez's "attack" on a middle-class necessity: higher education. Betancourt lauded the actions of university students in 1918 who were "persecuted, dissolved, offended, dispossessed of a profession—because the barbarian had closed the university seven years before..." (Gómez 1982, 83).[18]

AD, formally legalized in 1941, was the direct descendent of the illegal PDN. The PDN itself was formed in 1936 by the unification of several organizations: ORVE (*Organización Venezolana*, Organization for Venezuela); PRP (*Partido Republicano Progresista*, Progressive Republican Party);[19] BND (*Bloque Nacional Democrática*, Democratic National Bloc); and FEV (*Federación de Estudiantes de Venezuela*, Federation of Venezuelan Students). The *Frente Obrero* and *Frente Nacional de Trabajadores* joined as well (Martz 1966, 34).

Leaders who shared early beginnings as opponents of the Gómez regime also formed the main parties that eventually opposed AD. Judith Ewell noted that the Generation of 1928, which emerged after the student revolt of that year, did not solely metamorphose into leaders of AD. Rather, they divided into different groups that "competed for the following which would ensure them the control of government" (Ewell 1984, 89).

The two main parties that were to oppose AD were COPEI and the URD. Both formed primarily in opposition to AD during the *trienio*. COPEI stemmed originally from a split in the FEV in which Catholic students, including Rafael Caldera, formed their own organization, UNE (*Unión Nacional Estudiantil*).[20] After various brief incarnations as Electoral Action (1938) and National Action (1942), COPEI was officially formed in 1946. The URD was created in 1945 (and was subsequently taken over by Jóvito Villalba, another member of the "Generation of 1928").[21] While the founders of these parties were also opponents of Gómez, they did not share many of the views of AD. The opposition parties differed in both their assessment of the troubles of the regime and appropriate strategy.

Many of those who would later become leaders in AD were at first attracted to more radical means of removing the dictator, Gómez, from power. Their analysis drew heavily from Marxism, and also led to their association with communists; this association later haunted leaders such as Betancourt.[22] In addition to organizing a week of student protests in 1928 that led to their expulsion from the country, the opponents of the regime made ill-fated attempts at direct invasion from exile before settling into a less adventurous approach. As Betancourt concluded, "[we are] convinced that the revolution is in Venezuela, in her masses, in the latent discontent, and, certainly, undeniably certain, in her multitudes; and not in those Garibaldian expeditions from the outside, that conclude in failure or in ridicule, which is more painful than the failures" (Gómez 1982, 345).[23] The exiles maintained close contacts with events in Venezuela and prepared for political action within the country.

This preliminary period (1928–1935) is what Martz (1966) called AD's period of "ideological inquiry." As suggested by their Marxist influences, Betancourt and other student leaders at first expected their greatest revolutionary support to come from workers. However, by 1931 Rómulo Betancourt and others had reached the conclusion that because the Venezuelan working and middle classes were too small for a sufficient basis of political support, the support of the peasantry would be critical (Hellinger 1991, 50). Mariano Picón Salas, a founder of ORVE and also exiled after 1928, wrote in 1933 that South America in general had not reached the proper historical stage for a revolution. "We cannot make isolated revolutions . . . we can only speak of an agrarian revolution in order to incorporate the masses who live at the margin of the nation" (Gómez 1982, 353).[24] Instead, as Betancourt later wrote, " . . . we proposed and organized a party with a broader base than that offered only by the proletariat . . . " (Betancourt 1982, 322).[25]

The evolution of AD strategy is evident in the published programs of the various political factions that preceded the formation of the AD party. An early predecessor of AD was an nebulous group formed by Rómulo Betancourt, Raúl Leoni, and others called ARDI (*Agrupación Revolucionaria de Izquierda*, Revolutionary Leftist Group); they issued the *Plan de Barranquilla* in 1931. The Plan pointed to the "discontent of the masses" and went on to state that "So far Venezuela has never had [a leader] . . . close to the masses, no politician identified with the necessities and ideals of the multitude" (Suárez Figueroa 1977, 101). Later AD themes are evident in the call not only for the removal of Gómez and the military from office, but also for guarantees of civil liberties, confiscation of Gómez's property for "use by the people," protection of the "producing classes," a massive literacy campaign, more control of foreign companies and capital in Venezuela, and a constituent assembly to reform the constitution.

Demands became more pointed as time went on. By 1936 the PRP (*Partido Republicano Progresista*) was calling for a government in which "sovereignty resides in the people": guarantees of civil liberties, universal suffrage for men and women over 18 years of age, proportional representation, and the creation of an impartial civil service. In addition to calling for the confiscation of property owned by Gómez's followers, they also called for restrictions on foreign investment, ownership, and trade in the oil industry; increased technical aid to agriculture; elimination of debts held by peasants; and the parceling out of *latifundios* to poor peasants. They also called for the protection of workers and indigenous peoples (Suárez Figueroa 1977, 134–5).

The PDN's program in 1936 was similar to that of the PRP: a call for universal suffrage, guarantees of civil liberties, proportional representation, and civil service reform. While not calling outright for the parceling of the *latifundio*, the PDN program called for legal size limits to *latifundios* and legislation that favored the breakup of large estates, as well as the distribution of Gómez's lands, a debt moratorium, and increased agricultural aid for peasants (e.g. provision of seeds, tools, credit, and irrigation). Furthermore, it called for a "radical struggle against illiteracy" (Suárez Figueroa 1977, 182–90).

López Contreras refused to legalize the PDN in 1937. This exacerbated tensions within the different opposition factions and led to the splintering of the opposition (Ewell 1984). A major opposition split occurred when a bloc of predominantly Catholic members followed Rafael Caldera, Víctor Giménez Landínez,[26] and others in the formation of the UNE. The two factions that resulted, *Acción Electoral* (Electoral Action) in 1938 and *Acción Nacional* (National Action) in 1942, were short-lived. In contrast to the previous organizations, their programs lack a specific political agenda other than attaining office. *Acción Electoral* essentially called for "effective elections" in the upcoming polls.

Acción Nacional offered more specifics. Its goals included a pledge to: "defend legitimate tradition," "support a concept of Social Justice that satisfies the demands of workers," promote national unity, and defend the Catholic church. The program also declared "a special concern for the improvement of agriculture and the peasant life." As part of its program, *Acción Nacional* advocated representative government, but did not concern itself with the actual form of such a government. Instead, the program declares, "the selection of honest and capable men, more than an election of theoretical systems, ... [is] the fundamental solution for the problem of government" (Suárez Figueroa 1977, vol. 2, 41–5). AN (*Acción Nacional*) did not have the same coherent program as the precursors to AD, who had already linked the establishment of a democratic regime to both universal suffrage and political support among the urban and rural "masses."

Meanwhile, the PDN continued a clandestine existence. In its public statements it presented a detailed analysis of the political and economic situation in Venezuela, plus a program of action.[27] The "enemies" of Venezuela, according to the PDN, were the continuation of Gomez's cronies in office, "medieval *latifundismo*," usurious banks, and foreign imperialism. The PDN program clearly spelled out the importance of the rural poor in the following excerpt:

> A peasantry with a tradition of independent social struggle does not exist in Venezuela. However, the peasantry has always joined all the armed revolts . . . to recover what is theirs. Given its nature as the most exploited Venezuelan sector, [the peasantry has been] submissive in the democratic revolution designed for its benefit, [and the peasantry] depends solely on the way in which our party undertakes its problems and on the efficacy with which it endeavors to organize them. Without the active and resolute collaboration of the peasantry the democratic transformation of our country will not be possible. (Suárez Figueroa 1977)

The PDN considered itself the party of the oppressed sectors of society, including workers, laborers, peasants, and "middle sectors." It also portrayed itself as the only party able to unify and represent the majority of Venezuelans, combat the enemies of the people, and solve the economic and social problems facing Venezuela. Furthermore, the PDN called itself "the only national party capable . . . of guiding the people in their struggle for the democratic and anti-imperialist revolution" (Suárez Figueroa 1977, 258–60). The party called for universal suffrage and the "liquidation of the *latifundio*" (Suárez Figueroa 1977, 267–9).

These themes emerged in Rómulo Gallegos's symbolic candidacy for the presidency in 1941. Gallegos did not expect to win the election; rather, he expected Medina to win the majority of congressional votes necessary. However, Gallegos took advantage of his opportunity to campaign around the country. His program consisted of a call for federalism and municipal autonomy; respect for individual rights; an intense literacy campaign; formation of political parties and exercise of suffrage; religious tolerance; and, in the economic sphere, encouragement of medium and small property, division of national lands, and limitations on foreign capital (Venezuela 1985, 85). He called for "fostering our wealth through an agrarian policy aimed at creating a peasant economy that ensures adequate parcels for all workers of the land" (Venezuela 1985, 17). These concerns formed the basis of AD's actions once it took office.

Suffrage During the *Trienio*

Upon achieving office, AD began securing the support of the "masses." The provisional government announced that its "immediate mission" was "to convoke general elections, so that through the system of direct, universal and secret suffrage, Venezuelans can elect their representatives, give themselves the Constitution that they desire, and choose the future president of the republic."[28] AD extended the franchise to all Venezuelan citizens over 18 years old, regardless of gender, literacy, or income.[29] AD also made balloting secret, and election of the president and Congress direct. These rights were written into the new Constitution of 1947 (Powell 1971, 67). As the Constitution said (Article 81), "All Venezuelans, men and women, more than eighteen years of age, not subject by a...sentence of civil interdiction or penal condemnation which carries in itself political disqualification, are electors" (Fitzgibbon 1948).

Furthermore, new citizens were encouraged to vote, and voting was made easy; voters simply chose between colored cards, which they placed in an envelope in the secrecy of the polling booth. Parties chose their own colors: AD was represented by white; COPEI by green; URD, tan; PCV, red (Fuenmayor 1980, 494).[30]

The new system also established proportional representation for the first time. This ensured the representation of minorities who had been shut out of elections in the years before the *trienio*. Thirteen political parties were legalized to participate in the elections (Martz 1966, 65). (Few of these parties actually received enough votes to gain seats.) However, AD did not support the direct election of governors. Fuenmayor (1981, 239) asserts that this is because Betancourt did not want COPEI to win the governorships of the states it was dominant in (principally Andean states). This was likely if direct, popular elections would have been held.[31]

Specifying the increase in voters after 1945 is problematic. So few people were allowed to vote in the indirect system (5 percent in 1941) that obviously many more would vote in a direct election with universal suffrage. However, the records are unreliable.[32] Participation was significant during the three-year period of AD rule, and the extension of suffrage to illiterates made an appreciable difference. The literacy rates in Venezuela at the time were low: in 1941, only 41.5 percent of the population over 15 years old was literate (Vanhanen 1975, 255). The mood as well was excited: "a general euphoria seized the whole population, . . . by the act of being able to vote in the broadest way known, since women, illiterates, and persons older than eighteen years participated" (Fuenmayor 1980, 489).

As table 4.1 indicates, 26 percent of the *total* population voted in 1947.[33] Fuenmayor (1980, 495) states that for the 1946 election, 1,752,000 were expected to register; 1,527,392, or 87 percent, actually registered. Out of *registered* voters, Margarita López Maya estimates that 84.6 percent voted in 1946 and 73.8 percent in 1947 (Molina 1989). This was above the typical rate of voter participation in other Latin American countries (at the time, less than 15 percent of the population voted in Colombia, and Chile; in Bolivia, that figure was less than 5 percent).

Less problematic is AD's position as the main beneficiary of the open political system. AD was clearly the majority party in Venezuela at the time, and easily out-polled COPEI and the URD. AD consistently polled at least 70 percent of the vote in elections between 1945 and 1948, while its nearest rival, COPEI, received no more than 22 percent. (See table 4.2.)

AD won over three-quarters of the vote and 86 percent of the seats in the Constituent Assembly (elected in 1946), and over 70 percent of the votes

Table 4.1   The Venezuelan Electorate, 1946–1948; 1958–1973[a]

Year	Population	Number Registered	% Total Population Registered	Voters	% Total Population Voting	% Registered Voting
1941[b]	3,851,000	—	—	192,550	5	—
1946	—	1,527,392	87	1,395,200	—	84.6
1947	4,500,000	—	—	1,183,764	26	73.8
1948	—	—	—	693,154	—	—
1958	6,785,000	2,913,801	43	2,772,053	40	93
1963	8,143,629	3,369,986	41	3,059,434	38	91
1968	9,686,484	4,134,928	43	3,901,687	40	94
1973	11,279,608	4,737,152	42	4,572,187	41	97

Notes
[a] 1958–1973 figures for presidential elections; less than 1% difference between turnout for presidential and legislative elections.
[b] Elections indirect.

Sources for 1946–1948: 1947 from Nohlen (1993, 668); Molina (1989); Fuenmayor (1980, 252, 254–5). *Sources for 1958–1973*: 1958 from Nohlen (1993, 660); 1963–1973 from Venezuela (1992, 835–6); *SALA* (1969, 179); Molina (1989, 15).

and 75 percent of the seats in the new Congress in 1947.[34] AD's Rómulo Gallegos won the presidential election of 1947 with 74 percent of the vote. Gallegos "began his presidential term on February 15, 1948, being the first chief executive to be elected by direct and popular vote in the history of Venezuela" (*HAR*, 1, no. 2; December 15, 1948). (See table 4.3.)

An important element of AD's electoral success was the vote of the rural poor. An estimated one-third of all of AD's votes during the *trienio* were from peasants (Powell 1969, 89). AD had expected peasant votes; this was the fruit of its efforts of the past decade to attract the support of the peasantry. Aggressive efforts at organization of the peasantry formed an important part of AD strategy because AD leaders did not want to lose peasant support to

Table 4.2   Share of Votes for Main Parties, 1945–1948,[a] in Percentages

Year	Type	URD	COPEI	AD	PCV
1946	CA	4	12	78	4[b]
1947	C	4	18	71	4
1947	P	—	22	74	3
1948	M	4	21	70	3

Notes
[a] Percentages are rounded off and may not add to 100%. The appendix includes a list of Venezuelan parties. Type of elections: CA, Constituent Assembly; C, Congressional; P, Presidential; M, Municipal.
[b] PCV and UPV.

Sources: Nohlen (1993, 667–75); Martz (1966, 75); Fuenmayor (1980, 496–7).

Table 4.3   Distribution of Seats in Chamber of Deputies, 1945–1948[a]

Year	Type	URD	COPEI	AD	PCV
1946	CA	2 (1%)	19 (12%)	137 (86%)	2 (1%)[b]
1947	C[c]	4 (4%)	16 (15%)	83 (75%)	3 (3%)

Notes
[a] Percentages are rounded off and may not add to 100%.
[b] PCV and UPV.
[c] Other parties: UFR received 3 (3%) and PLP 1 (1%). Both (plus PLT) ran in 1946 election but did not receive enough votes to obtain seats.

Sources: Nohlen (1993, 667–75); Martz (1966, 75); Fuenmayor (1980, 496–7).

other political parties, and organization facilitated the implementation of AD's planned land reform.

Competition and Rural Organization

AD's leaders capitalized on the expansion of suffrage and the support it had developed in the countryside to stay in power. Those opposing AD's rule and policies coalesced into the URD and COPEI, which joined in the competition for votes. As Betancourt later said in his 1959 inaugural address, "AD [and the other parties] were animated by the impulse that was generally conceived as the only . . . battlefield of a democratic party: the conquest of power by way of suffrage in order to put in place their own platform and their own personnel" (*El Nacional*, February 14, 1959). During the *trienio*, most of the competition from the URD and COPEI was in organizing and gaining the support of urban labor unions. AD was nearly without competition in rural areas (Powell 1971, 64).

The rural population had always been important to AD's political goals, and when in office AD encouraged organization of this population. The party already had an advantage over other parties in that the leaders had been building support in the countryside for almost a decade. AD helped to create the FCV (Venezuelan Peasant Federation) in 1947 and the Confederation of Venezuelan Workers or CTV (ICSPS 1968; Martz 1966). The number of peasant unions increased dramatically from 71 unions with 5,823 members in 1944 to 312 with 19,113 members in 1946. The numbers increased further to 515 unions and 43,000 members in 1948 (Powell 1971, 61, 79). The AD-created FCV was the umbrella group for most of the new unions.

The program of the FCV showed the strong links between the government and the organization. The FCV stated "Only the Nation . . . can mobilize the peasantry to create an agriculture without *latifundistas*" (Martz 1966, 275). Being organized made it more likely that the rural poor would participate in politics, and peasants organized with the help of AD activists and members of AD unions were more likely to support the AD at the polls. The AD worked hard to establish control over its affiliated unions, something that became even more apparent after redemocratization in 1958.

AD's success at organizing the rural population stands in contrast to the PCV. The PCV found "it [difficult] to mobilize the multitudes of rural workers, not only to defend the [Medina] land reform against its detractors, but, what was more important, to . . . organize the agrarian masses" (Fuenmayor 1980, 147). Part of the PCV's problem was its strict adherence to Soviet communist leadership. Hellinger (1991) argues, "The PCV had failed to develop a strategy that reconciled its loyalty to the Comintern with an effective strategy to compete with AD for leadership of the Venezuelan working class" (74).

Rural union organization was important to AD's land reform plan. As will be seen later, unions were the mechanism for distributing land; this strategy served to reinforce AD's political support among the peasantry. Organization of the rural poor meant organization of rural beneficiaries of AD policies, plus encouragement that these beneficiaries would return the favor at the polls.

Land Reform During the *Trienio*

Land reform was one of several policies that AD planned to implement, but it was one of the most important. AD's main base of support was in the countryside among the rural poor that it strove to organize. AD immediately started distributing land even before a new land reform law was officially passed. The government used decrees to seize some private lands and created the CVF (*Corporación Venezolana de Fomento*) to provide credit and other aid to peasants to increase agricultural production (Martz 1966, 276).

Most of the land distributed during the *trienio* was either public land or land that had been confiscated from officials in the former government (Hellinger 1991). The emphasis of the land reform law was first to use idle or public land, and then private lands (Fuenmayor 1981, 438). However, some farms were confiscated and distributed in this initial period (*HAR*, 2, no. 11).[35] Approximately 150,000 hectares were given to 75,000 beneficiaries (AID 1970a, 4).[36] On average, recipients also received 332 bolívars in credit (Powell 1969, 67). Most of the beneficiaries were union members and consequently, AD supporters (Powell 1971, 83; AID 1970a). The local leader of the peasant union was the one who decided who would get land (Powell 1969, 67). The control of the unions, and thus the beneficiaries, was clear.

AD ignored the Medina land reform of 1945 and a new land reform law was signed October 1948, the third anniversary of the coup (Martz 1966). Predictably, the new land reform was criticized by landowners for threatening their property rights, and by the communists as being too lax. The law exempted from expropriation lands that were cultivated rationally and directly. As one communist deputy, Jesús Faria, said, "I have come to the conclusion that [this reform] does not take as its fundamental condition the destruction of the *latifundio* in our country....We think that while in our country the *latifundio* is not destroyed, there is no guarantee of survival for democracy, because *latifundismo* not only appropriates the land, but also exerts a feudal control over rural workers, over the *campesinos* themselves"

(Fuenmayor 1981, 439). However, the land reform did call for payment in bonds (unlike the Medina law).

Little progress in land distribution was made after the law was signed, given that only a month later AD was ousted in another coup. However, since AD had begun distributing land upon taking power, it was able to make significant progress. AD's success indicates that the use of land reform as a means of improving political support worked. Fuenmayor thought it did: "In truth, with the granting of the vote to the most extensive popular sectors and with other measures benefiting the masses, [granting] the credits of 500 bolívars for peasants [alone] would have been sufficient to get the majority to give their vote to the partisans of Betancourt, in significant fashion" (Fuenmayor 1981, 337).

Politics and Land Reform Under the Dictatorship, 1948–1958

A military junta overthrew the AD government in November 1948. Part of AD's downfall came from alienating almost all major groups in the country. "The Church was repelled by the anticlericalism of educational reforms; landowners opposed agrarian reform; the business sector feared *adeco* radicalism; international oil interests fought government reforms; the military mistrusted the AD attitude toward the role of the armed forces; and opposition parties were harassed by the sectarian self-righteousness of the AD" (Martz and Baloyra 1976, 6). The same military officers that helped the party into office in 1945 removed AD from power.[37] Although not active participants in the event, COPEI, URD and PCV all opposed AD by this time and welcomed the coup.

The junta promised to reinstate democracy as soon as possible, but instead shut down participation by declaring martial law, dissolving the national, state, and municipal legislatures, outlawing AD, persecuting *adecos* and eventually, members of other parties. The government imprisoned, tortured, assassinated, and exiled many opponents during this period. The Central University was closed, the CTV (Confederation of Venezuelan Workers) was banned (most members were AD supporters), and the Constitution of 1947 was declared void (*HAR*, 2, no. 1–2).

Controlled elections for a new constituent assembly were held in 1952 and a new constitution was established (in which the military returned the voting age to 21 [Nohlen 1993, 656]). A presidential election also was held in 1952, but although the URD's Jóvito Villalba appeared to have won, the vote count was suspended and General Marcos Pérez Jiménez was declared president.[38] This marked the beginning of opposition to the regime on the part of AD's previous opponents, the URD and COPEI.

After the coup the military also reversed much of the land reform of the previous three years: expropriated land under government control reverted to its owners, and peasants were evicted from land they had recently acquired through the reforms. About 96 percent of the beneficiaries lost their land (King 1977, 149). The military did pass its own land legislation in 1949, but this law severely restricted the conditions for expropriation of land (Powell 1971, 91–3). Instead, the military concentrated mainly on colonization efforts (Wilkie 1974, 25) or directed its efforts at mechanization, building roads, housing, and irrigation, projects that entailed significant costs but benefited few (Carroll 1961, 190). The U.S. AID gives a modest figure of 1,500 families settled on land between the years 1950 and 1957 (AID 1970a, 4).

Persecution under the military regime led to increased opposition. Leaders of COPEI and the URD, who had supported the 1948 coup, began to oppose the dictatorship. Opposition to the regime led to cooperation between these parties and their former adversary, AD. This cooperation would shape political competition after the fall of the dictatorship.

Redemocratization: 1958

The Pérez Jiménez dictatorship ended in January 1958 in the face of united and almost universal opposition.[39] A provisional junta was formed, and all parties concerned formulated agreement on the transition to a democratic government through a series of pacts. Already in 1956 the four main parties, AD, COPEI, URD and PCV had agreed to overlook their own disagreements with each other and instead work together in toppling the Pérez Jiménez regime (Hillman 1994). Also, an initial Patriotic Junta (*Junta Patriótica*) had been formed in 1957 in which the AD, URD, COPEI, and Communist Party participated. Cooperation between the AD, COPEI, and URD was further cemented by the Pact of Punto Fijo, which the party leaders signed in October 1958 (the communists were excluded).[40] In the pact, the leaders agreed to recognize the result of the upcoming elections, no matter who won the presidency. They also agreed that the victor, regardless of party affiliation, would include representatives of all three parties in the new government. An interim government oversaw the holding of elections in December 1958.

Participation and Suffrage After 1958

The 1958 election was held under the resumed conditions of direct and universal suffrage, and universal suffrage was officially reinstated in the new 1961 Constitution. Again there were no literacy or property restrictions, and voting was secret: "All Venezuelans who have reached eighteen years of age and who are not subject to civil interdiction or political disqualifications are voters" (Article 111, Flanz 1971). As in most Latin American countries, candidates for office had to be able to read and write (Article 112).

Two main changes were made from the *trienio* system. The first was that presidential, congressional, and municipal elections were held simultaneously starting in 1958. The second was that voting became mandatory.

Daniel Levine suggests that simultaneous elections provided a "cooling off" period between elections (1973, 38). This was a contrast with the continuous electoral races of the *trienio*, in which a major election was held every year. Simultaneous elections have another effect: the tendency to increase voter participation (Molina 1989). When municipal elections were held separately from other elections starting in 1978, voter participation in those elections decreased substantially (Molina 1989).

Voting was made obligatory in 1958, and the requirement subsequently became part of the new constitution: "Voting is a right and a public function. Its exercise shall be compulsory, within the limits and conditions established by law" (Article 110). Those failing to vote were subject to fines and proof of registration and voting was necessary in order to do a variety of important activities, such as applying for public employment, entering a university, or getting a government contract (ICSPS 1968, 16). Molina (1989) points out that the mandatory vote was not enforced; however, he also notes that citizens assumed that the sanctions would be applied. In addition, subsequent Venezuelan surveys have found that the compulsory nature of the elections does have an effect. A survey conducted in 1973 found that 48.4 percent of respondents said they would not vote if it were not compulsory (Martz and Baloyra 1976).

Voting was also easy, especially for those who could not read. Ballots displayed only distinctive party colors and emblems, making voting a simple task of selecting one party ballot for president and one other party ballot for all other positions (ICSPS 1968, 43). Provisions were even made for the blind so that they could vote, by shaping ballot cards into geometric shapes (Myers 1971, 71–3). Until 1973, municipal elections were held simultaneously with national elections; so with one colored card voters chose the party that would represent them in all non-presidential elections: Chamber of

Deputies, Senate, State Legislative Assembly, and Municipal Council (Molina 1989).[41] Registration was easy and registration offices were open all day on weekdays, with extended hours on weekends and holidays in rural areas (ICSPS 1968, 42).[42]

The voting system obliged the voter to choose by party, not candidate. This greatly enhanced the influence of parties over individual candidates.[43] Voters were not able to choose individual candidates; they probably did not know who all the candidates running for a position were. Instead, they had to make their choice between parties.

Voter participation was high in Venezuela following the democratic transition. Political participation was actively encouraged (Levine 1988, 259). Table 4.1 gives the percentage of the *total* population voting. The percentages of *eligible* voters are higher. In 1963, 93.97 percent of an estimated 3,586,000 eligible voters were registered (Martz 1966, 393). Of those registered, 93 percent went to the polls in 1958, 91 percent in 1963. Molina (1989) points out that the rate declines to an estimated mean of 82.7 percent of the estimated eligible population from 1958 to 1988, rather than registered voters. This, he points out, is still a high rate of participation and is a rate that places Venezuela within the top 12 democracies.[44]

Initially, AD was the largest recipient of votes in newly redemocratized Venezuela. AD's Betancourt easily won the 1958 presidential election with 49 percent of the vote, beating Rafael Caldera (COPEI) and Admiral Wolfgang Larrazábel (supported by the URD and PCV).[45] (See table 4.4.)

However, AD's share of the vote was much lower than the 70 percent the party had received in the 1940s and the party did not return to the high vote levels of the *trienio* in either the presidential or congressional elections. Although AD won a majority of congressional seats in 1958, the party lost this majority in the 1963 contest. (See table 4.5.)

Rómulo Betancourt was inaugurated on February 14, 1959 and upheld his promise to form a cabinet that included members of all three parties. The Communist Party remained excluded from cooperation with the government. As Betancourt said in his inauguration speech, his government "would not seek the support of the Communist Party because the political philosophy of Communism does not serve the best interests of Venezuelan democracy" (*HAR*, 12, no. 2).

Cooperation and Competition

The pacted transition to democracy set up the cooperative nature of political competition after 1958. The new government faced many difficulties and

Table 4.4   Presidential Election Results, 1958–1978,[a] in Percentages

Year	AD	COPEI	URD	FDP	Others
1958	49	16	35[b]		
1963	32	20	19[c]	9	2 AD (Opp)
					16 IPFN
1968	28	29	22[d]	e	19 MEP
1973	49	37	3	f	5 MEP
					4 MAS
1978	43	47	.1	1	1 MEP
					5 MAS
					1 MIR

Notes
[a] Numbers do not total 100%—percentages rounded off and "Other" category includes only larger parties; appendix provides a list of parties.
[b] URD candidate supported by PCV (3% of vote) and MENI (1%).
[c] Includes support of PSV and MENI (together 1%).
[d] Includes FDP, MENI, and FND support.
[e] FDP supported URD candidate.
[f] FDP supported COPEI candidate.

Sources: Ruddle and Gillette (1972, 100); Nohlen (1993, 675–7); for 1978, SALA volume 20, table 3303, volume 34, table 3402.

Table 4.5   Election Results for Chamber of Deputies, 1958–1973,[a] in Percentages

Year	URD	COPEI	AD	PCV	Others
1958	27 (26)	15 (14)	50 (55)	6 (3)	
1963	17 (16)	21 (22)	33 (37)	—[c]	13 (12) IPFN
					10 (9) FDP
					3 (3) AD-OPP
					.7 (1) MENI
1968	9 (8)	24 (28)	26 (31)	3 (3)[d]	13 (12) MEP
					5 (5) FDP
					11 (10) CCN
1973	3 (3)	30 (32)	44 (51)[b]	1 (1)	5 (4) MEP
					5 (5) MAS
					1 (1) MIR
					4 (4) CCN

Notes
[a] Percentage of vote (percentage of seats).
[b] AD and PR.
[c] PCV banned.
[d] UPA, legal arm of PCV.

Sources: Nohlen (1993, 667–75); Martz (1966, 401); Venezuela (1992, 839).

threats (Guevara 1989), and guaranteeing the success of the new democratic endeavor in Venezuela was the primary concern of the regime. This meant that competition had to be relegated to second place within a cooperative framework in order to avoid a repeat of the coup of 1948. As Martz and Baloyra stated, AD was "badly seared by the results of the *trienio* experience [and] renounced its past narrow sectarianism" (1976, 7). The possibility of a coup was not abstract; several attempts were made during the early years to overthrow the government. Further challenges came from guerilla groups such as the MIR, which split away from AD in 1960, and the communists, who were banned from 1962 to 1969.[46] The precariousness of the situation was accentuated by an assassination attempt on the life of President Betancourt.[47]

Betancourt emphasized the lessons of history in his inaugural speech when he spoke of the recent cooperation between parties:

> Inter-party discord was reduced to a minimum and thus revealed that the leaders had learned the hard lesson that despotism gave all Venezuelans. Underground, in prison, in exile, or suffering a precarious liberty here at home, we understood that because of the open breach in... culture and civility, the way opened for the conspiracy of the 24th of November 1948... and that with good intentions some people supported the plot that brought down the legitimate government of... Rómulo Gallegos. (*El Nacional*, February 14, 1959)

Betancourt kept his preelection promise to form a coalition government, and COPEI and the URD cooperated. The first cabinet that Betancourt formed included members of AD, COPEI, and the URD, as well as independents. Members of COPEI and URD each received three cabinet posts, the AD two posts, and independents filled the rest. AD's incentive was to preclude removal from power as had occurred in 1948. The URD and COPEI also had incentives to cooperate, although the URD soon left the coalition government in 1960. COPEI continued its cooperation through the Betancourt administration.

COPEI's experience during the Pérez Jiménez dictatorship convinced its leaders to cooperate with AD. COPEI had cooperated with and supported Medina Angarita in the early 1940s, and initially cooperated with the *trienio* government. COPEI welcomed the coup that removed AD from power but after a brief period was also repressed by the Pérez Jiménez regime and went into opposition. COPEI's leaders recognized that a democratic regime provided the best guarantee of the political freedoms necessary for the party's continued existence.

COPEI benefited greatly from its cooperation with the AD government after 1958; its position within the AD government afforded opportunities to enhance its own electoral future. The three COPEI ministers occupied important posts: the ministries of Agriculture (Víctor Giménez Landínez), Development (Lorenzo Fernández), and Justice (Andrés Aguilar) (*El Nacional*, February 12, 1959; *HAR*, 12, no. 2). COPEI leader Rafael Caldera became vice president. Also, because of the collaborative effort, COPEI was included in the slates of elected officials for the labor unions (Herman 1980). Even when COPEI left the governing coalition in 1964, COPEI-dominated labor groups remained integrated in the labor movement (Powell 1969).[48] Eventually, COPEI narrowly won the 1968 presidential election (the party was helped by a factional split in AD before the election).[49]

The electoral situation following redemocratization remained uncertain, and the parties continued to compete for the support of previously excluded voters. Many voters (those who turned 18 between 1948 and 1958) were going to the polls for the first time. AD's leaders had been forced into exile, jailed, or killed after the military countercoup of 1948, and AD-affiliated organizations were outlawed and repressed. For example, esteemed member Andrés Eloy Blanco and labor organizer Valmore Rodríguez both died in exile. In addition, COPEI began to work with labor unions and peasant organizations after 1953, thus challenging AD's support in the countryside (Herman 1980, 44–5).[50] Thus, it was unknown at the time to what extent the political situation might have changed in the country as well as in the countryside since 1948.

The Land Reform Law of 1960

Land reform was high on the list of priorities of the new government. Not surprisingly, AD offered the same policies that it had offered during the *trienio* (albeit with more diplomacy in order to avoid another military coup). AD's traditional support was in the countryside, and land reform promised to solidify that support once again after ten years out of power. However, the AD-led government had to cooperate in order to guarantee the survival of democratic government.

The land reform law was written at the same time that the new constitution was being discussed. All Venezuelan parties participated in the formulation of both the constitution and the land reform law. While the 1947 Constitution served as the basis for the 1961 Constitution (*El Nacional*, February 24, 1959), the process of forming the constitution was much more cooperative than in 1947 (Kornblith 1991). Kornblith points out some major differences between the two periods.[51] In the first period, the 1947 debates were broadcast over the radio and the constitution was written by the entire Constituent Assembly, which also served as the ordinary legislature. This worsened tensions between the parties. By contrast, the bulk of the 1961 Constitution was written by a bicameral commission in which the major parties were represented. Many of the same individuals on the committee had been important participants during the *trienio*; their behavior was more moderated than it had been in the 1940s. While written and then revised with serious debate, the new constitution sparked little partisan tension. A similar spirit of cooperation prevailed in the drafting of the land reform law.[52]

Passed within a year of Betancourt's inauguration, the new law met with general approval.[53] The leaders of the three major parties spoke at the elaborate signing ceremony, and stressed the cooperative spirit of the legislation. Rafael Caldera stated:

> In spite of partisan discrepancies, the Law represents a grand convergence. It is an example of how opposite viewpoints can and must be harmonized, if one is to heed...the national interest. This is a time of truce; not in order to ready bows and sharpen arrows awaiting the signal for combat, but in order to build a real base without whose guarantee the quarrel between partisan interests would be foolish and chimerical. (Venezuela 1964, 49–50)

Like the new constitution, much of the preliminary writing of the law took place in a nonpartisan commission that President Betancourt appointed after his election (Venezuela 1960b).[54] The commission presented its bill to the legislature on July 23, 1959; it was approved in February 1960. The political parties had little trouble ensuring the support of members; individual votes of legislators are not even recorded in the transcripts of the proceedings (Venezuela 1960b).[55] Rómulo Betancourt signed the bill into law on March 5, 1960.

There was little outright opposition to the bill; although significant, the provisions of the land reform law were moderate enough to avoid provoking a reaction from landowners and the military. Members of the URD, as well as some members of AD, expressed concern over the law but nevertheless approved it; they expressed the belief that the law as written could lead to significant reform (Venezuela 1960b, 600–1). Amendments to the bill came primarily from Communist Party deputies and senators. AD and COPEI leaders fended off Communist proposals such as a limit on property ownership of 1,000 hectares for cultivated lands and 2,000–5,000 for grazing lands. According to AD peasant union leader Ramón Quijada, the peasant unions similarly had requested a limit on the size of property. The proposed amendments slowed down passage by extending the debate, but they did not alter the law (*El Nacional*, February 6, 1960; Venezuela 1960b, 725–72).[56] Quijada ultimately supported the law, stating that it "is an effective instrument" that would enable peasants to possess land and eliminate "the latifundist obstacle to progress" (Venezuela 1960b, 518–19).

The reform called for the expropriation of all land that did not comply with its social function.[57] The law specifically sought to expropriate lands in the following order of priority: (1) idle lands, including large properties and lands cultivated not by owners but by others (e.g. renters or sharecroppers); (2) lands that had been designated to be redistributed but had not yet been parceled out; (3) lands used for grazing (Article 27). The principal goal of the reform was to expropriate insufficiently utilized land, but the possibility remained that other lands, including efficiently exploited ones, could be expropriated if "no other recourse remained in order to solve an agrarian problem of evident gravity" (Article 27, in Venezuela 1960b, 939–40). As Agriculture Minister Giménez Landínez said, "whoever works the land and complies with the...social function...will have plenty of guarantees of work in Venezuela. Only in exceptional cases...when there is no other possibility...can one expropriate farms even when they comply with their social function" (*El Nacional*, February 24, 1960).

Ten percent of the national budget was earmarked for land reform in the first year (*El Nacional*, April 8, 1960, 1), and much of this money would be used to purchase land. Like other land reforms, the Venezuelan law called for landowners to be compensated in part in cash (up to $30,000) and the rest in bonds. The basis for compensation was the current market value (Carroll 1961).[58]

The land reform also used tax credits to provide incentives for farmers to use their land more productively, and called for the provision of credit, marketing, and other technical aid (Carroll 1961). The law was praised for going beyond simple land distribution into providing credit and marketing assistance, since "distribution of land by itself is not sufficient for increasing production and ensuring the well-being of peasants" (Salvador de la Plaza, *El Nacional*, February 17, 1960, 30).[59]

One criticism of the Venezuelan reform was that it relied too much on colonization efforts. As Ramón Quijada, argued, "Agrarian reform...is not the colonization of uncultivated lands in virgin forests. Its objective...is the division of the present *latifundista* property structure and its substitution by another" (*El Nacional*, February 19, 1960). However, the reform targeted public and private lands equally; between 1959 and 1963, a little over half of the lands affected by the reform were private lands (Venezuela 1964, 122–3).

While the land reform failed to significantly change landownership in Venezuela (Hellinger 1991, 105), the reform was a major attempt at redistributing land, and in the end, many rural inhabitants benefited. The reform was expected to provide land for 300,000 rural inhabitants in ten years, according to Agriculture Minister Giménez Landínez (*El Nacional*, February 20, 1960, 25), who called for 30,000 peasants to receive land in the first year (*El Nacional*, February 24, 1960, 29). Rural unions wanted faster results; Ramón Quijada called for the land reform to take place more quickly, within 4 years, with 87,500 families receiving land each year (*El Nacional*, February 19, 1960). Neither goal was accomplished, but the reform positively affected the lives of many beneficiaries.

During the first six months (between April and September 1960) the National Agrarian Institute granted over 13,000 titles and later claimed that 66,428 families had benefited from the reform between 1959 and 1964 (Venezuela 1964). By 1967, over 96,000 had become direct beneficiaries of the reform; this number equaled one-third of farm families who previously had either no land or less than 2 hectares (AID 1970a, 39). The U.S. AID report adds that, "this figure is rather large considering the period, the type of peaceful agrarian reform within the existing juridical norms, and the conditions of development of the process." A total of 117,286 families received titles to 3,898,302 hectares by 1969 (Wilkie 1974, 69, 72).

Reminiscent of the *trienio*, an important part of the 1960 land reform was rural unionization. Raúl Leoni, AD leader and future president, pointed out the importance of the rural poor and rural organization in his comments at the signing of the land reform law:

> This land reform will not be whisked away or impaired, because the Venezuelan peasant will [fulfill it] according to his own longing for justice. He can count on adequate means: a Government that is the direct result of popular will, a Peasant Confederation that, with its unions, associations, and leagues ... will maintain, from now on, a state of permanent vigilance ..., and democratic national parties, all promising ... concrete results. (Venezuela 1964, 48)

Competition for Rural Votes: Rural Organization in the 1960s

All Venezuelan parties recognized that the rural poor were an important source of political support. As a URD deputy noted, "for us the peasantry is no longer a quiet slave...the peasantry has become...a positive factor, not only in our economy, but in the whole life of the nation" (Venezuela 1960b, 600). Jóvito Villalba (URD) suggested the importance of peasantry when he had proclaimed that he was not going to adopt "a demagogic position in order to strive for the peasant vote for my party" (Venezuela 1964, 50). Such a stand may explain the eventual demise of the URD. Rafael Caldera, leader of COPEI, acknowledged the importance of the rural poor as he spoke of the progress of the land reform law through the Chamber of Deputies when he noted that the representatives had been "elected with the free vote of Venezuelans, among them...immense groups of peasants" (Venezuela 1960b, 611).

Initially, AD received the majority of support in rural areas after 1958. AD received almost 60 percent of the rural vote in 1958 compared to COPEI's 16 percent and the URD's 25 percent. AD's share of the rural vote subsequently decreased to 40 percent in 1963 while COPEI's increased to 23 percent (ICSPS 1968, 35 and 38). COPEI had consciously sought to increase its support among the rural population.

Repeating its *trienio* strategy, AD maintained its support in rural areas through revitalized unionization efforts. Union structures were resurrected after the end of the dictatorship's repression. The number of peasant unions increased dramatically from 130 unions with 4,586 members in 1958 to 782 unions and 39,090 members in 1959. The growth continued, with 3,476 unions and 171,299 members counted in 1965 (Powell 1971, 107). At first, AD's hegemony in the labor unions mirrored its support at the polls; AD or AD supporters controlled over 60 percent of the rural labor unions (Coppedge 1994a; Powell 1969). However, in time, COPEI challenged AD's lead in rural areas.

The most important union organization was the Peasant Federation of Venezuela (*Federación Campesina de Venezuela*, FCV), which AD had helped to create. The FCV was reinstated after redemocratization, and continued "under the hegemonic control of *Acción Democrática*," although slowly COPEI built up some support within the organization (Combellas Lares 1985).

Peasant organizations played a significant role in the land reform. Two members of the National Agrarian Institute's (IAN) five-member board of directors were to represent peasant organizations (Article 158). The members were to be named by the president, but in practice, this meant that they were named by the FCV. One FCV member, usually an AD member as well, occupied a position on the Board of Directors of the *Banco Agrícola y Pecuaria* (BAP), and the FCV was represented in the Ministry of Agriculture and the National Agrarian Coordinating Committee (Powell 1969, 86).

Furthermore, AD and the FCV together influenced the process of land redistribution. The land reform of 1960 relied on landless farmers initiating petitions for land that was not properly utilized ("not fulfilling its social responsibility") (Article 9). The petitioning process was designed to "stimulate the initiative that the peasantry, the principal beneficiary of the Land Reform, should have in the application of the law, and in the realization of the reform in general" (Senator Núñez Aristimuño, Venezuela 1960b, 728).[60]

According to the law's provisions, peasants had to: (1) name a committee (*Comité campesino provisional*); (2) each fill out an individual application; (3) have the committee fill out a collective application. This petition for land could be turned in directly to the agrarian bureau, or it could be submitted through the local peasant federation (Venezuela 1964, 53). Usually, the petitions were handled by the FCV; furthermore, the FCV often instigated the formation of the local committees that petitioned for land (Eckstein 1978, 36). It was to the FCV that the IAN directorate would turn in order to accelerate applications for land (*El Nacional*, April 6, 1960, 36). The petitions would be processed and approved by IAN, which would then purchase the land. The FCV oversaw distribution (*El Nacional*, April 30, 1960, 1).

Despite the formal procedures, in practice the local peasant union leader could decide who got land and the governmental assistance that went along with it, according to Powell (1969, 67). Almost all of the land that was redistributed was given to farmers who had been organized by the FCV (Eckstein 1978, 87). AD's close relationship with the FCV helped ensure that most land recipients would also be supporters of AD.

In the face of AD's dominant position in the government, the ability for COPEI to gain support among the peasantry appeared grim. However, COPEI exploited the opportunity presented by its presence in the government coalition to chip away at AD support. A cofounder of COPEI, Agricultural Minister Victor Giménez Landínez was a strong supporter of land reform (Herman 1980; Martz 1966) and personally presented the land reform bill to the legislature. While supporting the government's practices, Giménez Landínez also indirectly criticized the AD by suggesting that a land reform drafted by a solely COPEI government would have been "much more advanced" (*El Nacional*, February 24, 1960, 29).[61]

AD had the advantage of being able to use government resources to seek the support of targeted groups. COPEI did not have the same access to government largesse as the *adecos*, or AD members. Despite COPEI's high profile in the Agriculture Ministry, "Luis Herrera Campins complained the AD bypassed the COPEI minister of agriculture and worked through other institutions such as the *Instituto Agrario Nacional* (National Agrarian Institute, IAN)" and the BAP (Herman 1980, 56). These institutions were more favorable to AD; the IAN director was *adeco* Ildegar Pérez Segnini, a staunch supporter of land reform who had briefly been secretary of the ITIC (*Instituto Técnico de Inmigración y Colonización*, predecessor to IAN) in 1948 (*El Nacional*, February 17, 1960, 29).[62] Nevertheless, COPEI was able to get funds from governmental agencies, even from IAN and BAP, to finance projects; the party also used private funds when possible to support its own reform endeavors (Herman 1980).

When COPEI finally achieved control of the presidency, the party took its turn at "taking partisan advantage of... governmental programs and activities" (Herman 1980, 74). COPEI made political use of its peasant assistance programs: "First they would send technicians to work on a particular project; these were later followed by political activists, who asked the peasants to think carefully the next time they voted and reminded them of the improvements that had taken place under the COPEI government" (Herman 1980, 76).

COPEI also actively sought to win peasants to its own organizations. Despite COPEI's roots of support among the peasants of the Andean region, the party did not have significant rural support throughout the rest of the country. Supplying policies favorable to the rural poor fit in with COPEI's Christian Democratic ideology, which included concern for the plight of the rural poor, calls for equitable distribution of wealth, and modernization. However, the party initially had no plans to create a specific organization for *campesino* supporters of COPEI (Combellas Lares 1985). In time, COPEI challenged AD's superiority in organization in the countryside.

COPEI created a National Secretary for Agriculture in 1960 to coordinate its agrarian activities (Combellas Lares 1985). At first, COPEI incorporated its outreach to peasants through its worker organization, the FTC (*Frente de Trabajadores Copeyanos*), created in 1947 (Herman 1980); in 1965, a separate organization was created, the *Movimiento Agrario Socialcristiano*, or MASC (Combellas Lares 1985, 117; Herman 1980). Furthermore, while AD controlled the biggest peasant organization (the FCV), members of COPEI slowly infiltrated the regional and national management of the FCV. This process took time; the *copeyano* faction finally challenged *adeco* control in 1982 (Combellas Lares 1985, 118–19).[63]

Parties in opposition to AD cut into AD's political support through their own support for land reform. COPEI especially was able to take advantage of this situation by making inroads into AD's traditional support in the countryside. In the 1963 presidential campaign, COPEI lauded its own contribution to land reform, and focused its criticism of the AD government on charges of corruption and bureaucratic inefficiency in AD's administration of the reform (Martz 1966). COPEI complained that "AD was paternalistic and demagogic in manipulating the illiterate peasants" (Herman 1980). COPEI increased its share of votes in rural areas from 16 to 23 percent between 1958 and 1963, while AD's support declined from 59 to 40 percent (ICSPS 1968, 35, 38). COPEI's support for land reform was an effective way to compete for votes with the AD—and it paid off in 1968 when COPEI's Rafael Caldera narrowly beat AD's candidate, Gonzalo Barrios, in the presidential election (29 to AD's 28 percent). The margin of victory was so narrow that the announcement of the final vote count was delayed for a week while the ballots were counted (Gorvin 1989, 392). The COPEI government continued its support of land reform once it had won the presidency. The amount of land distributed during the early years of the Caldera administration compared favorably to amounts distributed under the previous AD governments (Wilkie 1974, 69, 72).

Conclusion

As occurred in Chile, land reform legislation was undertaken in Venezuela to attract support in the countryside. In both the mid-1940s and in 1960 land reforms were initiated at the same time as a sudden expansion in voters occurred. Both times, the same party, AD, championed land reform and the expansion of suffrage. AD had first turned to the rural poor as a potential source of support when laboring to overthrow the repressive Gómez regime. When the party took power in 1945 with the help of the military, it instituted both universal suffrage and a land reform. AD used the peasant organizations it had created and promoted to award land titles.

When AD came back into power through an election after the fall of Pérez Jiménez, the party once again sought to solidify its support among the rural poor. However, AD moderated its politics in order to avoid a repeat of the military coup of 1948. Its main contender, COPEI, took advantage of the cooperation between parties by seeking its own share of support from the rural poor. Eventually, COPEI evolved from paying vague attention to the rural poor in the 1940s to actively soliciting their support in the 1960s. The URD, which did not seek rural support, eventually declined.

As in Chile, the competition between strong, programmatic parties in Venezuela increased the attention paid to the rural poor. Party discipline made passage of land reform legislation easier, and after 1958 this discipline kept members in line when compromises had to be made to avoid jeopardizing the new democratic regime. Cohesive and efficient party institutionalization also enabled AD to effectively organize the rural poor, and the extremely simple voting procedure instituted by AD made it easier for the uneducated rural poor to show their support for the party.

Venezuelan politics changed dramatically in the 1990s with the election of Hugo Chávez in 1998 and the adoption of a new constitution in 1999. Dissatisfaction with the traditional parties' control of politics fueled support for Chávez's "revolution." Nevertheless, the Venezuelan case illustrates the importance of institutionalized parties in ensuring the representation of the rural poor. In contrast, the next case study examines the negative effect a system of weak parties can have on the representation of the rural poor.

CHAPTER 5

Brazil: The Land Reform that Wasn't[1]

Introduction

I n contrast to the countries heretofore examined, significant land reform did not occur in Brazil despite promises by most governments since the mid-twentieth century. As expected, however, the timing of land reform proposals coincided with proposed or enacted expansions of suffrage. This chapter examines two periods of expansion of suffrage and land reform. During the early 1960s, President João Goulart attempted both the extension of suffrage to illiterates and land reform. Upon redemocratization in 1985, President José Sarney decreed the extension of suffrage to illiterates and a new land reform plan. Further legislation followed in the Constitution of 1988. The land reform attempts did not succeed: the military coup of 1964 ended reform in the 1960s, Sarney's ambitious plan faltered, and the 1988 Constitution deferred significant reform.

The Brazilian case demonstrates that the expansion of suffrage is a necessary, but insufficient, condition for significant land reform in democratic countries. Politicians recognized the demand for reform, and believed that it could attract votes. However, politicians did not follow through on pledges of land reform; nor could the newly enfranchised rural poor punish representatives for ignoring their campaign promises. Basic features of the Brazilian electoral system including open-list PR and negligible party discipline diminish accountability of politicians to the electorate. Citizens, particularly poor, rural voters, cannot effectively evaluate candidates based on broad policy agendas. Instead, politicians forsake party programs and seek support through more concrete benefits: through the pork barrel.

Neither significant land reform nor meaningful incorporation of the rural poor occurred.

After a brief discussion of land reform in Brazil, this chapter explains the features of the Brazilian political system that ultimately reduced the potential of the rural poor as a new source of political support. A description of expanding suffrage and attempts at land reform in the 1960s and 1980s follows. The chapter concentrates on the Northeast, the region of Brazil most likely to be affected by the expansion of suffrage to illiterates, and the 1986 elections, the first major elections held after the end of the military period and illiterate suffrage.[2] These elections also determined who would write the 1988 Constitution.

Land Reform in Brazil

The same underlying pressures for reform found in other Latin American countries also existed in Brazil. Notoriously maldistributed land and protests by landless and land-poor peasants confirmed demand. Substantial demand for land reform existed in Brazil in both the 1960s and 1980s. Brazil of the 1960s was mostly rural; only 28 percent of the population lived in cities of 20,000 or more. After nearly three decades of migration to the cities, the proportion of city dwellers increased to 62 percent of the population in 1990 (see table 2.2). Some regions remained more rural than others. In the Southeast, home of São Paulo and Rio de Janeiro, only 12 percent of the population was rural, while the South and Center-West regions more closely matched the national average at 32 percent and 23 percent, respectively. However, one-half of the population of the Northeast (50 percent) and North (48 percent) lived in rural areas in 1988 (IBGE 1992, 207).

Based on 1985 IBGE (*Instituto Brasileiro de Geografia e Estatística*) figures, landownership was highly concentrated: .8 percent of landowners owned 44 percent of Brazilian land, and 53 percent of farms occupied only 2.7 percent of the land. Almost 40 percent of landholdings were under 5 hectares, over one-half under 10 hectares (IBGE 1985). In 1985, nearly 2,642,000 rural producers had either no land or little land; this totaled 15 percent of Brazilians employed in agriculture (ranging from 27 percent in the Northeast to 6 percent in the Center-West).[3] Depending on the region, a large percentage of the population still earned their living through agriculture: 27 percent in the Northeast; 16 percent in the North; 19 percent in the South; 6 percent in the Center-West; but only 1 percent in the Southeast.

Organizations representing the rural poor, such as the Peasant Leagues (*Ligas camponeses*) in the 1950s and 1960s and the Landless Workers'

Movement (*Movimento dos Trabalhadores Rurais Sem Terra*, MST) after the 1980s actively pursued land reform. However, organizations in the 1960s were primarily created by outside leaders and had little grassroots impetus (Hewitt 1969); once this leadership withdrew in the wake of military repression, peasant organization faded. A sizeable grassroots movement arose in the 1980s that achieved limited local success, primarily through land occupations: 80 in 1989, 49 in 1990, 77 in 1991, and 81 in 1992 (CPT 1993). Land occupations took place throughout Brazil. For example, in 1992, 13 occupations occurred in the North, 18 in the Northeast, 13 in the Southeast, 23 in the South, and 14 in the Center-West. The operations involved up to 16,000 families (CPT 1993). The MST continues to be the most effective advocate for land reform and leads land occupations and protests to call attention to the land reform issue.[4]

Violent conflicts over land occurred throughout the 1980s and into the 1990s, including the period of the transition to democracy, expansion of suffrage, and attempted land reform. The CPT (*Comissão Pastoral da Terra*, Pastoral Land Commission) documented 637 rural conflicts in 1985, 634 in 1986, and 582 in 1987. The conflicts in 1987 involved 667,177 people, and included 109 assassinations, 143 death threats, and 37 assassination attempts (CPT 1988).[5] Land conflicts continued in the 1990s: 500 in 1989, 401 in 1990, 383 in 1991, and 361 in 1992 (CPT 1993).

Table 5.1 below provides regional information on land conflicts. While conflicts took place in all parts of Brazil, the Northeast experienced the greatest number of conflicts each year.

Demand failed to spark a significant nationwide or regional land reform. Nor did international pressure prompt the passage of a land reform law in democratic Brazil. Although Brazil was the biggest beneficiary of Alliance for Progress–era aid, the United States opposed President Goulart and his reform

Table 5.1 Rural Conflicts in Brazil, 1985–1988

	1985	*1986*	*1987*	*1988*
North	121	117	139	141
Northeast	245	250	197	199
Southeast	99	112	103	78
South	61	55	41	88
Center-West	111	100	102	115
Brazil	637	634	582	621

Source: ABRA (*Associação Brasileira de Reforma Agrária*).

attempts and cut off aid to his government. In turn, Goulart and members of his administration criticized the Alliance for Progress; Paulo de Tarso, the Brazilian education minister, considered the Alliance "an instrument to prolong the privileges of minorities that persist in putting their own interests above the national interest... the Charter of Punta del Este should consider our true sentiment regarding social revolution; on the contrary, it has not had any benefit for our peoples" (*Corrêio da Manhã*, August 7, 1963).

The military government, swiftly recognized by the United States after the 1964 coup, soon passed its own land reform law. However, this law did not lead to significant reform despite nearly $2.5 billion in economic assistance from the United States between 1961 and 1969 (see table 2.3). The United States, while supporting reform, could not control Brazilian policy, nor is it clear that it wanted to. The priority of the United States was stopping communist expansion in Latin America; social reforms held secondary importance.

According to many analysts, the traditional landowning elite blocked land expropriation and distribution, despite the apparent need for reform in Brazil. The elite supported the military coup that halted reform attempts in the early 1960s.[6] Similarly, Sarney's proposed land reform in 1985 and land reform legislation in the 1988 Constitution were thwarted, it is argued, by large landowners and their allies, including the military that continued to exercise influence during the transition to democracy (Gomes da Silva 1989 and 1987; Graziano da Silva 1986; Ferreira and Teixeira 1988; Veiga 1990).

Conservative interests were well represented in the national legislature and executive, while grassroots efforts at land reform did not translate into sufficient representation at the national level. According to Maria Conceição d'Incao (1990), those who would most benefit from land reform were not directly involved in the discussion of reform, though they had been involved indirectly from the beginning. In Brazil, it seems, the legislature became the "graveyard" that Huntington described. However, what is not clear is why Brazil is different from other cases, such as Chile and Venezuela. Landowners in these countries also opposed land reform, but they did not succeed in stalling reforms. Differences in the electoral systems of these countries help explain the disparity in outcomes.

Political Competition: Expansion of Suffrage and the Search for Political Support

Brazilian politicians promised land reforms at the same time as the extension of the franchise to illiterates, but significant land reform did not occur.

Politicians did not follow through on their promises: they did not have to, despite the increase in poor, illiterate, rural voters. Politicians could not and did not believe they would be punished for abandoning pledges of reform.

To hold representatives accountable, the electorate must assess their performance. For this, voters need information. Information on elected officials often proves costly to obtain, and requires more than cursory attention to news sources. The average voter, even in affluent nations, does not know each candidate's background or voting record. However, parties provide a guide for the electorate; party affiliation supplies general information for the voter who does not even need to know the candidate's name to make a reasonable choice at the polls. At the least, voters can punish an incumbent party by voting for opposition candidates.

Identification with parties, or party ID, performs an important role in countries like Brazil, where the electorate lacks education and access to information. Few Brazilians read newspapers: 36 percent of registered voters in 1988 and only 20 percent in the Northeast read a paper weekly (IBGE 1988a).[7] Much of the population was unable to read at all: in 1980, 32 percent of the total population and 53 percent of the rural population was illiterate (IBGE 1992, 358).[8] Most Brazilians obtained information via television and radio. Seventy-seven percent of Brazilian voters watched television, and 75 percent listened to the radio; in the Northeast, only 58 percent watched television and 68 percent listened to the radio weekly (IBGE 1988a). In the more economically prosperous regions of Brazil, televisions and radios were common. In the Southeast, 89 percent owned a radio and 84 percent owned a television set; in the Northeast, 67 percent of the population owned a radio, and only 44 percent a television (IBGE 1988b).[9]

Party ID helps voters overcome the difficulties of obtaining information about candidates. Voters need only a basic understanding of which party has been in office and a general determination of whether they approve or disapprove of what that party accomplished. In Brazil, however, party ID provides little assistance at the polls, because of characteristics of the electoral system that weaken parties and complicate the voting system.

Weak Brazilian Parties

Brazilian parties are notoriously weak or "inchoate." Many analysts attribute this weakness to features of the Brazilian electoral system, such as Brazil's brand of open-list PR, privileges for small parties, and preferences for incumbents (e.g. Mainwaring 1991; Ames 1996; Hagopian 1996). The factors that contribute to weak parties also decrease the ability of voters to use party ID as a guide. Weak parties do not present a coherent party program, in part because they cannot compel their members to adhere to the party line. Brazilian politicians frequently switch parties, further decreasing the value of party ID. According to Scott Mainwaring, "Mechanisms of accountability are vitiated because the electorate cannot keep track of the performances of all of the deputies and senators, nor can it infer much about their performances and positions on the basis of party affiliation" (Mainwaring 1991, 40).

Open-list PR tends to weaken parties and foster individualistic campaigns. The number of votes each party receives determines the number of seats the party wins, but the candidates' rank on the list depends on votes for each individual. Elections resemble a combined party primary and general election, and pit party members against each other as well as against members of other parties.

The open-list system decreases party control over members. In closed-list PR systems, where party leaders determine the order of candidates, party members who provoke the displeasure of the party can be placed low on the party list, eliminating all chance of election. Voters have no choice of individual candidate. In contrast, in open-list PR, voters choose among all names on the party list. The system reduces parties' ability to reward and punish, and therefore control, party members. At the same time, the system encourages candidates to differentiate themselves from other members of the same party because they compete for votes (Geddes and Ribeiro 1992).

Open-list PR alone does not explain the anomalies of the Brazilian system; Chile also uses the system but has stronger, more disciplined parties. However, other features of the Brazilian system magnify its centrifugal tendencies. Brazilian parties wield little control over their own membership. The Brazilian practice of *candidato nato* guaranteed that an incumbent could run again no matter which party he or she joined (Mainwaring 1991).[10] Members of Congress switched parties without penalty after redemocratization; nearly 40 percent of deputies elected in 1986 switched parties by 1990 (Ames 1995, 331). Before the 1986 election, many politicians from the former promilitary party switched to the opposition PMDB to avoid association with the military regime.[11] This would have important consequences for the fate of land reform in the 1988 Constitution.

Brazilian electoral rules also encourage a large number of parties and reduce incentives for politicians to abandon small parties. To register, a party need only receive 3 percent of the vote in a national election (Geddes and Ribeiro 1992). Brazil's high district magnitude (discussed later) increases the chances of small parties winning seats (Mainwaring 1995, 375). Free television time for campaign advertisements is divided among parties; politicians in smaller parties have fewer candidates with whom to share their time

(Geddes and Ribeiro 1992). Leaders of small parties (with at least six seats) also receive the privileges of larger parties: free use of telephones, mail services, an official car, extra time to speak in Congress, and the ability to nominate candidates for committees (*Latin American Regional Reports: Brazil*, November 29, 1990, 2). This contributes to a large number of Brazilian parties; nearly 20 parties won seats in the 1990 election.

Lacking mechanisms for disciplining and regulating their membership, Brazilian parties only weakly control members on the campaign trail and in the legislature. Weak parties cannot present a clear and coherent platform or make credible promises of reform. With so many parties, low discipline, and frequent party switching, party ID provides little information for voters; consequently, 62–76 percent of registered voters surveyed base their decision to vote on the candidate rather than party (IBGE 1988a).[12]

Campaigns in Brazil

The above-mentioned practices contribute to personalistic election campaigns. Parties do not control candidates, and candidates cannot rely on party ID for help in getting elected. One of hundreds seeking office, a politician must distinguish himself or herself from all other candidates, but is unlikely to be rewarded or punished at the polls for broad, redistributive policies.

Barry Ames emphasizes the importance of Brazilian electoral districts. Although politicians seek election in a large multimember district (the state), they typically do not solicit state-wide support. Instead, they raise support in smaller regions within the state: electoral strongholds, or *redutos eleitorais* (Ames 1995). Politicians can win office by parlaying local office into a national career, or by making deals with leaders in the targeted areas. Since campaign laws allow federal deputies to finance state races, federal deputies can also form alliances with state candidates to increase local support (Ames 1996).

With a specific geographical region of support to please and few limits imposed by parties, individual politicians have an incentive to provide particularistic goods, rather than to promote broad policies such as land reform. They will not benefit if the rural poor in other areas receive land; even if their party received credit for providing land reform, benefits to the party as a whole will not necessarily help their own election. As a group, the rural poor in their own district is unlikely to be able to reward or punish them because of the complicated electoral system and absence of party ID.

Instead, Brazilian politicians focus on the provision of benefits specifically targeted for their areas of support: pork and patronage. Building roads and clinics in a *reduto*, or bestowing jobs and construction contracts, reward the local areas that support the candidate and the big donors who help him or her win office. This support, based on personal provision of goods, reinforces the weakness of party ID; politicians retain support regardless of party affiliation.

Furthermore, politicians tend to leave the federal legislature to run for state and local executive office (mayor or governor), or to bureaucratic posts. These are positions that offer opportunities to dispense benefits to political supporters: jobs, contracts, and public works. Only 36 percent of the members of the Chamber of Deputies were reelected in 1986 (*O Estado de São Paulo*, December 3, 1986, 2), and a little less than 40 percent in 1990 (*Latin American Regional Report: Brazil*, November 29, 1990, 2). As seen later in the discussion of the 1986 election, most of those elected went to the Chamber from other elected office (governor, state deputy, mayor) or a position in the state bureaucracy.

Local support for candidates is exemplified in the region where the enfranchisement of the rural poor could matter most: the Northeast, home to the greatest proportion of illiteracy and poverty. The Northeast is also known for the politics of the "*coronéis*" or colonels. According to Martins (1981), "*coronelismo* is characterized by rigid control by political bosses over the electorate's votes, constituting '*currais eleitorais*' ['electoral corrals'] and producing the so-called '*voto de cabresto*' ['halter vote']. That is, the elector and his vote are under the tutelage of the *coronéis*, who dispose of them as if their own" (46). The *coronel* directed dependents how to vote, and used other kinds of fraud, such as the use of illiterates (before it was legal) and the dead (never legal) as voters (Love 1970).

The world of the "old colonels" has changed from the time when they were the undisputed lords of their own fiefs. However, methods of controlling the vote have evolved and continued under "new colonels" (Palhares 1985). Political power still equals "economic power, a guarantee of employment, one's own survival" (*O Estado de São Paulo*, November 9, 1986). Citizens trade their votes for concrete goods, from health care to money. According to José de Souza Martins, people in rural areas vote for politicians who give them stuff, for example, a job, a pair of shoes, or a place in school.[13] "The *cabo eleitoral* [electoral corporal] sells, in the political market, the votes of his clients. The price obtained includes the expenses of transporting the electorate (to register and to vote), the costs of medical consultations, operations, dental work and the most sundry aid, given to the voters and relatives (to pay for light bills, water, rent, eyeglasses, dentures, milk and other foods, etc.)" (Paiva 1985, 264). Among other gimmicks, candidates in the

Northeast handed out straw mattresses to the poorest voters in 1986 (*Jornal do Brasil*, November 4, 1986, 2).

In summary, the Brazilian electoral system decreases accountability to the electorate and fosters individualistic campaigns that focus on personalistic support through pork-barrel policies. Instead of policies that broadly aid less privileged members of society, representatives engage in selective distribution of benefits to political supporters. However, given the demand for land reform and the numbers of potential illiterate voters, politicians have used the promise of land reform at times to improve their political support.

Proposed Reforms in the 1960s

President Jânio Quadros's unexpected resignation on August 24, 1961, prompted the succession of his controversial vice president, João Goulart.[14] On an official trip to China when Quadros resigned, Goulart returned and assumed the presidency on September 7 under an arrangement making Brazil a temporary parliamentary system (Figueiredo 1987). He spent much of 1962 fighting to regain full presidential powers and seeking political support.[15]

Goulart faced opposition from the military and conservatives, but adding to his troubles, he was challenged as well from the left of his party, the Brazilian Labor Party (*Partido Trabalhista Brasileiro*, PTB). Challengers included his brother-in-law, Leonel Brizola. Goulart's "Basic Reforms" campaign sought to increase his political support. Two main goals of the reform package were the expansion of suffrage and land reform.[16]

Goulart called for extending the right to vote to illiterates. Voter participation had been rising; the number of voters more than doubled between 1945 and 1962. The increase followed the removal of the property requirement in the Constitution of 1946; voting also became obligatory. However, literacy requirements still barred a large percentage of the population from voting.[17] At the time, at least 40 percent of the Brazilian population was illiterate (ECLAC 1985, 125); up to 90 percent of the rural population was illiterate (Cehelsky 1979). Opposition by the rural elite to Goulart's proposal indicated their concern that the enfranchisement of illiterates threatened their influence (Love 1970) (see table 5.2).

Other reforms made the participation of illiterates and poor literates alike more meaningful. Although the act of voting had been officially secret since 1932, the lack of a single national ballot allowed undue influence by parties and local political bosses. An official ballot was introduced in 1955 for

Table 5.2   The Brazilian Electorate, 1945–1962 and 1978–1989

Year	Registered Voters	Voters	Population Voting (%)	Registered Population Voting (%)
1945	7,499,670	6,122,864	12	82
1955	15,243,246	9,097,014	16	60
1960	15,543,332	12,586,354	18	81
1962	18,528,847	14,747,221	20	80
1978	46,030,464	37,629,180	33	82
1982	58,871,378	48,466,898	38	83
1986	69,166,810	65,708,469	50	95
1989	82,074,718	70,260,701	48	87

Sources: IBGE (1989, 1992, 1993); Nohlen (1993, 99); Paiva (1985).

presidential and vice presidential elections (Law 2.582, August 20, 1955). The UDN (*União Democrática Nacional*, National Democratic Union) supported the law but PSD (*Partido Social Democrático*, Social Democratic Party) support was divided; many feared that a single ballot would reduce their rural votes. *Pessedistas* (PSD members) supported the measure with the condition that parties themselves could distribute the new official ballot (thus reducing the law's effectiveness), and that the ballot's use be restricted to majoritarian elections (Paiva 1985).

A single ballot for all other majoritarian elections (e.g. governor, vice governor, senator, mayor) was mandated in 1956 (Law 2.982, November 30, 1956). Not until 1962 was a single national ballot used for all elections, including proportional elections (Law 4.109, July 27, 1962). This consolidated the voting process and made rural fraud and intimidation more difficult. As Paiva (1985, 259) stated, "The single official ballot adopted in 1962 established a new advance in the electoral legislation of the country, since it favored the choice of the voter and his/her freedom, reinforcing, alongside the private voting booth, the secret vote."[18] The official ballots were provided at the polls, but voters could also get ballots either from party members, or bring their own ballots (ICSPS 1962).

As seen in table 5.2, the number of registered voters increased by 3 million, and votes increased by over 2 million between 1960 and 1962. The rise in voter participation coincided with an increase in the PTB's legislative representation. The PTB remained a minority party in the Chamber, but rose from 66 seats, or 20 percent, in 1958, to 116 seats, or 28 percent, after the 1962 congressional elections. The PTB apparently gained from

Table 5.3   Distribution of Seats in Chamber of Deputies, 1954–1962, in Percentages

Year	PTB	UDN	PSD	PSB	PSP	PTN	PR
1954	17	23	35	1	10	2	6
1958	20	22	35	5	8	2	7
1962	28	22	29	.1	5	5	5

Note: The appendix includes a list of Brazilian parties.
Source: Nohlen (1993, 116–24).

increasing participation, but conservative parties still held veto power in the legislature over Goulart's policies (see table 5.3).

Organization and Reform in the 1960s
Widely seen as an opportunistic politician, Goulart used the working-class unions to further his political ambitions (Skidmore 1967). He reached out to the rural poor upon legalization of rural unions in March 1963. This was a "take-off" year for rural organization in Brazil (Morães 1970). The Rural Worker Law established the right of rural workers to organize and provided other social welfare rights.[19] Goulart's government formed CONTAG (*Confederação Nacional dos Trabalhadores na Agricultura*, National Confederation of Agricultural Laborers).[20] The number of recognized rural worker unions exploded, increasing from 12 (unrecognized) unions between 1951 and 1960, to 1,052 between 1961 and 1970 (IBGE 1993, 2-251).

The Goulart administration also unified and supported rural union by creating SUPRA (*Superintendência de Política Agrária*) in October 1962. SUPRA was meant to achieve a variety of rural policy goals such as designating land for expropriation, supplying rural health care, and stimulating rural unionization (Welch 1995). It became a major force in the formation of unions and redistribution of land. Support included VW buses and guides on how to organize rural unions, and copies of the Rural Worker Law (Welch 1995). SUPRA also sought to register new voters: "... the Goulart administration wanted to use unions to register independent voters to help erode the influence of *coronelismo*, the patronage system that traditionally locked political power in the hands of the conservative planter and merchant class" (Welch 1995, 179).

Rural organizations provided alternatives for the rural poor, who were influenced by the *cabo eleitoral* because registration and voting still required documents such as a birth certificate, transportation, and ballots that could be provided by party workers and employers. "Through the unions, workers were becoming acquainted with and demanding their rights, received assistance, and felt protected in the presence of proprietors-employers. Consequently, an alternative situation arose, favorable to a '*voto contra*' the colonel, rich man, or traditional political boss" (Paiva 1985, 260).

Goulart concurrently proposed land reform. Goulart formally proposed a constitutional amendment to allow payment for expropriated property in bonds, rather than cash, in his March 1963 address to Congress (Figueiredo 1987). As he later said, "Land reform with prior payment for the unproductive *latifúndio* at once and in cash, is not land reform. It is a land transaction that interests only the *latifundiário*, [and is] radically opposed to the interests of the Brazilian people" (*Corrêio da Manhã*, March 14, 1964). Goulart's own land reform proposal depended on the passage of the constitutional amendment.

Other attempted land reforms had failed. Feder (1971) counted "forty-five major bills on land reform" that had reached the legislature between 1947 and 1962, including executive decrees and other measures. Cehelsky (1979) counted 12 major agrarian reform bills proposed in the 1960s (nine before the coup of 1964). President Quadros had established a "Special Commission for Agrarian Reform" in May 1961 headed by the conservative Milton Campos of the UDN. This commission eventually issued a report recommending land reform.

Meanwhile, violence increased in the countryside, with the Peasant Leagues continuing to organize and gain notoriety in the Northeast.[21] Competition over rural organization was fierce in Pernambuco, where the Leagues, Catholic Church, communists, state Governor Miguel Arraes and President Goulart all sought to attract members to their own organizations (Hewitt 1969). In addition, Brizola, Goulart's brother-in-law and rival, promoted rural unionization and land invasions in their home state of Rio Grande do Sul. Candidates who favored agrarian reform also won election as governors and legislators (Morães 1970).

A land reform bill sponsored by Senator Milton Campos passed the Senate in December 1962, but met defeat in the Chamber of Deputies in August 1963. Goulart's own land reform bill, presented to the Chamber of Deputies in March 1963, depended on the passage of his constitutional amendment. A constitutional amendment required a two-thirds majority, or a majority vote in favor for two years in a row, which Goulart's amendment did not receive. The amendment was rejected in October, primarily by the opposition UDN and PSD.[22]

At a political rally on March 13, 1964, Goulart called for revision of the constitution, which "is antiquated and no longer serves the longings of the people and the development of the nation" (*Corrêio da Manhã*, March 14, 1964, 5). He decreed a land reform (Decree Law 53.7000) in which underused land within six miles (ten kilometers) of "federal highways, railways, dams, irrigation or drainage projects" would be expropriated (Figueiredo 1987, 164).[23] A mild reform law, Goulart himself said that the " . . . decree is not a land reform" because the constitutional amendment allowing compensation in bonds had not passed. Goulart expected to eventually achieve "real" land reform. At the same time, he extended the right to vote to illiterates and enlisted servicemen by decree (Skidmore 1967).

Goulart's mass rallies, calls for land reform, and apparent circumvention of an obstructionist Congress led to the hardening of public, party, and especially military, opinion against him.[24] His handling of the naval mutiny of March 1964 proved the final straw that unified military opinion against him and precipitated the coup of 1964 (Stepan 1971).

Land Reform and Political Participation During the Military Regime

Ironically, a land reform similar to the "radical" reform that Goulart proposed and that contributed to his downfall was passed within months of the coup by the military regime that unseated him. President Humberto Castelo Branco, the new military leader, pushed through the *Estatuto da Terra* (Land Law), the strongest land reform law (on paper) in Brazilian history.[25] Constitutional Amendment No. 10, proposed in May 1964 and passed in November 1964, allowed payment for expropriated land in bonds. In 1969, the military further changed the law to allow the immediate possession of expropriated property instead of waiting for appeals by the land's owners, as had been the practice.[26]

However, the military did not use this legislation to expropriate and redistribute private property, focusing its efforts instead at colonization. Military governments planned to encourage utilization of the vast areas available in regions such as the Amazon. Overall agricultural policy remained confined to the goals of increased agricultural productivity and national security.[27]

The military government outlawed popular organizations, persecuted, jailed, and exiled politicians and activists, and suspended politicians' political rights for up to ten years. However, the Brazilian military did not dispense with electoral practices. Instead, in 1965 the military banned the existing Brazilian parties and created two official parties: ARENA

(*Aliança Renovadora Nacional*, National Renovating Alliance), the official pro-military party; and the MDB (*Movimento Democrático Brasileiro*, Brazilian Democratic Movement), the official opposition party. The legislature remained open for all but a couple of years throughout the dictatorship, and elections continued (Skidmore 1988). Presidential elections nominally took place indirectly through an electoral college, but in practice presidents were selected by a small group of military leaders.

Beginning in 1974, the military began a "slow road to democratization" (Skidmore 1989). Proscriptions on parties were removed in 1979 (in an attempt to divide the opposition). Most members of ARENA joined the PDS (*Partido Democrático Social*, Democratic Social Party), the new pro-military party, while the MDB transformed itself into the PMDB (*Partido do Movimento Democrático Brasileiro*, Party of the Brazilian Democratic Movement). Finally, the PMDB opposition candidate, Tancredo Neves, won the indirect 1984 presidential election by exploiting dissension over the military's choice for executive, Paulo Maluf. The military's selection of Maluf as its candidate caused part of the PDS to split from the party and create the PFL (*Partido da Frente Liberal*, Party of the Liberal Front). In August 1984, the PMDB and the PFL formed the Democratic Alliance (*Aliança Democrática*), which backed Neves's bid for president. The electoral college chose Neves in January 1985.[28]

Suffrage Expansion and Land Reform Proposals of the 1980s

In one of the ironies of the Brazilian transition, Tancredo Neves fell ill and died before taking office. His vice president and new leader of the country was a former leader of the military-backed party, José Sarney.[29] Land reform continued to command attention after redemocratization in 1985. The agreement between the PMDB and the PFL when forming the Democratic Alliance included land reform (Graziano da Silva 1986). President-elect Tancredo Neves had promised reform, and after Neves's death José Sarney proposed land reform as well. At the same time, restrictions on political participation were lifted.

Literacy in the 1980s

Literacy restrictions on voting were removed in July 1985.[30] Sixty-eight percent of the Brazilian population was literate in 1980 (IBGE 1992, 358), meaning that changing the election law would change the size and composition of the Brazilian electorate and would have a greater effect where literacy rates were lowest: in rural areas (47 percent literate) rather than urban areas

(78 percent literate) (IBGE 1992, 358). Literacy rates also varied widely between regions. Over one-half of the population of the North and Northeast were *illiterate* in 1980, compared to 22 percent in the Southeast, 21 percent in the South, and 33 percent in the Central-West region. In 1981, 61 percent of the rural population in the Northeast was illiterate, compared to 34 percent of the Southeast, 21 percent of the South, and 39 percent of the Central-West (IBGE 1989 and 1992). Therefore, removing the literacy requirement affected a large portion of the population throughout Brazil, with the greatest effect in the North and Northeast.

Less educated and less affluent rural voters are less likely to register to vote, let alone go to the polls. Eighty-seven percent of eligible rural voters registered in 1988 (IBGE 1988a, 26). Illiterates were less likely to register to vote, but over two-thirds of citizens with less than one year of instruction and thus apparently illiterate registered to vote. Registration increased with a small amount of education: with more than one but less than three years of education, only 9 percent failed to register (IBGE 1988a, 24). In the Northeast in general, registration increased from 11 to 29 percent over those registered in 1982.[31]

Voter Participation

Increasing participation followed the removal of the literacy restriction. The number of registered voters in Brazil increased by 10 million between 1982 and 1986; the number of those actually going to the polls increased by 17 million. The percentage of the population that voted increased from 33 to 50 percent. Only 5 percent of registered voters abstained in the 1986 election. However, participation subsequently decreased; in part, this may be because illiterates' vote was made voluntary in the 1988 Constitution,[32] making their participation in elections less likely and indicating disinterest in developing the rural poor as a source of political support. While compulsory voting does not guarantee full compliance with the law, a survey in São Paulo in 1987 found that 31 percent of those questioned would not vote if it were not obligatory.[33]

These figures suggest that the change in the suffrage law would lead to a shift in the composition of the electorate in favor of the rural poor who would, in turn, favor policies like land reform. The over-representation in the legislature of the poorer, rural North and Northeastern states would accentuate the shift. Although a majority of the population of Brazil lives in the Southeast and South, the North and Northeast command a disproportionate share of seats in the legislature. While in 1982 the North and Northeast had less than one-half of the country's voters, the regions occupied 56 percent of the Senate and over 40 percent of the Chamber of Deputies (Wesson and Fleischer 1983, 80).[34] The relative overrepresentation increased as a result of the 1988 Constitution (Geddes and Ribeiro 1992, 655)

Sarney's Land Reform: The PNRA

President-elect Tancredo Neves had pledged to fulfill promises of land reform, and indicated his resolve by appointing well-known advocates Nelson Ribeiro as Agricultural Minister and José Gomes da Silva as president of INCRA (*Instituto Nacional de Colonização e Reforma Agrária*, National Institute of Colonization and Agrarian Reform). José Sarney was a less likely candidate to conduct a land reform; a Conservative landowning Northeasterner, he had served as president of the pro-military PDS from 1979 to 1984. However, Sarney surprised the country by announcing his own land reform.

At the fourth Congress meeting of CONTAG in May 1985, President Sarney proposed an extensive National Plan for Land Reform (*I° Plano Nacional de Reforma Agrária*, PNRA).[35] The PNRA envisioned benefiting over 7 million rural workers in the next 15 years (D'Incao 1990). At the same time, Sarney submitted a bill to Congress that included the extension of suffrage to illiterates and the change to direct elections.[36] The Communist Parties, the PCdoB (*Partido Comunista do Brasil*) and PCB (*Partido Comunista Brasileiro*), were also legalized (Baaklini 1992). Sarney found himself in a position like that of Goulart over 20 years earlier: a president from a minority party who unexpectedly became president. Although a conservative politician, he proposed land reform and the expansion of suffrage to broaden his chances of political survival.

The PNRA did not result in significant land reform. Proposed and essentially written by the "progressive" technocrats in the Ministry of Agrarian Reform and Development (*Ministério da Reforma e do Desenvolvimento Agrário*, MIRAD) and INCRA (Graziano da Silva 1986),[37] the PNRA's main support came from the National Campaign for Agrarian Reform (*Campanha nacional pela reforma agrária*, CNRA). The CNRA included CONTAG, parts of the Catholic Church such as the National Confederation of Bishops (*Confederação Nacional dos Bispos*, CNBB) and the CPT (Pastoral Commission on Land), as well as the ABRA (*Associação Brasileira de Reforma Agrária*), the Indianist Missionary Council (*Conselho Indigenista Missionário*, CIMI), and IBASE (*Instituto Brasileiro de Análises Sociais e Econômicas*).[38]

A swift response to the strongly pro-reform plan ensued. Landowner associations, including the SRB (*Sociedade Rural Brasileira*), the CNA (*Confederação Nacional da Agricultura*)[39] and the OCB (*Organização das*

Cooperativas do Brasil), protested the absence of landowner representation in the formulation of the plan; they organized their own Land Reform Congress (*Congresso Brasileiro de Reforma Agrária*) in June 1985 to lobby against the PNRA and promote their own vision of agricultural development and reform (Baltar 1990; D'Incao 1990).

Rewritten 12 times between June and October (D'Incao 1990), the PNRA became law on October 10, 1985 (Decree Number 91.766). Landowner associations and parts of the military became involved in the revision of the original plan (Veiga 1990). Among the changes were the prohibition of expropriation of *latifúndios* solely on the basis of size, and the removal of specific designations of priority areas targeted for land reform. The revision of the PNRA led to the almost immediate resignation of both Nelson Ribeiro and José Gomes da Silva.

The PNRA proposed settling 1,400,000 families on 43,090,000 hectares between 1985 and 1989. However, including land obtained prior to March 1985, only 515 settlement projects encompassing 4,537,983 hectares, with the capacity for 89,950 families were settled in that time (Brazil 1990, 50).[40] This represented 11 percent of the goal, and only .3 percent of the rural population of Brazil. Sarney's home state of Maranhão ranked high among those in which land was expropriated, and had 10 percent of all landless workers who received land (*Jornal do Brasil*, February 19, 1990, 3). Critics claimed that the land that was expropriated by executive decree was done so as a favor to the owners, who stood to gain from its compensation.

It is not surprising that President Sarney proposed a significant land reform proposal at the same time he advocated changes in the electoral system. The inclusion of illiterates into the electorate represented a substantial change in the composition of the electorate; millions of poor rural voters could participate in elections. The issue of importance to this segment of the population was land reform, and this preference was expressed through protests and rural violence, as well as through technocrats favorable to land reform in the government (the MIRAD and INCRA). However, neither Sarney nor the political parties followed through on the promise of reform.

The 1986 Election

The 1986 elections illustrate many of the issues raised in this study. The first major elections after the extension of suffrage and the end of military rule, the 1986 elections also determined who would write the new Brazilian constitution. Candidates supported land reform on a rhetorical level, but later withheld support in the Constituent Assembly. Party ID provided little information for voters; politicians switched parties, and many ex-military supporters joined the ranks of the main opposition party. While not incumbent deputies, most of the 1986 winners were long-time politicians who cemented their support through deals with local leaders. Again, this section focuses on the Northeast, the region most likely to be affected by changes in suffrage.

Complicated Ballots

In addition to eliminating party ID's usefulness, Brazilian electoral rules contributed to a complex voting procedure that further subverted accountability. A huge number of candidates and a difficult ballot impeded voters from effectively using their vote to reward and punish politicians.

The Brazilian voter faced a long list of candidates in 1986. Brazilian states serve as multimember districts; the number of members ranges from 8 to 70 federal deputies (Ames 1995), and from 12 to 84 state deputies (Mainwaring 1995). In combination with the large district magnitude, parties can field one and one-half as many candidates for each opening (Mainwaring 1991). With upwards of a dozen parties competing in an election, the number of candidates for federal deputy can range from 150 in smaller districts to over 1,000 in São Paulo. This results in a complicated system, particularly for illiterates, although the law stipulates that the Brazilian ballot should take into account the needs of voters who do not read or write (*Visão*, October 22, 1986).[41]

Illiterates participated in a major election for the first time in 1986, the first general elections since the end of the military regime.[42] Voters chose governors, senators, federal deputies, and state deputies. Candidates for majoritarian offices (governor and senator) were listed on the ballot, but candidates for proportional offices (federal and state deputies) were not (the ballot could not list all the names). Voters marked an "X" next to one candidate for governor and two candidates for senator, but had to write out the name or number of their chosen candidate for federal and state deputy. Voters could consult separate lists (also provided in newspapers) to make their choice. Alternatively, voters could choose one of the parties listed on the ballot by marking an "X" in the box next to the party's initials. All of this was to be accomplished in one minute (*O Estado de São Paulo*, "Jornal do Eleitor," November 14, 1986). Voting booth attendants (*mesários*) were not allowed to help voters with their selection. The vote for any of the ballot sections was annulled if the voter picked more than one candidate for governor, more than two for senator, marked an "X" outside of a box, or marked more than one party label.

The high number of blank and null votes cast in 1986 suggests the difficulty of the ballot (*O Estado de São Paulo*, November 25, 1986). Blank and null votes for the Chamber of Deputies rose from 15 percent in 1982 to 42 percent in 1986 (Moisés 1993); they reached particularly significant proportions in areas of the Northeast. Around 50 percent of votes were blank or null in Pernambuco (*Jornal do Brasil*, November 22, 1986); in some parts of the state, such as the Agreste, only 15 percent of the votes for state deputy were *valid*. In Piauí, blank and null votes topped 40 percent; in Alagoas, the blank votes could have elected five of the 27 state deputies (*Veja*, November 26, 1986). The most likely segment of the population to cast invalid votes were less informed, less educated voters, thus reducing the impact of the enfranchisement of the rural poor.

The difficult ballot provided the opportunity for the kinds of manipulation feared by those who had long opposed giving illiterates the right to vote: that local political patrons would dictate electoral choices, thus benefiting traditional and conservative politicians, such as those in the PDS and the PFL, over more leftist and urban-based parties such as the PT (*Partido dos Trabalhadores*, Workers' Party). As a waiter at a restaurant in Rio Grande do Norte said:

> This year, that illiterates are going to vote, we will get even more votes for the PDS and the PFL. I'm going to vote for João Faustino [PDS-PFL candidate] for governor because my wife got a job [emprego de servente] in the Centro Administrativo de Pau dos Ferros and already they promised to fit her in as a teacher next year... The ballot is complicated and the illiterate is like a blind person. He doesn't see the name or the number of the candidate. He's going to need help. I fill out a model, with my candidates, for him to take in his pocket and copy when he votes. This isn't prohibited. (*Jornal do Brasil*, November 4, 1986, 2)

Faustino lost the election for governor, but the PFL and the PDS together won the majority of the seats for federal deputy and senator, and the delegation voted against land reform (6 against, 4 in favor, 1 absent).[43] Anecdotal evidence indicates that many illiterates relied on others' help to vote, although "[f]urnishing sample ballots or prepared ballots for voters is an electoral crime" according to the electoral tribunal TRE (*O Estado de São Paulo*, November 9, 1986, 16).

Parties and the 1986 Campaign
Riding the wave of opposition to the military regime, the PMDB won all but one of the governorships in the country and half of all seats in the Chamber

of Deputies (see table 5.4). However, many of those elected under the PMDB label had switched to the PMDB from the pro-military ARENA or its successor, the PDS, in a successful strategy for reelection. Former ARENA or PDS politicians were still joining the PMDB as late as April of 1986. According to David Fleischer, "the extinct ARENA party 'won' the elections, that is, a plurality of the New Republic's newly elected deputies and senators were once members of ARENA" (Hagopian 1990, 161).

Fleischer's observation is borne out in the elections in the Northeast: the PMDB won one-half of the deputy seats (49.7 percent), the PFL 40 percent and the PDS 7 percent. Nearly 35 percent of all of the elected deputies had previously held office as members of the ARENA, and nearly one-half had served under either the ARENA or the PDS. Of the senators elected in 1986, 55 percent had been in ARENA.

In the PMDB itself, nearly 31 percent of its deputies and 55 percent of its senators elected in the Northeast were former ARENA politicians. Five of the nine PMDB candidates for governor had, "in some way or another, served the military government" (*O Estado de São Paulo*, November 9, 1986, 21). The winning PMDB gubernatorial candidate in Paraíba, Tarcísio

Table 5.4 Distribution of Seats in Chamber of Deputies, 1986–1994,[a] in Percentages

Party	1986	1990	1994
PMDB	55	21	22
PSDB	—	7	12
PFL	23	18	18
PDS	7	8	10[b]
PDC	1	4	[b]
PTB	3	7	5
PL	1	3	1
PDT	5	9	6
PT	3	7	11
PCdoB	1	1	2
PCB	1	.6	[c]

Notes
[a] Does not include smallest parties.
[b] PDS combined with PDC in 1993 to form PPR.
[c] PCB became PPS in 1992, and won 2 seats, or .5%.

Sources: *Folha de São Paulo* (January 19, 1987, B-8); *Latin American Regional Reports: Brazil* (November 29, 1990, 2; October 27, 1994, 6).

Burity, had served as governor, appointed by the military in 1978. Many, though not all, of these former-ARENA *peemedebistas* opposed land reform in committees and the Constituent Assembly votes, like Jorge Vianna (PMDB-BA) on the Land Reform Subcommittee.

Party ID provided a meager guide for voters. Instead, voters cast their ballots for well-known politicians with extensive ties to the local elite. Lula's São Paulo campaign speech in 1982 still applied:

> We tried to show that conventional politics, the politics of money, the politics of privilege, wouldn't work any more in this state or in Brazil ... that the PDS and the PMDB are flour out of the same sack and that they won't change the situation of the Brazilian working class. This is even more visible when we go to the interior of São Paulo and see the landowner candidate from the PDS running against the landowner candidate from the PMDB. In both parties, yesterday one was in the PMDB and today he's in ARENA, and yesterday one was in ARENA and today he's in the PMDB, changing parties with no respect for the people who elected them. (quoted in Keck 1992, 147–8)[44]

"Incumbents" in the Northeast

In the Northeast, only 46 percent of the deputies and 22 percent of the senators were reelected to the same office in 1986 (see table 5.5); but this simple reelection figure masks the continuation of long-time politicians. Less than 10 percent of senators and deputies had no discernable experience. Almost 70 percent of the deputies elected from the Northeast were serving in some elected office (federal or state deputies, governor, mayor or councilman) when elected. Of the senators, 67 percent were either reelected senator, had just served as federal deputy, or had just served as governor of the state.

The remaining 21 percent of senators and deputies had either held elective office previously, held important government posts, or were related to established politicians. For example, the five new senators (excluding the one elected senator with no previous electoral experience) were as follows: Teotônio Vilela Filho (AL), the son and apparent heir of a recently deceased senator; Cid Sabóia de Carvalho (CE), a radio personality who had been elected substitute state deputy in 1982; Mauro Benevides (CE), a man who had had a long electoral career but immediately prior to the 1986 election was president of the Banco do Nordeste do Brasil;[45] Chagas Rodrigues, who had been federal deputy and governor in the 1950s and 1960s and had been the most-voted-for candidate for senator in Piauí in 1982, but lost the election because his party did not receive enough votes; and Lavoisier Maia,

Table 5.5 Previous Experience of Northeastern Deputies and Senators

	Deputies (#)	Deputies (%)	Senators (#)	Senators (%)	Both (%)
Incumbent[a] (Reelected to Same Office)	70	46	4	22	
Incumbent (Any Office)	105	70	12	67	69
Non-Incumbent with Experience[b]	33	21	5	28	23
No Experience[c]	13	9	1	6	8

Notes

[a] Incumbent senators were federal deputies, senators, or state governors when elected in 1986.

[b] The text describes the five senators. Deputies had previously held office or a government position, had a relative in office, or had made previous attempts at election.

[c] Not elected previously, nor a relative of other elected officials.

Sources: Brasil (1987/1988); Martins Rodrigues (1987); DIAP (1988); *Veja, Jornal do Brasil, O Estado de São Paulo*, various dates.

who had previously been governor of Rio Grande do Norte and whose family had dominated politics in the state for more than a decade.

Long-time politicians who were connected with the military government were able to stay in office by adapting to different party circumstances while maintaining their control of local politics.[46]

Local Politics in the Northeast

The 1986 campaigns in the Northeast continued to rely on local support cemented through the provision of patronage and pork. Political careers were likely to hinge on political, and especially family, connections. As Airton Soares, PMDB, said, "The *caipira* [hick] electorate prevailed in this election. Those who had the support of mayor, councilman, municipal manager [*diretório municipal*] did well" (*Jornal do Brasil*, November 30, 1986, 16).

For example, in Rio Grande do Norte, four political families "together control[led] six parties and present[ed] eighteen candidates for everything except governor" (*Jornal do Brasil*, November 1, 1986, 8). The Maia family had controlled the governorship for over a decade, and had distributed its share of pork. The Maia family's career in state politics began when the military appointed Tarcísio Maia governor in 1975. He in turn named his cousin Lavoisier Maia his successor, who in due course picked Tarcísio's son, José Agripino Maia, who in turn named Lavoisier's wife as Secretary of Employment and Social Welfare in Rio Grande do Norte. The Maia family benefited from federal ties and claimed to have provided "1,022 new class-rooms, 30,000 public housing units, 1,438 wells, 1,300 km paved roads . . . But the most important is that it was the Maias, in the last decade, that distributed the municipal, state and federal public jobs" (*Jornal do Brasil*, November 1, 1986, 8).

The other main family in Rio Grande do Norte, the Alves, joined with the other major families (the Rosado and Muniz families) against the Maias.[47] The Maia candidate for governor lost to the Alves-supported PMDB candidate, Geraldo Melo—but the Maias were still able to elect three direct relatives, José Agripino Maia and cousin Lavoisier Maia as senators, and the latter's wife, Wilma Maia, as federal deputy.[48] Wilma Maia had lost her bid for mayor of the capital in 1985, but became the most-voted-for candidate of her party in the 1986 election, "helping the PDS-PFL coalition elect three more deputies." The Alves were able to elect two deputies and the Rosados one. The reason given for the PMDB's partial success in Rio Grande do Norte was that "various electoral '*currais*' of the PFL-PDS coali-tion in the interior voted for the opposition, which was not expected even by the PMDB" (*Jornal do Brasil*, November 22, 1986, 4).

In Pernambuco, Miguel Arraes reclaimed the governorship from which the military had ejected him after the 1964 coup. Arraes's immense popular-ity ensured his success in the race; but he supplemented the PMDB's usual support in urban areas by seeking the support of local leaders in the interior. Hundreds of city council members (*vereadores*) and at least 10 mayors left the PFL in order to support Arraes's campaign (*Jornal do Brasil*, September 8, 1986). In the end, the interior of Pernambuco voted for Arraes, ostensibly "the biggest surprise of the 1986 elections" (*Jornal do Brasil*, November 18, 1986, 7). His campaign also helped the PMDB's senators get elected, includ-ing one with a long history in ARENA.

Despite Arraes's victory at the top of state politics, only one candidate from a leftist party, the PCB, won a seat as federal deputy, and the PMDB won just over one-half of the 25 federal seats (13 to the 11 won by the PFL) (*Jornal do Brasil*, November 22, 1986). The PMDB did not obtain a majority in the state legislature, and only four of the 22 state deputies were considered leftist; the majority had belonged to pro-military parties and only recently joined the PMDB (*Jornal do Brasil*, November 28, 1986). Neither the PCB nor the PCdoB elected anyone to the state assembly (*Jornal do Brasil*, November 25, 1986). The most-voted-for deputy in Pernambuco was a PFL candidate who was ex-mayor of Recife and previously had been the state Secretary of Employment and Social Action (*Jornal do Brasil*, November 17, 1986). "Some urban candidates nicknamed the delegation the '*bancada de caipira*,' referring to the upcountry origin of the majority of the deputies" (*Jornal do Brasil*, November 28, 1986, 8).[49]

Arraes's main opponent and the PFL gubernatorial candidate in Pernambuco, José Múcio Monteiro Filho, attempted to attract support away from the popular Arraes by declaring himself in favor of land reform. He went so far as to sign a pact, the *Pacto da Galiléia*, with sugar mill owners in which they promised to donate 10 percent of their lands for redistribution if Múcio won the governor's race. Francisco Julião, leader of the Peasant Leagues of the 1950s and 1960s, helped to orchestrate the pact, supported Múcio for governor, and was himself supported by Múcio in Julião's bid for senator on the PDT ticket (*Veja*, October 1 and 29, 1986; *Visão*, September 10, 1986; *O Estado de São Paulo*, October 19, 1986).

Campaign coalitions formed that underscore the lack of cohesive, programmatic party distinctions. In Piauí, the PMDB aligned with the PDS. In Sergipe, the PCB and the PCdoB supported the PFL's winning candidate (*Veja*, November 26, 1986).[50] In another example from Pará (in the North), a PDS candidate, "an assertively intransigent anticommunist" supported the election of the PMDB candidate for governor, and in turn was being supported by the PCB, the PCdoB, as well as the UDR (*Visão*, September 10, 1986).

In Bahia, the PMDB candidate, Waldir Pires, "opened a fan of alliances considered 'strange' by the more traditional *peemedebistas*" (*O Estado de São Paulo*, November 16, 1986, 35) in order to hand Antônio Carlos Magalhães his first electoral defeat in 20 years. The cost was that "the PMDB absorbed so many *Malufistas* [it was] incapable of a single position on, for example, agrarian reform" (*O Estado de São Paulo*, December 28, 1986, 4). It was seen as necessary, according to the successful PMDB candidate, Waldir Pires, "because we needed to defeat the last piece of dictatorship still existing in Brazil" (*O Estado de São Paulo*, December 28, 1986, 4). Even so, Magalhães's son, Luís Eduardo Magalhães, won a seat as federal deputy and joined the 43 percent of the Bahian delegation that voted against land reform in the Constituent Assembly.[51]

Left-wing candidates did not fare well in the Northeast. Even the communists who won election were well-known incumbents. While the PCB and the PCdoB elected few federal deputies in the country (*Jornal do Brasil*, November 28, 1986, 9), over half of those elected were elected from the Northeast. Three deputies from the PCdoB (one-half of the six elected in the country as a whole) and two from the PCB were elected from the Northeast.

Rather than campaign under their own party labels, most of the communist parties also sought shelter under the PMDB umbrella. Most of their success occurred in Bahia, where two PCdoB candidates and one PCB candidate won their seats. The other PCdoB candidate, Eduardo Bonfim, won in Alagoas, and the other successful PCB candidate, Roberto Freire, won on the PCB label in Pernambuco. All of these candidates were incumbents with long careers in politics.

The PT campaigned in the Northeast, but with limited results: no PT candidates won a federal deputy seat, but one was elected state deputy in Bahia, and two each in Ceará and Sergipe. The elected deputy in Bahia and the next-highest PT vote-getter, who ended up as a substitute, were two former priests, who "acknowledged that a good part of the electorate became inclined toward them due to the work that they continue to develop in the ecclesiastic communities." One was a labor lawyer of significant prestige in the state, and the other a teacher "dedicated principally to the education of children of rural workers" (*Jornal do Brasil,* November 28, 1986, 7).

In Ceará, the PT candidate for governor, Haroldo Coelho, was "shipwrecked" with less than 5 percent of the vote (*Jornal do Brasil,* November 17, 1986). The PT mayor of the capital, Fortaleza, predicted that the PT would win four of the 22 seats in the federal Chamber of Deputies; even more realistic observers predicted that the party would win two seats (*O Estado de São Paulo,* October 19, 1986). They won no seats. Their plans to use election-day propaganda and enticements ("*boca de urna*"), as they had done in Fortaleza in 1985, were frustrated by a ban on *boca de urna* (*O Estado de São Paulo,* November 16, 1986, 37). Likewise, the PT ran candidates for governor in Rio Grande do Norte and Sergipe "only to keep its place and divulge the party's platform," according to the PT's candidate for governor in Sergipe (*O Estado de São Paulo,* October 26, 1986).

Several prominent Northeastern politicians, considered as good as elected by the press until election day, went down in defeat. However, even these surprises highlight the general trend. Wilson Braga of Paraíba lost his senatorial battle in what was called "the biggest surprise of the elections in Paraíba" (*Jornal do Brasil,* November 22, 1986, 2). However, his wife received the most votes of the PFL in the state in her successful bid for federal deputy. Wilson Braga may have been unable to overcome the PMDB's popularity in the top races (the PMDB won the governorship and both senate seats). However, he may have been undone by scandal; his alleged involvement in the assassination of a journalist led the journalist's paper to retaliate by publishing all possible accusations of corruption and scandal involving Braga (*Jornal do Brasil*, November 22, 1986, 2).

The 1986 election results were mixed. The PMDB was the main winner throughout the country, but in gaining office it also acquired many unlikely allies: former members of the conservative military party that had switched to the PMDB. Leftist candidates, the most genuinely in favor of land reform, did poorly throughout the country. All in all, winners were incumbents or otherwise connected to the traditional elite. As Hagopian said, "...viable opposition parties welcomed defenders of the old regime in order to enhance their vote totals in founding elections. By blurring the distinctions between previous military supporters and opponents, these partisan conversions allowed those who 'should have' been weakened electorally to resurface with a good deal of their power and prestige intact" (1990, 159–60). The "defenders of the old regime" then participated in the writing of the new constitution.

Support for Land Reform

Elected representatives supported land reform rhetorically. Most of the Assembly favored some sort of land reform; only 4 percent of the body stated that they were against any land reform in principle (Martins Rodrigues 1987, 113). Only 3 percent of the federal deputies elected from the Northeast declared themselves to be *against* land reform. Two-thirds (66 percent) said they were in favor of a land reform affecting nonproductive lands, and almost one-third (31 percent) favored a more radical land reform (Martins Rodrigues 1987, 115).[52]

One concern about the Martins Rodrigues study is that half of the 36 deputies (out of 487) *not* interviewed for the study were from the Northeast (Martins Rodrigues 1987, 21). In turn, half of these deputies (a total of 9) voted against land reform, 6 in favor, one abstained, and two left the Constituent Assembly before voting on the issue. Therefore, Northeastern deputies may have been initially less supportive of land reform than the survey indicated. This became clearer during the Constituent Assembly.

The UDR and Its Impact

The UDR, an interest group representing landowners, became another important factor in the 1986 election that requires mention. Although the left considered the PNRA a failure (Gomes da Silva, 1987), the proposal triggered an alarmed response by landowners, and the formation and subsequent dramatic rise of the Democratic Ruralist Union (*União Democrática Ruralista*, UDR). The UDR was one element of the successful mobilization of landowners in opposition to land reform in Brazil, and was possible in part because of the weakness of political parties. Their success is evident in the 1986 elections and in the drafting of the Constitution of 1988.

A handful of landowners founded the UDR in May 1985 in reaction to the PNRA.[53] The group's first goal was to influence the elections of November 15, 1986. Denying that it gave money directly to specific candidates, the UDR ran its own independent campaign for candidates that adhered to UDR principles, the most important being the inviolability of private property.[54] The UDR financed its campaign activities in part by sponsoring well-publicized cattle auctions.

The UDR grew quickly. Within a year, various reports estimated its membership at 50,000–60,000.[55] The UDR successfully unified the various rural groups in one nonpartisan entity, and gained the support of small and medium, as well as large landowners. Its organization spanned most regions of the country, whereas the support of other major agricultural organizations was regionally concentrated: the SRB in São Paulo and the SNA in Rio de Janeiro (Baltar 1990, 146).[56]

The UDR supported candidates of various parties, including the PFL, the PDS, the PL, the PDC and parts of the PMDB and the PTB. The UDR, the SRB, the CNA and others formed the *Frente Ampla da Agropecuaria* in October of 1986 (before the elections). The *Frente* helped elect up to 80 candidates to the Constituent Assembly. Some of these members would become key players in the struggle over land reform legislation in the *Constituinte* (Constituent Assembly), like Alysson Paulinelli (PFL-MG), Roberto Cardoso Alves (PMDB-SP), and Arnaldo Rosa Prata (PMDB-MG). The UDR continued as an influential lobby group throughout the Constituent Assembly.[57]

Land Reform and the Constituent Assembly

Land reform proved one of the more contentious issues addressed during the Constituent Assembly (*Assembléia Nacional Constituinte*), which met from February 1987 to October 1988. Fierce arguments and violence marked the debates.[58] As will be seen later, the most combative issue was the possible expropriation of productive land.

The Constituent Assembly divided its work into eight main thematic committees, each of which was responsible for developing a draft of a main chapter of the constitution.[59] Each of these committees, in turn, had three subcommittees that developed a draft of a particular section of the chapter. Positions on the committees were assigned proportionately according to party representation in the Congress, while satisfying the personal preferences of congressional members. By prior agreement, the presidencies of the subcommittees were assigned to members of the PFL, and the position of rapporteur (*relator*, the person who prepared the proposals) was given to members of the PMDB. After the subcommittees and committees did their work, the drafts went to the Integration Committee (*Comissão de Sistematização*),[60] which organized the various proposals to present a coherent draft to the full Assembly for discussion and amendments. The Assembly voted twice on the full draft.[61]

The issue of land reform was dealt with in the *Subcomissão da Política Agrícola e Fundiária e da Reforma Agrária* (hereafter referred to as the Land Reform Subcommittee), and the *Comissão da Ordem Econômico* (the Economic Order Committee) (Brazil 1987a). The rapporteur of the Land Reform Subcommittee, Oswaldo Lima Filho (PMDB-PE), had been João Goulart's agricultural minister (*Jornal do Brasil*, May 7, 1987) and prepared a draft report (*anteprojeto*) for the constitutional chapter on land reform that proved unacceptable to many conservative committee members. The proposal in large part conformed to the recommendations of the CNRA; MIRAD and INCRA also presented similar proposals. The proposal called for: the adoption of the "social obligation" of owning land, a more stringent requirement than simply "social function" (Soriano and Freitas);[62] payment for both expropriated land and infrastructure in bonds (called TDAs, *títulos da dívida agrária*), with the price based on the value of the property as declared for taxes; a fixed limit on the number of hectares that could be owned by any one person; special judicial tribunals to settle disputes; and the immediate possession by the state of targeted land.

In response, conservative members proposed a more conservative bill, named after its sponsor, Arnaldo Rosa Prata (PMDB-MG).[63] An attempt to thwart land reform, the counterproposal planned to leave most of the issues to be defined in ordinary legislation rather than specify the process of land reform in the constitution. Still, proponents of land reform expected to narrowly approve Lima Filho's draft, since they could count on a bare majority of 13 to 12 votes.

However, on the day of the vote, May 23, 1987, one expected supporter, Benedito Monteiro (PMDB-Pará), was inexplicably missing from the meeting. A substitute from the PL (*Partido Liberal*), conservative Oswaldo Almeida took his place.[64]

The balance thus changed, the Rosa Prata bill passed, 13 to 12. However, Monteiro was located in Belém, and retrieved at considerable expense by private jet. He returned to the meeting around 2 a.m., in time to vote on amendments (*destaques*) that removed five of the original seven articles of Rosa Prata's substitute. Consequently, the Land Reform Subcommittee sent little to the Economic Order Committee: confirmation of the right to own property subject to fulfilling its social function, a vague explanation of "social function,"[65] and provisions for the creation of special judicial entities to settle land conflicts in rural areas.[66]

The vote on the committee divided primarily along ties to agriculture. Of the 13 members of the subcommittee voting against the land reform proposal, 11 stated in the *Repertório biográfico* that their occupation involved agriculture (e.g. *agropecuarista, agricultor, extensionista rural, engenheiro agrônomo*). Three of those in favor stated their occupation as agricultural: *relator* Oswaldo Lima Filho, Percival Muniz, and Santinho Furtado (see table 5.6).

Those who voted in favor of Lima Filho's proposal belonged to more leftist parties that favored land reform: the PMDB, the PDT, the PT, the PCdoB, and the PCB. Those against were affiliated with the more

Table 5.6   Land Reform Subcommittee: Members' Votes

In Favor of Lima Filho Proposal	Opposed to Lima Filho Proposal
Amaury Müller, PDT-RS	Mauro Borges, PDC-GO[a]
Irma Passoni, PT-SP	Edison Lobão, PFL-MA[b]
Aldo Arantes, PCdoB-GO	Maluly Neto, PFL-SP[a]
Fernando Santana, PCB-BA	Jonas Pinheiro, PFL-MT[a]
Percival Muniz, PMDB-MT[a]	Alysson Paulinelli, PFL-MG[a]
Raquel Capiberibe, PMDB-AP	Rosa Prata, PMDB-MG[a]
Ivo Mainardi, PMDB-RS	Jorge Viana, PMDB-BA[a]
Vicente Bogo, PSDB-RS	Cardoso Alves, PMDB-SP[a]
Oswaldo Lima Filho, PMDB-PE[a]	Rachid Saldanha Derzi, PMDB-MS[b]
Benedito Monteiro, PMDB-PA	José Egreja, PTB-SP[a]
Santinho Furtado, PMDB-PR[a]	Victor Fontana, PFL-SC[a]
Marcio Lacerda, PMDB-MT[a]	Virgílio Galassi, PDS-MG[a]
Valter Pereira, PMDB-MS	Oswaldo Almeida, PL-RJ, substitute[a]

Notes
[a] Employed in agriculture (Brazil 1988; DIAP 1988).
[b] Also identified as member of rural business elite by Baltar.

Sources: Baltar (1990); Gomes da Silva (1989); DIAP (1988); Brazil (1988).

conservative PFL, PDC, PTB, PDS, and PL. However, the PMDB split. Four PMDB members voted against the proposal; two were former members of ARENA.

Furthermore, three *peemedebistas*, Marcio Lacerda (PMDB-MT), Santinho Furtado (PMDB-PR), and Valter Pereira (PMDB-MS), voted for the Lima Filho proposal only after a compromise in which infrastructure would be compensated in cash, the limit on ownership raised from 100 "model" hectares (*módulos fiscais*, basic unit of measure) to 200, and expropriation appeals heard through normal judicial channels without immediate possession of the land (Baltar 1990, 216).

Economic Order Committee

The process of drafting the constitutional chapter on land reform went next to the Economic Order Committee. Rapporteur Severo Gomes (PMDB-SP) used the defeated Lima Filho report for much of his proposal (Martínez-Lara 1994, 240); once again this draft met defeat, this time by a counterproposal from Jorge Vianna (PMDB-BA) similar to the Rosa Prata amendment (*Folha de São Paulo*, June 14, 1987, A-7). The first article of the chapter on agrarian reform retained similar language on the fulfillment of the social function of property. However, rather than being fulfilled when a property "is rationally utilized," it is fulfilled when the property "is, or is in the process of being, rationally utilized." This makes fulfilling the social function of property easier, since a determined owner can find a way to be in the process of putting his or her land to good use.

The draft also called for such measures as the "prior and just" compensation for expropriation of land, the placement of all expropriations under the purview of the president of Brazil, and restricting land reform to defined areas of priority. Other issues were left for definition in ordinary legislation, and the general tone of the document downplayed land reform and emphasized promoting agriculture through policies on prices for agricultural products, credit, research, and even rural electrical projects (*Folha de São Paulo*, June 5, 1987, 5).

Productive Property and Expropriation

The rapporteur of the Integration Committee, Bernardo Cabral (PMDB-AM), disregarded much of the Economic Order Committee's proposal while producing multiple drafts of the constitution for approval in the full Constituent Assembly. Key issues were worked out, usually by agreements between party leaders. Final compromises included payment for barren land in bonds, infrastructure and improvements in cash, and the exemption from expropriation of small and medium properties. No cap on the amount of land any one person could own was included, and productive land would not be subject to expropriation as long as it fulfilled its social function. This last issue remained contentious and led to an important episode in May 1988. The particular passage in question appears here in full (and in the original Portuguese in the appendix):

> **Art. 185.** The following are ineligible for expropriation for the purpose of agrarian reform:
> I—small and medium rural properties, as defined in law, so long as the owner does not possess any other;
> II—productive property.
> *Sole paragraph.* The law shall guarantee special treatment for productive property and shall establish norms for the compliance of requirements related to its social function <u>whose disregard shall permit its expropriation, under the terms of article 218.</u> [underlining added]

The conservative group sought to have productive property removed from any threat of expropriation: "Productive land is sacred, and can never be expropriated," according to Ronaldo Caiado of the UDR (*O Estado de São Paulo*, November 1, 1987). They wanted the underlined stipulation removed from the text, maintaining that the vague definition of "social function" and the unknown measure of "productive property" would leave productive farms open to expropriation. Proponents of land reform refused to remove the phrase, believing that too many compromises had already been made.

The conflict climaxed during the first round of voting on the full constitution. The *Centrão* once again presented a substitute bill. Neither Cabral's draft nor the *Centrão*'s substitute received the necessary absolute majority (280 votes). The entire chapter on land reform risked being left out of the constitution altogether; the chapter fell into a so-called *buraco negro* (black hole) because of the conflict over this one issue (*Correio Brasiliense*, May 7, 1988; *Folha de São Paulo*, June 6, 1988). That this was the only part of the new constitution threatened with this fate underscores the contentious nature of the issue.

In backroom discussions, a deal was proposed in which conservatives agreed to vote for the chapter, as long as they could attempt to remove the underlined passage in a *destaque simples* (amendment, DS) after the vote.[67] A DS, according to the internal rules of the Constituent Assembly, entailed voting for the entire text first and subsequently voting to remove passages that had been designated prior to the vote. A DS required an absolute majority of the votes of the Congress, 280 votes, since the passage had already been approved by a majority of the Congress within the main text. The DS request had to be presented and approved before the vote, but would be voted on after the main vote (Brazil 1987a).

According to Nelson Jobim, who was involved in forging the agreement with José Lourenço (PFL-BA), the PT refused to compromise.[68] As Plínio Arruda Sampaio (PT-SP) wrote in the *Folha de São Paulo* (May 9, 1988), the PT would rather face the "black hole" than cut a deal. Faced with this refusal, José Lourenço decided to vote in favor of the draft only if permitted a *destaque para votação em separado*, or DVS.[69] According to the internal rules, a DVS request required 187 signatures before the main vote, which they obtained.

The difference is significant, particularly in hindsight. With a *destaque simples* or DS, those who wanted to remove the contested clause would have had to get an absolute majority. However, for a DVS, the passage in question is removed from the text beforehand and voted on separately after the entire text has been approved. In this case, those who wanted the passage to *remain* in the constitution had to get an absolute majority of 280 because the Congress had not yet approved the passage.

The basic text was approved on May 10, 1988 by a vote of 528 to 4 (Brazil 1988b, 10303). The DVS vote followed. Those who wanted to keep productive property open to expropriation had to receive an absolute majority or 280 votes. The result of the vote was 267 yes, 253 no, and 11 abstentions (Brazil 1988b, 10318). The pro-reform members were 13 votes short of the 280 majority needed.[70] The irony, of course, is that a majority of the Assembly approved of the stricter language, and the vote was lost because of the strategic disadvantage of the DVS.

Party Support for Land Reform

Despite declared support for land reform, fewer representatives followed through in the Constituent Assembly. In the defining vote on land reform, 47.8 percent of the representatives from the Northeast voted in favor, while 45.5 percent voted against. The remaining 6.7 percent either abstained or missed the critical vote. Because an absolute majority (over 50 percent) was necessary, the vote failed. Vote totals for Northeastern representatives appear in table 5.7.[71] Land reform was supported by just under half of the politicians from the Northeastern who were elected in 1986.

Party label gives an indication of how members would vote, but was not a perfect indicator of how a representative would vote on land reform.

Table 5.7 Votes on Land Reform: Northeastern Members

	For	Against	Absent	Abstain	Total
PMDB	65	18	2	3	88
PFL	12	52	4	1	69
PDS	1	10	2	—	13
PDT	1	—	—	—	1
PTB	1	1	—	—	2
PCB	2	—	—	—	2
PCdoB	3	—	—	—	3
Total	85	81	8	4	178

Sources: DIAP (1988); Brazil (1988a,b); Martins Rodrigues (1987).

Overall, PMDB candidates were more likely to support land reform than conservative parties, but one-fifth (20.5 percent) of the PMDB representatives voted against land reform and another 6 percent did not vote. This mirrors the votes of PMDB members who opposed land reform provisions in the subcommittees. Members of the PFL and the PDS were more likely to vote against land reform, although 17 percent of the PFL representatives voted in favor of land reform and 7 percent avoided voting. Only one PDS member voted in favor of land reform.

Furthermore, individuals who played a large part in blocking land reform came from the Northeast, including: the president of the Land Reform Subcommittee, Edison Lobão (PFL-MA); the president of the Economic Order Committee, José Lins (PFL-CE); Jorge Vianna (PMDB-BA); and head of the PFL, José Lourenço (PFL-BA).

Aftermath of the Constituent Assembly

The Constituent Assembly left many issues to be defined by legislation. The Constituent Assembly broadly defined land reform, but two issues of importance were left to be decided. The first was the actual definition of small, medium, and productive property. The second was the procedure to be followed during expropriations (the *rito sumário*).

These definitions were of critical importance because land could not be expropriated unless a measure for productivity was available. Since small, medium, and productive properties were excluded, expropriations could not proceed until it was learned how large these properties were, or until it was learned if they were productive. The *rito sumário* established the actual legal procedure to be followed in expropriation proceedings, and was also necessary before expropriations could be realized under the new constitution.

Leaving these matters for ordinary law resulted in a long delay. The commission charged with writing the legislation was installed in November 1989.[72] However, the issues were not resolved until 1993. On February 25 of that year, Law no. 8.629 defined "small," "medium," and "productive" property.[73] On July 6, Lei complementar no. 76 established the *rito sumário*, the legal procedures for expropriation. Without these laws, land reform through expropriation was essentially halted from 1988 to 1993.[74]

Many other progressive measures were included in the new constitution, such as increasing rural workers rights. Rural workers gained the same rights as urban workers, their workweek was shortened from 48 hours to 44 hours, and the amount of overtime pay was increased. However, on the issue of land reform, relatively little resulted; as one advocate said, the "UDR gave [land reform] a fatal blow during the Constituent Assembly" (*Jornal do Brasil*, February 19, 1990, 3).

Conclusion

Events in Brazil contrast with those in other cases examined in this study. As in Chile and Venezuela, Brazilian politicians furthered their political careers through the extension of the franchise and the promise of land reform. However, not only did significant reform fail to materialize, but politicians and parties differed in their approach to the expansion of suffrage. Rather than aggressively seeking and organizing the support of the rural poor while making credible efforts at land reform, politicians instead focused on "buying" support through the provision of pork for influential constituencies. The rural poor's strength lay in its numbers, but its collective vote was diminished by electoral rules that have encouraged weak, personalistic parties.

Unlike the strong parties found in Chile and Venezuela, Brazilian parties are notoriously weak. This weakness stems from electoral rules that reduce party control of members, such as open-list PR, high district magnitude, and other features that facilitate party switching and increase the number of candidates and parties contesting for office. Since parties exercise little control over, and assistance to, their membership (e.g. no campaign funds), politicians concentrate on developing personal support. Acquiring the backing of local elites and well-off campaign contributors takes precedence over serving the underprivileged, who are unlikely to effectively exercise their franchise because of the electoral system.

For voters, party ID cannot serve as a rule of thumb because of the circumstances noted earlier, circumstances that also contributed to a horrendously complex ballot in 1986. Voters who managed to cast unspoiled ballots could not reward or punish politicians on the basis of clear, programmatic choices between parties. Instead, they had to consider individual attributes when choosing between possibly hundreds of candidates. This reduced the ability of voters to choose those who promised and delivered broad social policies, and encouraged them to vote for those who delivered concrete benefits to themselves or their local community.

The differences between Brazil, Chile, and Venezuela highlight the importance of party as a link between politicians and society. Strong parties fortify this link because voters can hold politicians accountable via their parties. Strong parties present clear, programmatic choices, which allow voters to punish parties (and politicians) that do not deliver on campaign promises. Weak parties, however, reduce accountability to the electorate. As seen in Brazil, this most affects the traditionally underprivileged members of society.

CHAPTER 6

Conclusions

Introduction

Robert Bates has asked whether the enfranchisement of the rural majority matters (Bates 1987, 182). This study concludes that, under certain conditions, the extension of citizenship rights to the rural poor significantly influences government policies. In the cases presented here, increased participation at the polls sparked the implementation of land reform.

The right to vote is an important tool for traditionally disadvantaged groups; although society may be inherently inequitable in other spheres, the polling booth represents an arena in which the poor and the wealthy can approximate equality. The extent of empowerment occasioned by the right to cast a ballot, however, depends in part upon the particular institutional framework present at the time of suffrage expansion. Institutions shape the type of system in which parties compete for the vote of the newly enfranchised rural poor.

Expansion of Suffrage and Land Reform in Latin America

The premise of this study is that rational, self-interested politicians implemented land reforms in order to gain the support of the newly incorporated poor. Election laws had prohibited or discouraged voting by the rural poor through such restrictions as literacy requirements, property requirements, inconvenient voter registration procedures, and nonsecret ballots. When these laws were changed, the poor were more likely to participate in elections; in order to compete for their votes, politicians offered land reform.

Opposition politicians and parties, such as the Christian Democratic and Socialist parties in Chile and AD in Venezuela, have an incentive to extend the franchise when they believe new voters will be likely to vote for their parties. However, politicians and their parties already in power are often unwilling to approve such changes, since this might mean their own political decline. Now and then, the functioning of democratic politics provided the opportunity to change the rules that had excluded politicians or parties.

Democratic land reforms in Latin America occurred at the same time as the expansion of suffrage to the rural poor. In Bolivia, Brazil, Chile, Colombia (1936), Dominican Republic, Ecuador, Guatemala, and Venezuela (1948), land reforms accompanied the removal of voting proscriptions. In Costa Rica and Venezuela (1960) land reform followed the implementation of mandatory voting. In Mexico, land reform coincided with the implementation of effective suffrage with direct elections and mandatory voting.

The coincidence of these reforms was not serendipitous; instead, the same parties sought both the expansion of suffrage and the redistribution of land to increase their own political support. These parties, which believed they could benefit from the enfranchisement of excluded groups, could not attain office under the existing electoral rules; however, historical circumstances provided the opportunity for their accession to power. Or, as in Chile, opposition politicians made use of a sympathetic president to push through election law changes that undercut the dominant parties. Once in office, parties effected the changes that they believed would increase political support in the future. In the process, the parties also encouraged participation by organizing and mobilizing the rural poor.

Significant increases in voter participation, summarized in table 2.5, underscored the importance of the expansion of suffrage. Once barriers to participation lifted, parties that had not initiated electoral reforms nevertheless also responded by promoting the redistribution of land and by creating competing rural organizations. As noted in the chapters on Chile and Venezuela, opposing parties competed amongst themselves for the newly available support of rural citizens.

Although land reforms accompanied the expansion of suffrage, responses varied in Latin America. Three countries stand out as exceptions: Brazil, Ecuador, and Peru. Each demonstrated a high demand for reform through unequally distributed land, rural poverty, and peasant unrest; promises of land reform by democratic regimes also accompanied the expansion of suffrage. However, the demand for land is a necessary, but insufficient, condition for reform in democratic countries. Significant redistribution of land did not occur under democratic regimes in Brazil or Ecuador despite the passage of land reform laws, and no land reform law occurred when illiterates got the right to vote in Peru. Politicians in the three countries apparently did not view the rural poor as a promising new source of political support. Further emphasizing the disregard for the rural poor, the extension of suffrage occurred particularly late in the countries: not until 1979 in both Ecuador and Peru, and 1985 in Brazil. Nor is voting mandatory for illiterates in Brazil or Ecuador.

As noted in chapter 2, only military governments achieved significant land reforms in these countries. The Peruvian military embarked on a massive land reform program in 1969 that expropriated over 40 percent of the country's agricultural land and distributed land to more than one-third of rural families. The Ecuadorian military eliminated virtual serfdom in 1964 and eventually expropriated over 15 percent of Ecuador's farmland. The Brazilian military attempted an auspicious reform in the 1960s, but did not significantly redistribute land.

The differences between Brazil, Ecuador, and Peru on the one hand, and other countries such as Chile and Venezuela on the other, are best explained by institutional factors. Brazil, Ecuador, and Peru share many similarities in the weakness and volatility of their party systems that reduced the representation of the rural poor.

The Importance of Institutions

Political parties serve as a critical link between individuals and government. Parties coordinate governing coalitions, simplify electoral choices, and mobilize the electorate. For the rural poor, though, the most important party function is ensuring the accountability of politicians to the voters.

Politicians are held accountable when their constituents can reward or punish them for fulfilling campaign promises. To hold a politician accountable, voters must assess the politician's performance, but processing information on the accomplishments of elected officials is costly. Even in affluent countries, where literacy levels are high and information accessible, voters often arrive uninformed at the polls. The problem is more critical in countries with abysmal literacy rates and few convenient sources of reliable information.

Political parties reduce the cost of information for voters by providing an easy guide at the polls. Party affiliation imparts general information about candidates' positions and performance; voters do not need to inform themselves about individual candidates. This guide becomes more important where voters lack basic resources and education.

Political parties most effectively facilitate voters' choices at the polls when the parties are strong. Strong, institutionalized, parties present a coherent party program, continuity in party officials, and the ability to discipline party politicians. Coherence and cohesiveness decrease information costs and increase credibility, since all party officials heed the party program.

Party affiliation, however, provides little assistance at the polls in countries where parties are weak. In countries such as Brazil, Ecuador, and Peru, parties lack a coherent party program, stable affiliations, and discipline. Weak parties are not effective guides for the electorate, leaving poor voters unable to punish or reward politicians effectively. Furthermore, electoral rules that weaken parties also complicate the voting system. Unsurprisingly, politicians, in turn, cannot rely on the votes of the rural poor; politicians have little incentive to implement policies such as land reform or increase the participation of the rural poor.

Electoral features such as closed-list PR increase party strength and reduce difficulties experienced by voters; closed-list PR fosters party cohesion by encouraging party discipline. Party leaders determine the order of candidates on party lists and punish disobedient party officials by placing them low on the list, thus eliminating their chances of reelection. Closed-list PR has a second benefit: it permits a simpler ballot. Voters choose only between parties, not candidates.

Open-list PR, on the other hand, decreases party strength by diminishing a party's ability to discipline members. Party leaders do not choose the order of candidates; instead, the number of votes received by each candidate determines his or her position on the list. Open-list PR also tends to complicate the ballot by presenting more choices for voters.

In combination with other practices, open-list PR encourages weaker parties. As described in the chapter on Brazil, high district magnitude weakens party control; high district magnitude also increases the difficulty of voting. Instead of a simple ballot, Brazilian voters had to write in their chosen candidates' names in proportional races. In contrast, low district magnitude in Chile allowed all candidates' names to be printed on the ballot. Chilean voters simply drew a line next to the name and number of their preferred candidate.

The differences between outcomes emphasize the importance of parties in connecting politicians with the electorate. Where one party clearly dominated, party institutionalization was not critical. In Bolivia and Guatemala in the 1950s, and Mexico in the 1920s, the poor could easily determine which party or politicians promoted land reform. Where two parties competed, as in Colombia, again choices between the parties were clear.

Where more than two parties competed, however, institutions mattered most. Of the multiparty systems considered here, countries where the significant reform was thwarted had open-list PR: Brazil, Ecuador, and Peru. Of the remaining countries, only Chile had open-list PR. As noted in chapter 3, Chilean parties were institutionalized despite this feature. In addition, district magnitude was relatively low and the ballots could be simple enough for illiterates to manage. Where parties were not yet institutionalized since free and open competition had been suppressed, as in the Dominican Republic, closed-list PR still simplified the choices between parties for illiterate voters and presented the prospect of building long-lasting support within society.

This study thus highlights the role that parties play in representation of the rural poor. Laws that promote party discipline and cohesion have the additional effect of increasing the probability that traditionally underrepresented members of society will be adequately represented on issues of importance. Strong parties encourage accountability to the electorate by first holding individual politicians accountable to the party. Weak parties discourage accountability because party officials themselves are not beholden to the party program. The voters most impacted by the lack of accountability are those who have the fewest resources with which to judiciously use the franchise: the poor.

Throughout Latin America, the distribution of land remains a pressing issue. In Brazil, Ecuador, and other countries, land use and land reform are connected to ills as various as rural poverty, environmental degradation, and indigenous rights. Indigenous and landless workers groups continue to agitate for reform. Based on the conclusions of this study, however, the long-term and meaningful attention to the needs of the poor remains unlikely as long as the majority of the electorate cannot hold politicians accountable for their actions.

Appendix

The following list provides the abbreviations and names of the political parties discussed in the text; all official parties are not included.

Brazilian Political Parties

PMDB   *Partido do Movimento Democrático Brasileiro* (Party of the Brazilian Democratic Movement)

PSDB   *Partido da Social Democracia Brasileira* (Party of Brazilian Social Democracy)

PFL   *Partido da Frente Liberal* (Party of the Liberal Front)

PDS   *Partido Democrático Social* (Democratic Social Party)

PDT   *Partido Democrático Trabalhista* (Democratic Labor Party)

PTB   *Partido Trabalhista Brasileiro* (Brazilian Labor Party)

PT   *Partido dos Trabalhadores* (Workers' Party)

PCdoB   *Partido Comunista do Brasil* (Communist Party of Brazil)

PL   *Partido Liberal* (Liberal Party)

PDC   *Partido Democrata Cristão* (Christian Democratic Party)

PCB   *Partido Comunista Brasileiro* (Brazilian Communist Party)

PSB   *Partido Socialista Brasileiro* (Brazilian Socialist Party)

Brazilian Parties, pre-1964

PSD   *Partido Social Democrático* (Social Democratic Party)

PTB   *Partido Trabalhista Brasileiro* (Brazilian Labor Party)

UDN   *União Democrática Nacional* (National Democratic Union)

PR   *Partido Republicano* (Republican Party)

PSP   *Partido Social Progressista* (Social Progressive Party)

PL   *Partido Libertador*

Brazilian Parties, Military Era

ARENA   *Aliança Renovadora Nacional* (National Removating Alliance)

MDB   *Movimento Democrático Brasileiro* (Brazilian Democratic Movement)

PP   *Partido Popular* (Popular Party) 1980–1982

Chilean Political Parties

PCU	*Partido Conservador Unido* (United Conservative Party)
PL	*Partido Liberal* (Liberal Party)
PR	*Partido Radical* (Radical Party)
PDC	*Partido Demócrata Cristiano* (Christian Democratic Party)
PS	*Partido Socialista* (Socialist Party)
PCCh	*Partido Comunista de Chile* (Communist Party)
PAL	*Partido Agrario Laborista* (Agrarian Labor)
PADENA	*Partido Democrático Nacional* (National Democratic Party)
VNP	*Vanguardia Nacional del Pueblo* (National Vanguard of the People)

Venezuelan Political Parties

AD	*Acción Democrática* (Democratic Action)
COPEI	*Comité de Organización Política Electoral Independiente* (Independent Electoral Political Organizing Committee, Christian Social Party)
URD	*Unión Republicana Democrática* (Democratic Republican Union)
PCV	*Partido Comunista de Venezuela* (Communist Party of Venezuela)
FDP	*Fuerza Democrática Popular* (Popular Democratic Force)
IPFN	*Independientes para la Frente Nacional*
OPINA	*Opinión Nacional* (National Opinion)
MIR	*Movimiento de Izquierda Revolucionaria* (Movement of the Revolutionary Left)
MEP	*Movimiento Electoral del Pueblo* (People's Electoral Movement)
FND	*Frente Nacional Democrático* (Democratic National Front)
PSD	*Partido Socialista Democrático* (Democratic Socialist Party)
PRIN	*Partido Revolucionario de Integración Nacional* (Revolutionary Party of National Integration)
BND	*Bloque Nacional Democrática* (Democratic National Bloc)
ORVE	*Organización Venezolana* (Organization for Venezuela)
PDN	*Partido Democrático Nacional* (Democratic Nationalist Party)
PRP	*Partido Republicano Progresista* (Progressive Republican Party)

Text of Brazilian Constitution Regarding Land Reform

Capítulo III
DA POLÍTICA AGRÍCOLA E FUNDIÁRIA E
DA REFORMA AGRÁRIA

Art. 184. Compete à União desapropriar por interesse social, para fins de reforma agrária, o imóvel rural que não esteja cumprindo sua função social, mediante prévia e justa indenização em títulos da dívida agrária, com cláusula de preservação do valor real, resgatáveis no prazo de até vinte anos, a partir do segundo ano de sua emissão, e cuja utilização será definida em lei.

§ 1º As benfeitorias úteis e necessárias serão indenizadas em dinheiro.

§ 2º O decreto que declarar o imóvel como de interesse social, para fins de reforma agrária, autoriza a União a propor a ação de desapropriação.

§ 3º Cabe à lei complementar estabelecer procedimento contraditório especial, de rito sumário, para o processo judicial de deapropriação.

§ 4º O orçamento fizará anualmente o volume total de títulos da dívida agrária, assim como o montante de recursos para atender ao programa de reform agrária no exercício.

§ 5º São isentas de impostos federais, estaduais e municipais as operaçóes de transferência de imóveis desapropriados para fins de reforma agrária.

Art. 185. São insuscetíveis de desapropriação para fins de reforma agrária:
I—a pequena e média propriedade rural, assim definida em lei, desde que seu proprietário não possua outra;
II—a propriedade produtiva.
Parágrafo único. A lei garantirá tratamento especial à propriedade produtiva e fixará normas para o cumprimento dos requisitos relativos a sua função social.

Art. 187. A função social é cumprida quando a propriedade rural atende, simultaneamente, segundo critérios e graus de exigência estabelecidos em lei, aos seguintes requisitos:
I—aproveitamento racional e adequado;
II—utilização adequada dos recursos naturais diponíveis e preservação do meio ambiente;
III—observância das disposiçóes que regulam as relaçóes de trabalho;
IV—exploração que favoreça o bem-estar dos proprietários e dos trabalhadores.

Table A.1 Electoral Changes in Fourteen Latin American Countries

Country	Property Requirement Removed	Literacy Requirement Removed	Mandatory Vote	Secret Ballot[a]	Women's Suffrage[b]
Argentina	1912	1912	1912	1912	1947
Bolivia	1952	1952	1929	1952	1952
Brazil	1946	1985	1932[c]	1962 (1932)	1932
Chile	1874	1970	1925	1958	1949
Colombia	1936	1936	1991[d]	1853	1957
Costa Rica	1913	1913	1959	1925	1949
Dominican Republic	1865	1962	1963	1962	1942
Ecuador	1861	1979	1967[c]	1861	1929

Table A.1 *Continued*

Country	Property Requirement Removed	Literacy Requirement Removed	Mandatory Vote	Secret Ballot[a]	Women's Suffrage[b]
Guatemala	1945	1945	1945[c]	1956	1945
Mexico	1857	1857	1917[d]	1857	1953
Panama	1904	1904	1928	1904	1945
Peru	1931	1979	1931	1963 (1931)	1955
Uruguay	1918	1918	1918	1918	1932
Venezuela	1945	1945	1958	1945	1945

Notes

[a] When the implementation of an effective secret ballot occurs at a date other than the legal mandate, the official date is given in parentheses.

[b] Women's suffrage from Ochoa (1987, 904; Nohlen 1993);

[c] Illiterates not obligated to vote.

[d] Not enforced. *Argentina*: Changes first applied to 1916 election; *Bolivia*: Mandatory vote reintroduced in the 1940s (Nohlen 1993, 70); *Brazil*: Literacy requirement removed July 1, 1985 (Law 7.332), also in 1988 Constitution. The secret ballot originally introduced in 1932 (Nohlen 1993, 95) but single ballot not used countrywide until 1962; *Chile*: Property restrictions removed by law in 1874 (it was presumed that those who could read and write must meet the requirement (Torres Dujisin 1989). Widespread fraud ended in 1891 (J.S.Valenzuela 1985, 17); *Colombia*: Vote officially secret since 1853 (Nohlen 1993, 139). Although not enforced, Congress passed Law 403 of August 1997 that "established incentives for voters," *Political Database of the Americas* <www.georgetown.edu/pdba>. Article 258 of the 1991 Constitution states that "voting is a citizen's right and obligation" ("El voto es un derecho y un deber ciudadano"); *Costa Rica*: Direct elections began in 1913, and the mandatory vote originally introduced earlier and reintroduced in 1959 (Nohlen 1993, 185); *Ecuador*: Property and secret ballot dates from Nohlen (1993, 279). Literacy requirement removed in Constitution of 1979; *Guatemala*: Literate citizens were to vote secretly after 1945; the secret vote for illiterates came in 1956 (Nohlen 1993, 341; Yashar 1997, 122); *Mexico*: Elections were indirect until the Revolution of 1910. Article 36 of the 1917 Constitution stipulated that among the "obligations of a citizen of the Republic" was "to vote in popular elections in their electoral district," although the mandatory vote has not been enforced ("son obligaciones del ciudadano de la República...votar en las elecciones populares...") According to Inter-Parliamentary Union, women gained right to vote in 1947 and right to stand for election in 1953 <www.ipu.org/wmn-e/suffrage.htm>; *Panama*: Independence in 1903. Information from Nohlen (1993, 479); *Peru*: Information on property requirement, mandatory vote, and official secret ballot from Nohlen (1993, 519). Literacy requirement removed in Constitution of 1979, 1980 was first applicable election. A single ballot was introduced in 1963; *Uruguay*: changes made in the 1918 Constitution. *Venezuela*: Changes made in practice after 1945 coup, and written into 1947 Constitution.

Notes

Chapter 1   Introduction: Connecting Suffrage and Land Reform

1. Land distribution varies among individual countries; chapter 2 examines specific cases.

2. In developed countries such as the United States, land concentration facilitates economies of scale; large agribusinesses are indeed efficient. However, similar economies of scale have not been widespread in Latin America. Deininger (1999) notes potential "equity and efficiency benefits" of land reform.

3. Land reform might include compensation, or entail outright confiscation. Governments usually compensated landowners in part with bonds, whose value were often diminished by inflationary Latin American economies. For discussion of the definition of land reform, see Lipton (1974), Wilkie (1974), or Barraclough (1973).

4. Opponents of reform included those arguing that agricultural inefficiency arose not from land concentration, but from adverse agricultural policies produced by governments pursuing import-substitution industrialization.

5. This definition distinguishes between "land reform" and "agrarian reform," two possible translations of the Spanish term *reforma agraria* (Thiesenhusen 1989): "agrarian reform" encompasses all policies aimed at agricultural development, while "land reform" limits these policies to the expropriation and redistribution of land.

6. In many countries, establishing that land need fulfill a "social function" (be productively utilized) provided the legal basis for expropriating private land.

7. Successful land reforms depend not only on lawmakers' intentions, but also on factors not related to the timing of reform, such as financial resources and bureaucratic autonomy of land reform agencies. Poor bureaucratic organization or lack of technical competence could also hamper fulfillment of reform goals (Rueschemeyer and Evans 1985, 53).

8. This is the official estimate. Unofficial estimates placed illiteracy at 60% of the population (Nyrop 1983a, xiv). Chapter 5 presents more information on illiteracy in Brazil.

9. *Keesing's Contemporary Archives* (1956, 14660). This occurred despite "an electoral law...issued on April 21 making voting secret" (14959).

10. Political participation also declined as a result of the National Front agreement, in which the presidency alternated between the two major parties and all posts were divided equally regardless of vote outcomes. Voting became mandatory with the 1991 Constitution. Article 258 states that "voting is a citizen's right and obligation" ("El voto es un derecho y un deber ciudadano"), but it is not enforced.

11. Organizations of rural elites had been allowed in Brazil prior to 1963, but small landowners and rural workers did not have their own, independent organizations (Baltar 1990).

12. Exiting political leaders seeking a legacy often support reformist policies or gestures; I thank an anonymous reviewer for making this observation.

13. The Venezuelan regime held highly regulated, indirect elections prior to the coup. AD's fate illustrates the liability of achieving office in this manner; the military overthrew the government three years later.

14. A minor reform law was passed in 1928 during the Ibáñez dictatorship.

15. Two main Argentine laws regarding agriculture passed in the years after the extension of suffrage: a 1917 "Homestead" law that gave plots of land to settlers, and a 1921 law that regulated tenancy contracts (Remmer 1984). Argentina also had tenancy reforms instituted during Juan Perón's presidency, in addition to some colonization; colonization and attempts at reforming land taxation also occurred in Uruguay. Meyer notes that Argentina and Uruguay only implemented colonization projects (1989, 4).

16. Argentina and Uruguay are not included in the table because of the lack of demand for reform in those countries, particularly at the time of suffrage expansion (1912 and 1918 respectively). And, as explained above, land reform did not occur. More information on Argentina and Uruguay is given in the appendix.

17. The Venezuelan "ballot" originally consisted of colored cards from which voters could choose.

18. The 1964 election was an exception; the Conservative and Liberal Parties shifted their support to the Christian Democrat candidate, Eduardo Frei, who won with 56 % of the vote. This very exception reinforces the closeness of the elections: the Right supported Frei because it feared Allende would win the election.

Chapter 2 Cases of Reform: An Overview

1. "Latin America" for this study includes countries in the Western Hemisphere where the main language is Spanish or Portuguese.

2. The most inclusive operationalization of "democracy" serves to avoid problems associated with selection on the dependent variable because cases of democratic countries where the expansion of suffrage did not coincide with land reforms, or land reforms occurred in the absence of the expansion of suffrage, would undercut the argument of this study.

3. Some changes did occur earlier. Chile eliminated the property requirement in 1891, but direct elections for president were not instituted until 1925; in Peru,

the property requirement was ended in 1895, but elections were not free and fair until 1931 (and not always after that).

4. This work does not specifically consider women's suffrage, which has not had a significant relationship with the timing of land reform. Indeed, land reform programs often focus on male recipients to the exclusion of women (Deere 2003). Even so, the appendix includes dates of women's suffrage.

5. Some other countries' population density (population per square mile) for 1912: Colombia, 13; Costa Rica, 20; Ecuador 14; Guatemala, 27 (Banks 1971).

6. Arrivals less departures. See also Mitchell (1993, 90–6).

7. Prosterman and Riedinger (1987) provide an example of this argument: the relative deprivation suffered by the landless and land-poor peasants would make them likely supporters of revolutionary movements.

8. Levinson and de Onís reiterate that "By themselves these agrarian reform measures create conditions for increased production that benefit not the landless but those who already have productive farms." Apparently, the United States determined that Latin American governments could acquire land without having to use external funding; the countries could expropriate land with a small initial payment in cash and the remainder in long-term bonds. U.S. officials also rejected a 1965 proposal to create a fund to guarantee the Latin American bonds (1970, 230).

9. Brazilian President João Goulart attempted a land reform in 1964 just before the military coup; the U.S. government supported his ouster. The military government implemented a land reform in the 1960s primarily aimed at colonization rather than redistribution of land.

10. King gives similar figures: 8% of all holdings were on 95% of privately held farmland while 61% of all landholdings were under 5 hectares and took up 8% of cultivated area (.3% of total area) (King 1977, 117).

11. Paz Estenssoro received a plurality of the votes (45%) but needed an absolute majority. The election was to then go to the Congress, but the president resigned and gave control to a military junta to avoid Paz Estenssoro's selection (Patch 1960).

12. Chávez's political career floundered when he confronted Siles over economic policies and was forced out of his post (Patch 1960, 132).

13. Tannenbaum notes that 213 villages received land from Carranza between 1915 and 1920 (Tannenbaum 1950, 147).

14. By this time (April 1920), Emiliano Zapata was dead, having been assassinated in April 1919. For more information on Zapata, see Womack (1969).

15. Article 36 states "son obligaciones del ciudadano de la República:... III. Votar en las elecciones populares en el distrito electoral que le corresponda" (*Political Database of the Americas* <www.georgetown.edu/pdba>).

16. Partial expropriations pertained to farms measuring from 224 to 672 acres.

17. This is a conservative estimate based on a lower beneficiary figure of 89,000, the total (rather than rural) population in 1950 of 2,791,000, and an average of 4 persons per household.

18. Women were given the right to vote in 1949.
19. According to Bernard Thibaut, this was the reintroduction of the mandatory vote; voting had been mandatory in the mid-nineteenth century, but the requirement had lapsed (Nohlen 1993).
20. One-half of the Costa Rican population was under the voting age, which accounts for the wide difference in numbers.
21. Estimate does not include banana workers. Prosterman and Riedinger estimate that 15–16% of Costa Rica's total population were landless in the early 1980s (1987, 27).
22. In addition, the number of deputies in the Costa Rican legislature increased from 45 to 57 deputies between 1958 and 1962 (CAPEL 1986). This opened up electoral competition for new seats and increased the importance of attracting the votes of the newly participating rural poor in order to maintain a majority.
23. Seligson is highly critical of the law, primarily because it compensated owners for expropriated land (1980, 125–7).
24. The official PLN candidate was Francisco Orlich Bolmarcich; Jorge Rossi Chavarría split from the PLN in 1956 and ran for president in the newly formed Independent Party (*Partido Independiente*, PI) (Nelson 1983).
25. AD was legalized in 1941, but previous to 1941 many of its members and leaders had organized and participated in other opposition organizations.
26. Trujillo officially took power in 1930. The United States may have known of and supported the assassination (McDonald and Ruhl 1989, 322). U.S. support for Trujillo declined after his involvement in an assassination attempt on Venezuelan President Rómulo Betancourt in 1960 (Haggerty 1991).
27. McDonald and Ruhl suggest that Trujillo increased vote totals and created fake opposition parties to bolster his legitimacy.
28. The lack of reform cannot be considered a result of a contented rural population, particularly given the rise in indigenous organization and demand for reform. For example, a massive uprising occurred in 1990 (Zamosc 1994).
29. This was the first real Peruvian land reform (No. 14444), although an earlier decree law (No. 14238) was the first land reform law, "and marked a legal recognition of the existing land tenure problem" (Kay 1983, 205).
30. This event led APRA to oppose subsequent reformist measures (Cotler 1990, 11).

Chapter 3   Chile: Accelerating Reforms from Alessandri to Allende

1. The Liberal Party was also a conservative party.
2. A short undemocratic interregnum occurred in the 1920s and early 1930s.
3. Property restrictions on voting were removed by law in 1874 (it was presumed that anyone who could read and write must therefore meet the property requirement [Torres Dujisin 1989]), then by constitutional amendment in 1888, but it

was in 1891 that widespread vote manipulation by the government ceased (Valenzuela 1985, 17).

4. John Thompson, "The Third Congressional District Election of March 23," *Hispanic American Report*, 11, 3, 160–5, describes the voting process as well as instances of fraud. In this case, the party member would "somehow get a fraudulent ballot envelope. A party member would then submit his ballot in the fraudulent envelope and retain the proper envelope—this in turn is given to another individual with a ballot already filled out. This person submits the ballot and then retains the proper envelope to exchange for money [approximately an amount four times the usual daily wage]."

5. A Santiago election held on March 23, described in John Thompson's special *Hispanic American Report* report cited in the previous footnote.

6. The FRAP was made up of the Communist, Socialist, and *Demócrata Nacional* parties.

7. This is a short-lived National Party that supported Ibáñez; it is not the same National Party that formed as a result of the PCU and PL's merger in the late 1960s (Cruz-Coke 1984). Yet another National Party was active from 1821 to 1924: the *Partido Nacional Monttvarista* (Urzúa Valenzuela 1992, 378).

8. After supporting Gabriel González Videla in the 1946 presidential race and participating in his government, the Communist Party was banned in 1948 (Gil 1966).

9. When the president submitted a bill considered "urgent," it had to be acted upon within 30 days. (Gil 1966, 102). There was significant debate in the Senate over whether the "urgency" request was valid in this case (debate in *El Mercurio*, April 30, 1958, 23 and 25).

10. Published in *Diario Oficial*, August 1, 1958. A minor revision was made in August.

11. Gandrillas (1968) gives a description of voting rights and procedures in the aftermath of these changes.

12. Proposed by Frei in January 1969 (*Facts on File*, March 6–12, 1969); the illiterate vote provision was added later (Quezada Lagos 1984).

13. The new law also added the stipulation that deputies and senators be able to read and write (Article 27 of the constitution).

14. The Alessandri reform was the first democratic land reform. A minor reform law was passed in 1928 during the Ibáñez dictatorship; this law did not result in significant redistribution of land.

15. Juan Antonio Ríos in 1942 had been the last president to win the election by an absolute majority (56% of the vote). As prescribed by law, elections in which no candidate received an absolute majority were decided in Congress, which had traditionally selected the candidate who had won a plurality of the vote.

16. The Christian Democratic Party, which began as a youth movement of the Conservative Party, split off from it in 1938 and operated as the *Falange Nacional* until 1957. At this time, they fused with many of the members of another offshoot of the Conservative Party (the Socialchristian Conservative

Party), the Agrarian Labor Party, and some other small parties. The PDC experienced a dramatic rise in electoral successes after 1957 (Cruz-Coke 1984, 57–9).

17. Furthermore, as Gil (1966) explains, the house that originated a bill can "insist on modification by a special vote of two-thirds, in which case the other chamber may in turn reject the amendments only with a two-thirds majority" (116).

18. Francisco Bulnes, "Discurso a la Directiva General," *Diario Ilustrado*, Santiago, June 13, 1963, 2, cited by Kaufman (1967, 13).

19. King (1977, 164). Kaufman (1967) gives a smaller number: 700 beneficiaries in 1963 and 1964, out of an "active rural population of 600,000" (19).

20. Article 1 of the law states that "Every agricultural proprietor is obligated to cultivate the land, increase its productivity and fertility, conserve its natural resources and effect the investments necessary in order to improve its operation or improvement and conditions of life of those that work on it . . ." Chile. *Reforma Agraria y sus Reglamentos, Ley No. 15.020, Promulgada 27 November 1962.*

21. "Three agencies were deemed necessary so that each of the parties in the governmental coalition could control aspects of the reform program and provide employment for supporters. CORA was to be under control of the Conservative party, INDAP of the Radical party, and CONSFA of the Liberal party" (Loveman 1976a, 232). Later, left-wing members of the PDC would head both INDAP and CORA.

22. The text of the reform is in, "Reforma Constitucional Será Votada Hoy En Sesión Conjunta de Cámara y Senado," *El Mercurio*, September 29, 1963, 55.

23. Muñoz (1991, 163) states that as a result of this mission, the United States determined that the Alessandri government would not be sufficiently willing to carry out reforms. As a result, the United States decided to back the PDC.

24. Quote by Sr. Chelen: The "riñón oligarquico más poderoso de la reacción chilena," *El Mercurio*, May 1, 1964, 35.

25. Also a quote by Chelen, *El Mercurio*, May 1, 1964, 35; a similar statement was made by Allende. The candidate backed by the right lost to the FRAP candidate, 39.5% to 32.5% (Gil and Parrish 1965, 31–2). In 1961, the Democratic Front had won 55% of the vote (Francis 1973, 13).

26. "Partido Conservador Acordó Apoyar a Don Eduardo Frei Sin Pactos ni Compromisos," *El Mercurio*, May 1, 1964.

27. Durán reentered the race as only the Radical Party candidate (Alexander 1973, 101). He won 5% of the vote.

28. As Kaufman (1967, 27) notes, the PDC was "still two votes shy of the crucial one-third mark in the Senate."

29. Alessandri proposed several reforms: the possible use of a plebiscite in cases of conflict between the executive and legislature; a simplified legislative process; limits on legislative initiative regarding economic policy; a four-year presidential term with reelection allowed; and some sort of run-off in cases where no presidential candidate received a majority (*El Mercurio*, October 2, 1963). *El Mercurio* (December 2, 1964) gives a critical comparison of the two proposals.

30. Text of the constitutional reform proposal printed in *El Mercurio*, December 1, 1964, 23–5.
31. The PDC, of course, had other reforms that it pursued: chileanization (part-ownership) of copper, reforming the tax system, solving the housing shortage, and improving education.
32. A larger number of 480 fundos and over 8,000 families, is given in King (1977) and Kaufman (1972, 69). The discrepancy is probably due to different periods of measurement, ending in March rather than November as for King and Kaufman.
33. The text of Frei's speech upon proposing the law is included with the text of the law in Chile, *Ley de Reforma Agraria, Ley No. 16.640*, 1967.
34. A timeline of the legislation's progress is provided in Chile, *Ley de Reforma Agraria, Ley No. 16.620*, 1967.
35. Examples of the positions of the Liberal and Conservative parties, and the SNA are found in "Declaraciones de los Partidos Liberal y Conservador sobre Proyecto de Reforma Agraria," *El Mercurio*, December 4, 1965, 37; December 3, 1965, 21.
36. Text of law in Chile, *Ley de Reforma Agraria, Ley No. 16.640*, 1967.
37. The standardized hectares were based on hectares near Santiago; owners were allowed to keep larger units of land in less fertile areas.
38. The terms of the bonds varied according to the degree of use of the land that was expropriated.
39. Efforts to evaluate whether production dropped because of the reform were complicated by a severe drought in 1968 and 1969 (Swift 1971). The winter of 1967 was the Chile's driest in over 100 years (*New York Times*, July 17, 1967, 14).
40. Eckstein (1978, appendix A, 6). Kaufman gives a similar figure (1972, 98). Other estimates are 28,000 (Francis 1973), and 35,000 (Loveman 1976b, 259). In all, it seems clear that only a quarter of the proposed recipients received land. Swift (1971) notes that the original goal was probably unrealistic.
41. The rural unionization law also allowed land owners to organize, which they did in opposition to land reform.
42. Strikes in the countryside began to rise, from only 3 strikes in 1960 and 39 strikes in 1964, 648 strikes in 1968 and 1,580 in 1970 (Valenzuela 1978, 336). In 1971, the number of strikes remained high at 1,758 (Silva 1992, 219). Similarly, while 68 farms had been invaded by workers in 1968, 368 were taken over in 1970 (Valenzuela 1978, 337). Land seizures increased to 1,278 in 1971 (Silva 1992, 219).
43. A sample of criticisms from the right, including the SNA (*Sociedad Nacional de Agricultura*) can be found in: "Declaración del Consejo de SNA Frente a Proyecto de la Reforma Agraria," *El Mercurio*, April 19, 1967, 27; "Ley de Reforma Agraria," *El Mercurio*, April 28, 1967, 27.
44. While 18–21 year olds could vote for the first time in April 1971 and could have resulted in a half million more voters, only 230,000 registered; the short period of time after the change in Article 104, and the coincidence of the

registration period with school exams, were blamed for the low registration rate (*El Mercurio*, February 8, 1971, 21).

45. Blind citizens also voted for the first time in this election.

46. *El Mercurio* reproduced the ballot on page 37 of its March 3, 1973 issue. Voters were to make only one selection. A ballot would be annulled if both a party and a candidate were chosen, even if the candidate was on that same party's list (*El Mercurio*, March 4, 1973, 36). Depending on the location, voters could use up to three ballots: a sky-blue-colored one for senators, yellow for deputies, and pink for councilmen (regidores) (*El Mercurio*, March 3, 1973).

47. Much higher estimates exist. King estimates that about 75,000 campesino families benefited directly from the reform, and that 50,000 more benefited indirectly through such avenues as increased opportunities for part time employment (King 1977, 171).

48. MAPU accelerated its instigation of land seizures after the March 1973 elections, making "fifteen seizures and dozens of unsuccessful attempts in Llanquihue" alone in the month after the election; they were afraid the Allende government would be "willing to compromise with bourgeois elements." The Allende government, for its part, said it would not accept illegal seizures of land (*New York Times*, April 9, 1973, 18).

49. A good exposition of the MIR perspective is given in "Discurso de Miguel Enríquez, Secretario General del MIR" (*El Mercurio*, November 3, 1971, 9).

50. Cruz-Coke argues that the conservative parties had undergone three periods of decline in the past, and that their decline in the 1960s was not due to the emigration of the rural population to the cities, the expansion of the electorate, the elimination of bribes, nor the agrarian reform.

51. The CODE was made up of the Christian Democrats, the National Party, the PIR, PADENA and Democracia Radical. The UP coalition was made up of the Communists, Socialists, Radicals, API, Izquierda Cristiana and MAPU (*El Mercurio*, March 3, 1973). The USP, *Unión Socialista Popular*, fielded its own list on the March 1973 ballot.

Chapter 4   Venezuela: Democratization and Reforms

1. Ramón Quijada helped organize the campesino movement and was a major opposition figure in 1936 (Martz 1966).

2. Landowners feared that the government would give the title to land that the tenants cultivated.

3. Wilkie (1974) gives a lower estimate of beneficiaries in 1959 (table 9).

4. Gonzalo Barrios was a member of the "Generation of 1928" and was AD's candidate for president in 1968.

5. A 1989 reform allowed the option of voting for individual candidates, for state and local elections only (Hellinger 1991). The Venezuelan system changed substantially with the approval of a new constitution in 1999.

6. From 1936 to 1945 there were direct state and municipal elections (CAPEL 1986).

7. Illiterate men over 21 years of age could vote until 1936, but the voting process was extremely limited and indirect. In 1936, suffrage was limited to literate men (Martz 1966, 39).

8. Gómez's rule began in 1908. He died of natural causes.

9. Juan Bautista Fuenmayor was a leader of the communist party in Venezuela.

10. The electoral college met April 28, 1941. Gallegos received 13 votes, Isaías Medina Angarita received 130 votes (Serxner 1959).

11. In "El caso de Venezuela y el destino de la democracia en América," 1949.

12. AD leaders had traveled to Washington to meet with Escalante and were satisfied with his positions. Fuenmayor disagreed with the assertion of Escalante's "neutrality."

13. Fuenmayor continued to support Medina in his memoirs and thought that Medina's only error was not to have had a direct election for president (1979, 413–23). Kornblith (1991, 65) believed that, among other motives, the main reason for the military coup "was Medina's unwillingness to transfer power through an open electoral process."

14. Fuenmayor considers the Medina law to have been a much stronger law than AD's 1948 land reform law (Fuenmayor 1981, 435–42).

15. Other accounts state that Escalante suffered a nervous breakdown.

16. There is some disagreement over the extent of AD's involvement with the planning of the coup. Betancourt apparently started meeting with the military officers in July 1945 (Serxner 1959).

17. From the declaration of the junta that took power in 1948 (Fuenmayor 1981, 544).

18. José Rafael Pocaterra quoted by Betancourt in correspondence in Gómez (1982).

19. The PRP was essentially a communist party (Ewell 1984, 90).

20. Rafael Caldera helped to form and became leader of COPEI; he ran for president several times, became president in 1968, and was again president from 1994 to 1999. For his second presidential campaign, however, he ran as an independent.

21. Some accounts state that Villalba founded the URD (e.g., Myers 1973, 250); he did not, although he subsequently took over the party (Martz and Baloyra 1976, 6).

22. Although Betancourt helped found the communist party in Costa Rica during his first exile, he eventually disassociated himself with them to the point that he supported José Figueres over the communists during the 1948 civil war (Gómez 1982, 13).

23. Written in a letter to Mariano Picón Salas on February 10, 1932.

24. Letter to Betancourt dated November 20, 1933.

25. Written in 1949, "El caso de Venezuela y el destino de la democracia en América."

26. Various spellings of this name have been observed: Jiménez and Geménez.
27. PDN statements taken from "Political Thesis and Program of the *Partido Democrático Nacional* ('PDN ilegal,' 1939)" and the "First National Conference of the *Partido Democrático Nacional* (September 30, 1939)," in Suárez Figueroa (1977, 235–75).
28. "Comunicado de gobierno provisional a la nación (19 de octubre de 1945)" in Suárez Figueroa (1977, vol. 2, 70–3). The signatories of the declaration were Major Carlos Delgado Chalbaud, Captain Mario Vargas, and AD members Rómulo Betancourt, Raúl Leoni, Luis B. Prieto F., Edmundo Fernández, and Gonzalo Barrios.
29. Via Decree 216, March 15, 1946.
30. These were the main parties. Other parties also participated in the elections, and had their own colors, such as the UFR (Mérida), blue, and the Partido Social Cristiano, purple. Also, the communists had split into "red and black" factions (Fuenmayor 1980, 494).
31. The question of governors was highly disputed. Although it was decided that the president would appoint the governors, the 1947 Constitution called for plebiscites to decide whether or not to switch to direct elections for governors. The 1961 Constitution set up a more vague solution that allowed the delay of direct elections until 1989 (Kornblith 1991, 85–6).
32. Martz and Baloyra report that "Electoral figures for the trienio elections were faultily recorded, and detailed returns were destroyed during the Pérez Jiménez government" (1976, footnote 15, 274).
33. Ochoa gives as similar estimate of 26.6% (1987), Hellinger (1991) a higher one of 36% (60).
34. The communists had hoped to win 15 seats in the Constituent Assembly and only won 2 (Fuenmayor 1980, 496).
35. Some of these lands were reinstated to their owners by the 1947 constitutional assembly because of errors that had been made in confiscation (*HAR*, 2, no. 11).
36. Powell (1971, 77) gives a similar figure of 125,000 hectares distributed to 73,000 beneficiaries. Hellinger (1991) gives a much smaller number: 6,000 receiving 73,770 hectares confiscated from Gómez's family and another 1,130 families receiving 29,350 hectares through colonization of public lands (61).
37. The immediate excuse for the coup was Gallegos's refusal to accede to military demands regarding military representation in the cabinet and demands for the exile of Betancourt. Apparently the military did not expect their demands to be met and used them as an excuse for the coup (Hillman 1994; Martz and Baloyra 1976). There had been various attempted coups between 1945 and 1947 (Herman 1980).
38. A military junta of three persons originally took power in 1948; Pérez Jiménez consolidated his own power, particularly after the assassination of fellow junta member Carlos Delgado Chalbaud on November 13, 1950. Some suggest that Pérez Jiménez himself plotted the assassination. The third member of the junta, Luis Felipe Llovera Páez, was subsequently exiled (Hellinger 1991, 84–5).

39. The catalyst for Pérez's downfall was his manipulation of a plebiscite in December 1957 intended to extend his presidency beyond his promised five-year term, rather than hold a true election as promised. This led to an abortive coup attempt a couple weeks later, followed by the successful coup of January 23, 1958. Pérez Jiménez also lost support in the military by ignoring merit considerations for advancement and by imprisoning and torturing officers (Levine 1973).

40. The Communist Party had been banned from 1950 to 1957; it was again banned from 1962 to 1969 for supporting guerrilla warfare (Gorvin 1989, 391).

41. After 1973, and until 1984, municipal elections were held six months after the other elections; this may account for a decline in voter participation rates in the municipal races that occurred after 1973 (Molina 1989).

42. One problem is that voters could not register or vote on an absentee basis (Myers 1973, 71–3).

43. The card system was replaced after 1968 by a single ballot based on the same principles of voting by color and party list (Martz and Baloyra 1976).

44. Molina (1989) gives the following percentages of *eligible* population voting in elections: 1958: 80.44%; 1963: 75.12%; 1968: 92.02%; 1973: 89.58%.

45. Larrazábel was the popular admiral who, after Pérez Jiménez fled into exile, eventually led the junta that oversaw the transition to democratic elections. He stepped down to run in the 1958 election.

46. Three major splits occurred in AD in the 1960s: MIR (*Movimiento de Izquierda Revolucionaria*) in 1960; AD (Opp) in 1962; and MEP in 1967. The MIR split in disapproval over Betancourt's policy of conciliation; the AD (Opp) and MEP splits centered on disagreements over presidential nominations (Myers 1973, 54–5).

47. Betancourt was seriously hurt and nearly killed by a bomb in June 1960 (Hellinger 1991, 108).

48. In contrast, when the URD left the coalition in 1960, its labor members also left the official labor movement (Powell 1969).

49. A split in AD over the presidential nominee made Caldera's victory possible. AD split nearly in half, with the rebels forming the People's Electoral Movement (*Movimiento Electoral del Pueblo*, MEP) and supporting Luis Beltrán Prieto as its own presidential candidate. Prieto received 19% of the vote in the election.

50. At first, COPEI's primary source of peasant support was in its traditional strongholds in Andean states.

51. The rest of this paragraph, unless otherwise noted, is based on Kornblith's article.

52. The presence of President Betancourt and his ministers at the presentation of the land reform bill to Congress in 1959 highlights the importance given to the law. Venezuela (1960b) described this as an exceptional occurrence.

53. Land distribution had begun as AD took office, even before the official land reform law was passed in 1960.

54. The debates of the commission were published in Venezuela, Ministerio de Agricultura y Cría, Comisión de Reforma Agraria, *Reforma agraria*, vols. I–IV, Caracas, 1959.

55. Party members give a summary of their parties' views at the end of discussions of the bill in the Chamber of Deputies in Venezuela (1960b, 595–603).

56. Another minor Communist Party criticism was that the law "did not set a specific deadline for answering petitions brought by the peasant, nor did it accept the proposition of the different communist worker and peasant organizations that 40% of the land reform organs be staffed by those who belonged to the rural masses." See also *El Nacional*, February 6, 1960, 35 and February 7, 1960, 29.

57. As per Articles 19 and 20 of the law, social function was fulfilled when the land was worked in such a way as to efficiently use all applicable factors of production; the owner personally and directly worked and oversaw the use of the land; natural resources were conserved; all worker-related laws were complied with; and the land was properly registered with the *Oficina Nacional de Catastro de Tierras y Aguas*. Idle, uncultivated, or indirectly worked land did not fulfill its social function (Venezuela 1960b, 937).

58. There were different types of bonds, with different interest rates and maturities (*El Nacional*, February 24, 1960, 29). According to Article 178, land worth up to 100,000 bolívars (estimated at $30,000 at the time by Carroll 1961) would be paid in full with cash. For properties of greater value, a percentage would be paid in cash; the portion decreased as the value of the land increased. Property worth over one million bolívars received a 10% cash payment (Venezuela 1960b, 991).

59. Salvador de la Plaza was an early communist organizer (1920s) who was exiled after participating in protests. Hellinger considers him "an independent communist thinker whose ideas were not widely embraced by the party" (Hellinger 1991, 209 [note 41]).

60. Those who denounced the idle land did not get preference in allocation; an amendment (proposed by Communist Senator Márquez) which would have given them preference was defeated (Venezuela 1960b, 728).

61. Giménez Landínez later became IAN director during the early Caldera government. Giménez, with the help of others, created organizations aimed at helping rural workers and landowners such as the *Instituto de Servicios Rurales* (ISER), founded in 1963, and the *Fundación para el Desarrollo Rural y la Educación Campesina* (FUNDECA) in 1968 (Herman 1980).

62. Segnini spent the years 1948–1958 in exile.

63. This led to a major split in the FCV. Almost half of its affiliated organizations switched to the newly created *Federación Nacional Campesina* (FEDENACA).

Chapter 5   Brazil: The Land Reform that Wasn't

1. Title inspired by a Fernando Homen de Mello newspaper article, "*A reforma agrária (que não houve)*."

2. The Northeast consists of nine states: Maranhão (MA), Piauí (PI), Ceará (CE), Rio Grande do Norte (RN), Paraíba (PB), Pernambuco (PE), Alagoas (AL), Sergipe (SE), and Bahia (BA).

3. Regional figures vary from 16% in the North, 7% in the Southeast, and 10% in the South. Figures calculated from MST and INCRA data compiled by ABRA, using the number of people with "no land" or "little land" (less than 5 hectares, considered little land in Brazil) in 1985 and the number employed in agriculture in 1988. Prosterman and Riedinger similarly estimate that 28–34% of the Northeast's population and 18% of Brazil's population were "landless agriculturalists" (1987, 31).

4. For example, a march of at least 40,000 *sem-terra* converged on Brasília in April 1997 (*Veja*, April 16, 1997 and April 23, 1997).

5. These figures exclude conflicts not directly related to land (e.g., labor and mining disputes).

6. However, Goulart's overthrow owed much to strategic mistakes he made while attempting to increase his own political power (Figueiredo 1987), including interference with the military (Stepan 1971).

7. Like many IBGE surveys, the survey does not include the rural population of the North.

8. Ages five and older. The IBGE survey defined literacy as the ability to read and write a simple note in one's native language.

9. Figures for the other regions were as follows: in the South, 90% had radios, 79% had televisions; in the Center-West, 77% had radios, 68% had televisions; in the North, 71% had radios and 74% had televisions.

10. The *candidato nato* law was overturned in 2002.

11. Another means of party control is through money; where parties fund candidates' campaigns, they also exert some control over candidate behavior. Brazilian parties do not finance their candidate's campaigns; candidates must find their own sources of funding. Brazilian candidates do not risk losing campaign funds when disobeying party leaders; instead, they must please other "bosses," campaign contributors that help them raise the estimated $1 million necessary to get elected to the Chamber of Deputies (Ames 1995).

12. Survey of heads of households. The breakdown by region was as follows: North 70%; Northeast 62%; Southeast 66%; South 76%; and Center-West 72%.

13. Interview with José de Souza Martins, August 30, 1993. For history and effects of clientelism in Brazil see Leal (1977), Cammack (1982), and Hagopian (1992).

14. Brazilian presidents and vice presidents were elected separately. Quadros's "chosen" vice presidential candidate lost to Goulart, the PTB candidate.

15. Members of the military and others opposed Goulart's accession to the presidency. A return to the presidential system was approved in a plebiscite held in January 1963.

16. The reforms also included "banking, fiscal, . . . university" changes and the legalization of the Communist Party, illegal since 1947 (Figueiredo 1987, 62–3).

17. For a short period of time in the nineteenth century illiterates and the poor were allowed to vote, but both were prohibited again in 1889 (Lamounier and Muszynski 1989). Income (*renda*) was not specifically required after 1889, but Brazilian constitutions excluded "beggars" until 1946.

18. Information on the single ballot is from chapters 3 and 4 in Paiva (1985). According to Paiva, while previous law mandated that each voter booth contain ballots for all candidates, this was impossible until the adoption of a single ballot.
19. Decree law 8127 of October 24, 1945 legalized rural organization, but did not allow a distinction between landowners and workers. Rural workers could not legally form their own separate organizations.
20. Through decree law 53.516. At the same time, the CNA (*Confederação Nacional da Agricultura*) formed to represent the landowners (Baltar 1990).
21. The Peasant Leagues first began to organize in 1955 and received domestic and international notice (Figueiredo 1987; Hewitt 1969). The prominent leader of the Leagues was Francisco Julião.
22. Goulart attempted a compromise with the PSD, but members of the PSD from Minas Gerais and members of the PTB refused. The PSD deputies from Minas Gerais refused to vote for any constitutional amendment; however, many of them later voted for the Castelo Branco amendment (Cehelsky 1979). Figueiredo (1987) describes the amendment's failure.
23. According to Figueiredo (1987, 164–7), Goulart had this decree prepared by December 1963 but had delayed signing it. The text is in *Corrêio da Manhã* (March 14, 1964, 5).
24. Figueiredo (1987) describes the lack of compromise between the PSD, the UDN, the PTB and Goulart leading up to the coup.
25. The military government negotiated the law's provisions with the leadership of the PSD, the UDN, the PSP, and the PDC (Teixeira and Tavares de Araújo 1992).
26. Castelo Branco also proposed a limited right to vote for illiterates (not compulsory and only for municipal elections). The measure was opposed by the UDN, the PRP, the PSP, and parts of the PSD and the proposal was dropped without contest (Rodrigues 1965, 161–2).
27. See, e.g., Joseph Love on the military's land reform (1966, 100) and Gomes da Silva (1987).
28. Keck (1992, chapter 2), and Hagopian (1996) describe the events surrounding the democratic transition and the election of Tancredo Neves.
29. Sarney became vice president as part of the deal that secured Neves's election. Sarney filled in as acting president from March 15 until Neves's death on April 21, 1985, and was inaugurated on April 22.
30. Law 7.332 of July 1, 1985 states "*As eleições serão realizadas por sufrágio universal e voto direto e secreto*" (Article 12).
31. Calculated from registered voters by state, 1982 and 1986.
32. Article 14. Voting by those who are 16, 17, or over 70 years old is also voluntary. As in many Latin American countries, illiterates are not allowed to run for public office.
33. IDESP survey provided by the COSEP at UNICAMP. Surveys conducted in November 1982 and June and July 1987.

34. The Southeast has 47.7%, the Northeast 26.4%, the South 16.3%, the Center-West 6.7%, and the North 3% of the electorate (IBGE 1988a, 38).

35. The plan operated under the prevailing law, the military *Estatuto da Terra*, which was superceded by the 1988 Constitution.

36. The bill also legalized all political parties, and allowed the direct election of mayors of state capitols and national security zones (*Keesing's Contemporary Archives*, 1985, 33648). Congress unanimously approved the bill (Bruneau and Smith, 270).

37. MIRAD asked for public suggestions in crafting the plan. The Arquivo Edgard Leuenroth at UNICAMP houses the records of the suggestions.

38. The CNRA formed on April 28, 1983. Information from Herbert de Souza, "10 anos de campanha, 500 anos de luta," *Democracia na terra*, no. 8 (January/February 1993, 2).

39. As described by Graziano da Silva (1986), the CNA was the legal representative of the large landowners, and was "encrusted with the most backward, retrograde and reactionary of the Brazilian agrarian bourgeoisie" (4).

40. According to an interview with an INCRA official, INCRA did not know how many families were settled on expropriated land. Their data are presented as "capacity" rather than actual numbers. Graziano da Silva (1987) also charged that government figures included not only families that received land as part of the land reform but also those whose titles were recognized during the period but had nothing to do with the PNRA.

41. Newspapers at the time reported criticism of the 1986 ballot (e.g., *Estado de São Paulo*, November 9, 16 and 22, 1986, 2; *Jornal do Brasil*, November 18, 1986, 10).

42. Illiterates had voted in the 1985 elections mayoral elections. With only one office contested, the ballot was simple; voters had to mark an "X" by one candidate's name (*Visão*, October 22, 1986).

43. The absent deputy, Jesse Freire, was ill throughout the Constituent Assembly and missed the vote on land reform.

44. After three unsuccessful bids for the presidency, Luiz Inácio "Lula" da Silva of the Workers' Party won the 2002 presidential election.

45. Benevides also had been director of SUDENE and Public Works, lucrative positions for the distribution of pork.

46. The figures include only politicians who previously held public office. Thus, they underestimate the continuation of traditional politicians by excluding those with less obvious ties to the established political elite.

47. The "patriarch [of the Alves], Aluizio Alves, was governor in 1960 . . . but was *cassado* [banned] in 1969 and as PMDB candidate for governor was defeated by José Agripino Maia." Alves was named Minister of Administration by Tancredo Neves, "taking from the Maias a good part of the federal jobs in Rio Grande do Norte" (*Jornal do Brasil*, November 1, 1986, 8).

48. The Maia family influence also extended into Paraíba with the election of two federal and one state deputy (*O Estado de São Paulo*, December 27, 1986, 4).

49. Fraud was another possible factor. In Jaboatão, Pernambuco, 143 blank ballots were found to have been altered in favor of a PFL candidate for state deputy (*O Estado de São Paulo*, December 13, 1986).

50. In 1985, the PMDB, the PFL, the PDT, the PT, the PCB and the PCdoB all backed the left-leaning PMDB candidate for mayor of the capital, who won overwhelmingly. However, in 1986, the alliance broke down over the choice of candidates and other factors, which led to the PFL, the PDT, the PT, the PCB and the PCdoB supporting the winning candidate, Antônio Carlos Valladares (*Jornal do Brasil*, November 4, 1986).

51. Both the younger and elder Magalhães successfully continued their political careers. Luís Eduardo headed the Chamber of Deputies until February 1997, the same month that Antônio Carlos Magalhães became leader of the Senate.

52. Responses to a questionnaire. The question: With regard to reform, with which of the following sentences do you most agree? (1) Instead of a land reform entailing the distribution of land, the government should stimulate and protect farmers and rural producers; (2) A land reform is necessary but the distribution of land should be limited to nonproductive properties; (3) A radical land reform is necessary in order to change the structure of rural landowning in Brazil and to correct social injustice (Martins Rodrigues 1987, 159).

53. Interview with UDR founder and president Ronaldo Caiado in the *Folha de São Paulo* (June 8, 1986, 6).

54. Interview by the author with Ronaldo Caiado in Brasília, October 5, 1993. The UDR's philosophy stressed free enterprise and less government involvement as well. See, e.g., interview with Ronaldo Caiado in *Visão* (October 22, 1986). UDR members also denied pervasive rumors that some of the money was used to purchase arms for vigilante squads that violently forced land-invading peasants off their lands.

55. The former estimate from *Jornal do Brasil* (November 1, 1986); the latter from *Gazeta Mercantil* (November 17, 1986).

56. According to the UDR, the organization spread to 16 states and a majority of its members owned between 200 and 1500 hectares (*Visão*, October 22, 1986, 16).

57. The UDR used the media, airing weekly ten-minute segments on the Banderantes channel. In April 1987, UDR hired Multi-Consultoria de Comunicação Ltda., a lobbying firm (Tavares 1989, 20).

58. Sessions were suspended because of heckling from the audience, fights broke out, and a security guard was threatened by an onlooker with a gun.

59. Information on the structure of the Constituent Assembly based on Vânia Lomônaco Bastos and Tânia Moreira da Costa, ed., *Constituinte: Questões polêmicas*. Caderno CEAC/UnB Ano 1-N°2 Universidade de Brasília.

60. I thank Javier Martínez-Lara for this translation.

61. One of the early victories of the *Centrão* (the Big Center) was to alter the procedures for the first vote to allow voting section by section, instead of a simple yes or no vote on the complete draft of the constitution as originally

intended. The *Centrão*, a diverse group of more conservative members of the Constituent Assembly, united across party lines to oppose the leftist direction of proposed constitutional measures. See Baaklini (1992) for a fuller explanation of its membership and objectives.

62. The Constitution of 1946 established the "social function" of owning property, which permitted expropriation for land reform. However, the Constitution also guaranteed property rights and stipulated that "prior and just compensation" be paid for expropriated land (Brazil 1987c).

63. This was in spite of an argument over procedures that appeared to prohibit such a measure. The internal rules (*regimento interno*), particularly Art. 23 §2 as pointed out by Irma Passoni and other members of the subcommittee, appeared to prohibit the presentation of an alternate draft rather than simply amendments to portions of the subcommittee draft.

64. Although PMDB leader Mário Covas had designated Monteiro's substitute to be Antero de Barros, also from the PMDB and someone expected to join the pro-reform side on this vote, Almeida was approved by the president of the sub-committee, Edison Lobão (PFL-MA), and confirmed by the president of the Constituent Assembly, Ulysses Guimarães. The argument was that in the inter-ests of proportionality, the accepted practice of having the party leader appoint a substitute of the same party was waived. Instead, the first person to sign in was chosen: Oswaldo Almeida. The session had to be recessed briefly but various times because of the general turmoil that resulted from this decision. Meanwhile, members frantically searched for the missing Benedito Monteiro. (His absence has not been explained. Some speculated that conservative members either bribed or intimidated him into not appearing at the meeting.)

65. More or less as it remains in Art. 187 of the 1988 Constitution and loosely trans-lated as the following: Land is fulfilling its social function when (a) it is ration-ally utilized; (b) conserves renewable natural resources and preserves the environment; (c) observes worker legislation; and (d) its use favors the well-being of its owners and the workers who depend upon it.

66. The official record of this session can be found in the *Diário da Assembléia Nacional Constituinte (Suplemento)* July 1987, 126–74.

67. Interview with Nelson Jobim, Brasília, October 7, 1993.

68. Interview with Nelson Jobim, Brasília, October 7, 1993.

69. Interview with Nelson Jobim, Brasília, October 7, 1993. See also *Correio Brasiliense* (May 10, 1988) and *Senhor* (May 16, 1988).

70. The Centrão and the UDR considered the vote a great victory. Ronaldo Caiado exclaimed, "we have avoided having the inconsequentials take the country toward a social cataclysm!" Caiado's supporters carried him from the Congress on their shoulders (*Folha de São Paulo*, May 11, 1988, 1). Caiado sought to con-tinue his political career with an unsuccessful run for the presidency of Brazil in 1989, and then became a senator. His political career is a good example of the unimportance of parties and the individualistic nature of politics in Brazil.

71. Vote totals include substitutes for deputies and senators who left the Assembly. If the votes of the nine senators elected in 1982 are removed, then 49.1% of the delegates voted in favor of reform, and 43.8% voted against. Of senators elected in 1982, 7 voted against land reform and 2 in favor.
72. *O Estado de São Paulo* (November 26, 1989, 45). The rapporteur of the commission, Fábio Luchési, helped to rewrite the decree law for the PNRA in October 1985. This was the version that caused the president of INCRA and the Minister of Agriculture to resign.
73. Small properties were considered to be between 1 and 4 *módulos fiscais* (basic units of measure), medium-sized properties between 4 and 15 *módulos fiscais*.
74. Interview with INCRA official Ivanilson Guimarães.

Bibliography

Adams, Richard N. 1960. *Social Change in Latin America Today: Its Implications for United States Policy*. New York: Harper and Brothers.

AID (Agency for International Development). 1970a. *Land Reform in Chile, Colombia, Venezuela*. Washington, DC: Department of State.

AID (Agency for International Development). 1970b. *Land Reform in Bolivia, Ecuador, Peru*. Washington, DC: Department of State.

AID (Agency for International Development). 1970c. *Land Reform in Brazil, Northeast, Cuba, Guatemala, Mexico*. Washington, DC: Department of State.

AID (Agency for International Development). *U.S. Overseas Loans and Grants and Assistance from International Organizations*. Washington, DC: Department of State, various years.

Alexander, Robert. 1973. *Latin American Political Parties*. New York: Praeger Publishers.

Altimir, Oscar. 1982. *The Extent of Poverty in Latin America*, World Bank staff working papers no. 522. Washington, DC: The World Bank.

Ames, Barry. 1995. "Electoral Rules, Constituency Pressures, and Pork Barrel: Bases of Voting in the Brazilian Congress." *The Journal of Politics* 57 (May): 324–43.

Ames, Barry. 1987. *Political Survival: Politicians and Public Policy in Latin America*. Berkeley: University of California Press.

Ames, Barry. 1994. "The Reverse Coattails Effect: Local Party Organization in the 1989 Brazilian Presidential Election." *American Political Science Review* 88 (March): 95–111.

Ames, Barry. 1996. "Soft Theory, Hard Evidence: Rational Choice and Empirical Investigation in Brazil." *The Latin American Program Working Paper Series*. Woodrow Wilson International Center, no. 217 (March 1996).

Ayres, Robert. 1976. "Unidad Popular and the Chilean Electoral Process." In *Chile: Politics and Society*, ed. J. Samuel Valenzuela and Arturo Valenzuela. New Jersey: Transaction Books.

Baaklini, Abdo I. 1992. *The Brazilian Legislature and Political System*. Westport, Conneticut: Greenwood Press.

Bagley, Bruce. 1989. "The State and The Peasantry in Contemporary Colombia." *Latin American Issues*. 6.

Bagley, Bruce. 1979. "Political Power, Public Policy and the State in Colombia: Case Studies of the Urban and Agrarian Reforms During the National Front, 1958–1974." Ph.D. diss. UCLA.

Baloyra, Enrique and John Martz. 1979. *Political Attitudes in Venezuela: Societal Cleavages and Political Opinion.* Austin: University of Texas Press.

Baloyra, Enrique and John Martz. 1976. *Electoral Mobilization and Public Opinion: The Venezuelan Campaign of 1973.* Chapel Hill: University of North Carolina Press.

Baltar, Ronaldo. 1990. *Os empresários rurais e a reforma agrária no governo de transição (1985–1988).* Master's thesis, UNICAMP.

Banks, Arthur S. et al. 1971. *Cross-Polity Time-Series Data.* Cambridge, MA: MIT Press.

Barraclough, Solon. 1973. *Agrarian Systems in Latin America.* Lexington, MA: Lexington Books.

Barraclough, Solon and Arthur L. Domike. 1970. "Agrarian Structure in Seven Latin American Countries." In *Agrarian Problems & Peasant Movements in Latin America*, ed. Rodolfo Stavenhagen. Garden City, NY: Anchor Books.

Bassols Batalla, Narciso. 1967. *El pensamiento político de Álvaro Obregón.* Mexico: Editorial Nuestro Tiempo.

Bates, Robert H. 1987. "Agrarian Politics." In *Understanding Political Development*, ed. Myron Weiner and Samuel P. Huntington. Glenview, Ill.: Scott, Foresman and Company.

Bates, Robert H. 1981. *Markets and States in Tropical Africa: The Political Basis of Agricultural Policies.* Berkeley: University of California Press.

Berry, R. Albert. 1984. "Land Reform and the Adequacy of World Food Production." In *International Dimensions of Land Reform*, ed. John D. Montgomery. Boulder, CO: Westview Press.

Berry, R. Albert, Ronald G. Hellman, and Mauricio Solaún, eds. 1980. *Politics of Compromise: Coalition Government in Colombia.* New Brunswick, NJ: Transaction Books.

Betancourt, Rómulo. 1982. *Rómulo Betancourt: memoria del último destierro, 1948–1958.* Caracas, Venezuela: Ediciones Centauro.

Betancourt, Rómulo. 1959. *Posición y Doctrina.* Caracas: Editorial Cordillera.

Betancourt, Rómulo. 1951. *Rómulo Betancourt: Pensamiento y Acción.* Mexico, DF: Impresores Beatriz de Silva.

Blutstein, Howard I. et al. 1970. *Area Handbook for Costa Rica.* Washington, DC: Department of the Army.

Bond, Robert. 1977. *Contemporary Venezuela and Its Role in International Affairs.* New York: New York University Press.

Booth, John and Mitchell Seligson, eds. 1995. *Elections and Democracy in Central America, Revisited.* Chapel Hill: University of North Carolina Press.

Booth, John A. and Mitchell A. Seligson, eds. 1978–1979. *Political Participation in America*, 2 vols. New York: Holmes and Meier.

Borón, Atilio A. 1971. "Movilización política y crisis política en Chile (1920–1970)." *Aportes*, no. 20 (April): 41–69.

Boucher, Phillip. 1979. *U.S. Foreign Aid to Latin America: Hypotheses and Patterns in Historical Statistics, 1934–1974.* Ph.D.diss. UCLA.

Brazil. MIRAD (Ministério da Agricultura e Reforma Agrária) and INCRA. 1990. *Avaliação do Plano Nacional de Reforma Agrária—1987/89* (Estudos de Reforma Agrária, no. 4 ano II-1989). Brasília (May).

Brazil. Câmara dos Deputados. 1988a. *Assembléia Nacional Constituinte–1987/88: Repertório Biográfico dos Membros da Assembléia Nacional Constitutinte de 1987.* Brasília.

Brazil. Câmara dos Deputados. 1988b. *Diário da Assembléia Nacional Constituinte.* Brasília.

Brazil. Câmara dos Deputados. 1987a. *Regimento interno da Assembléia Nacional Constituinte.* Brasília.

Brazil. Câmara dos Deputados and Tribunal Superior Eleitoral. 1987b. *Eleições de 15 de novembro de 1989: candidatos e votos obtidos.* Brasília: Centro de Documentação e Informação, Coordenação de Publicações.

Brazil. INCRA (*Instituto Nacional de Colonização e Reforma Agrária*). 1987c. *Evolução da estrutura agrária do Brasil.* Brasília.

Brazil. INCRA. 1987c. *Evolução da estructura agrária do Brasil.* Brasília.

Bresser Pereira, Luiz. 1992. *Economia Brasileira: Uma Introdução Crítica* (10th ed.). São Paulo: Editora Brasiliense.

Brockett, Charles D. 1991. "The Structure of Political Opportunities and Peasant Mobilization in Central America." *Comparative Politics* 23 (April): 253–74.

Brockett, Charles D. 1988. *Land, Power, and Poverty: Agrarian Transformation and Political Conflict in Central America.* Boston: Unwin Hyman.

Bruneau, Thomas C. and Anne-Marie Smith. "Brazil." *Latin America and Caribbean Contemporary Record,* vol. IV: 265–86.

Caballero, José María. 1980. *Agricultura, reforma agraria y pobreza campesina.* Lima: Instituto de Estudios Peruanos.

Cambranes, Julio Castellanos. 1992. *500 años de lucha por la tierra: estudios sobre propeidad rural y reforma agraria en Guatemala,* vol. 1. Guatemala: FLACSO.

Cammack, Paul. 1982. "Clientelism and Military Government in Brazil." In *Private Patronage and Public Power,* ed. Christopher Clapham. New York: St. Martin's Press, 53–75.

Camp, Roderic Ai. 2003. *Politics in Mexico: The Democratic Transformation* (4th ed.). New York: Oxford University Press.

Campbell, Angus, Philip Converse, Warren Miller, and Donald Stokes. 1976. *The American Voter.* Chicago: University of Chicago Press.

CAPEL (*Centro de Asesoría y Promoción Electoral*). 1988. *Legislación electoral comparada: Argentina, Bolivia, Brasil, Chile, Ecuador, Paraguay, Perú y Uruguay.* San Jose, Costa Rica: Ediciones CAPEL.

CAPEL (*Centro de Asesoría y Promoción Electoral*). 1986. *Legislación Electoral Comparada: Colombia, México, Panamá, Venezuela y Centroamérica.* San Jose, Costa Rica: Ediciones CAPEL.

Carroll, Thomas F. 1961. "The Land Reform Issue in Latin America." In *Latin American Issues: Essays and Comments*, ed. Albert O. Hirschman. New York: Twentieth Century Fund, 161–201.

Carvalho, Abdias Vilar de and Maria da Conceição D'Incao, eds. 1982. *Reforma Agrária: Significado e viabilidade*. Petrópolis, Brasil: Editora Vozes.

Castelblanco de Castro, Beatriz, ed. 1988. *La Reforma Agraria de 1988: Ley 135 de 1961 modificada y adicionada por la Ley 30 de 1988*. Bogotá, Colombia: Editorial Publicitaria.

Castillo, Leonardo and David Lehmann. 1983. "Agrarian Reform and Structural Change in Chile, 1965–79." In *Agrarian Reform in Contemporary Developing Countries*, ed. Ajit Kumar Ghose. New York: St. Martin's Press.

Cehelsky, Marta. 1979. *Land Reform in Brazil: The Management of Social Change*. Boulder, CO: Westview Press.

Cheibub, José Antônio Borges. 1988. "*O voto do analfabeto: limites de participação e cidadania*." São Paulo: Instituto de Estudos Economicos, Sociais e Politicos de São Paulo.

Chile. 1969. *Ley general de elecciones; ley no. 14.852*. Publicado en el Diario Oficial no. 25.245, de 16 de mayo de 1962, modificado por leyes 16.094, 16.250 y 17.030. Santiago de Chile.

Chile. 1967. Ley no. 16.640, de 16 de julio de 1967. *Ley de reforma agraria publicada en el Diario Oficial de 28 de Julio de 1967*. Santiago: Editorial Nascimento.

Chile. 1963. *Reforma agraria y sus reglamentos, ley N 15.020, promulgada 27 November 1962*. Santiago, Chile: Ediciones Gutenberg.

Christodoulou, Demetrios. 1990. *The Unpromised Land: Agrarian Reform and Conflict Worldwide*. London: Zed Books.

Christodoulou, Demetrios. 1977. "Agrarian Reform in Retrospect: Contributions to its Dynamics and Related Fundamental Issues." *Land Settlement and Cooperatives*. 2.

Cline, William. 1970. *Economic Consequences of a Land Reform in Brazil*. Amsterdam: North Holland Publishing Company.

Coelho, João Gilberto Lucas and Antonio Carlos Nantes de Oliveira. 1989. *A nova Constituição. Avaliação do texto e perfil dos constituintes*. Instituto de Estudos Sócio-Econômicos, INESC. Rio de Janeiro: Revan.

Cohen, Suleiman I. 1978. *Agrarian Structures and Agrarian Reform*. Leiden and Boston: M. Nijhoff Social Sciences Division.

Collier, David and James Mahoney. 1996. "Insights and Pitfalls: Selection Bias in Qualitative Research." *World Politics* 49 (October): 56–91.

Collier, Ruth Berins and David Collier. 1991. *Shaping the Political Arena: Critical Junctures, the Labor Movement, and Regime Dynammcs in Latin America*. Princeton, NJ: Princeton University Press.

Colombia. DANE. 1972. *Colombia Política, Estadísticas 1935–1970*. Bogota: Departamento Administrativo nacional de Estadística.

Colque Huayllaro, Jorge. 1966. *La reforma agraria peruana: un estudio sobre los problemas sociales del campo*. Rome: Universidad Pontificia "Santo Tomás de Aquino in Urbe."

Combellas Lares, Ricardo. 1985. *COPEI: Ideología y Liderazgo.* Caracas: Editorial Ariel.

Coppedge, Michael. 1994a. "Prospects for Democratic Governability in Venezuela." *Journal of Interamerican Studies and World Affairs* 36 (2): 39–64.

Coppedge, Michael. 1994b. *Strong Parties and Lame Ducks: Presidential Partyarchy and Factionalism in Venzuela.* Stanford: Stanford University Press.

Coppedge, Michael. 1993. "Parties and Society in Mexico and Venezuela: Why Competition Matters." *Comparative Politics* 25 (3): 253–74.

Costa Rica. Ministerio de economía y comercio. 1984. *Anuario estadístico de Costa Rica 1982.* San José, Costa Rica: Dirección General de Estadística.

Cotler, Julio. 1990. "Segmentación Social, Fragmentación Política y la Cultura de la Violencia en el Perú." Columbia University Conference Papers, no. 41.

Cotler, Julio. 1978. "A Structural-Historical Approach to the Breakdown of Democratic Institutions: Peru." In *The Breakdown of Democratic Regimes: Latin America*, ed. Juan J. Linz and Alfred Stepan. Baltimore, MD: The Johns Hopkins University Press.

CPT. *Conflitos no campo. Brasil '92.* 1993. Goiânia, GO: *Comissão Pastoral da Terra*, Setor de Documentação.

CPT. *Conflitos no campo. Brasil/88.* 1989. Goiânia, GO: *Comissão Pastoral da Terra*, Setor de Documentação.

CPT (*Comissão Pastoral da Terra*, Pastoral Land Commission). 1988. *Conflitos no campo. Brasil/87.* Goiânia, GO: *Comissão Pastoral da Terra*, Setor de Documentação.

Crisp, Brian. 2000. *Democratic Institutional Design: The Powers and Incentives of Venezuelan Politicians and Interest Groups.* Stanford: Stanford University Press.

Cruz, María Elena. 1992. "From Inquilino to Temporary Worker; From Hacienda to Rural Settlement." In *Development and Social Change in the Chilean Countryside: From the Pre-Land Reform Period to the Democratic Transition*, ed. Cristóbal Kay and Patricio Silva. Amsterdam, The Netherlands: CEDLA (Centre for Latin American Research and Documentation).

Cruz-Cole, Ricardo. 1984. *Historia electoral de Chile, 1925–1973.* Santiago, Ediorial Jurídica de Chile.

Dahl, Robert A. 1971. *Polyarchy: Participation and Opposition.* New Haven: Yale University Press.

de Janvry, Alain. 1981. *The Agrarian Question and Reformism in Latin America.* Baltimore: The Johns Hopkins University Press.

Deere, Carmen Diana. 2003. "The Gender Asset Gap: Land in Latin America." *World Development* 31 (6): 925–48.

Deere, Carmen Diana. 1987. *The Peasantry in Political Economy: Trends of the 1980s.* University of Massachusetts, Amherst. Latin American Studies Program Occasional Papers no. 19.

Deere, Carmen Diana. 1985. "Rural Women and State Policy: The Latin American Reform Experience." *World Development* 13 (9).

Deere, Carmen Diana. 1984. "Agrarian Reform and the Peasantry in the Transition to Socialism in the Third World." Kellogg Institute for International Studies University of Notre Dame Working Paper no. 31.

Delury, George E., ed. 1987. *World Encyclopedia of Political Systems and Parties* (2nd ed.). New York: Facts on File Publications.

D'Incao, Maria Conceição. 1990. "Governo de transição: entre o velho e o novo projeto político de reforma agrária." *Lua nova* 20 (May) São Paulo.

Diamond, Larry Jay, Juan J. Linz, and Seymour Martin Lipset, eds. 1989. *Democracy in Developing Countries: Latin America*, vol. 4. Boulder, CO: Lynne Rienner Publishers, Inc.

DIAP (*Departamento Intersindical de Assessoria Parlamentar*). 1988. *Quem foi quem na constituinte: nas questões de interesse dos trabalhadores*. São Paulo: Cortez, Oboré.

Deininger, Klaus. 1999. "Making Negotiated Land Reform Work: Initial Experience from Colombia, Brazil and South Africa." *World Development* 27 (4): 651–72.

Dorner, Peter. 1992. *Latin American Land Reforms in Theory and Practice: A Retrospective Analysis*. Madison: Wisconsin.

Downs, Anthony. 1957. *An Economic Theory of Democracy*. New York: Harper & Row.

Drake, Paul W. and Eduardo Silva, eds. 1986. *Elections and Democratization in Latin America, 1980–1985*. San Diego: Center for Iberian and Latin American Studies and the Center for U.S.-Mexican Studies Institute of the Americas, University of California, San Diego.

Duff, Ernest A. 1985. *Leader and Party in Latin America*. Boulder: Westview.

Duff, Ernest A. 1968. *Agrarian Reform in Colombia*. New York: Frederick A. Praeger, Publishers.

ECLAC. 2001. *Statistical Yearbook for Latin America and the Caribbean*. Santiago, Chile: ECLAC.

ECLAC. 1985. *Statistical Yearbook for Latin America and the Caribbean*. Santiago, Chile: ECLAC.

Eckstein, Shlomo et al. 1978. *Land Reform in Latin America: Bolivia, Chile, Mexico, Peru and Venezuela*. Washington, DC: The World Bank.

Ellis, Frank. 1992. *Agricultural Policies in Developing Countries*. Cambridge: Cambridge University Press.

Ellner, Steve. 1993–1994. "The Deepening of Democracy in a Crisis Setting: Political Reform and the Electoral Process in Venezuela." *Journal of Interamerican Studies and World Affairs* 35 (4): 1–42.

Ellner, Steve. 1989. "Organized Labor's Political Influence and Party Ties in Venezuela: *Acción Democrática* and its Labor Leadership." *Journal of Interamerican Studies and World Affairs* 31 (4): 91–129.

Enríquez, Laura. 1991. *Harvesting Change: Labor and Agrarian Reform in Nicaragua, 1979–1990*. Chapel Hill: University of North Carolina Press.

Evans de la Cuadra, Enrique. 1970. *Relación de la Constitución Política de la República de Chile*. Santiago: Editorial Jurídica de Chile.

Ewell, Judith. 1993. "Venezuela in Crisis." *Current History* (March): 120–5.

Ewell, Judith. 1984. *Venezuela: A Century of Change*. London: C. Hurst & Company.

Falcão, Joaquim, ed. 1985. *Nordeste: Eleições*. Recife: Fundação Joaquim Nabuco, Editora Massangana.

Falcoff, Mark. 1989. *Modern Chile 1970–1989*. New Brunswick, NJ: Transaction Publishers.

Feder, Ernest. 1971. *The Rape of the Peasantry: Latin America's Landholding System*. Garden City, NY: Anchor Books.

Fernández y Fernández, Ramón. 1965. *Reforma agraria y crédito agrícola en Ecuador*. Chapingo, Mexico: Escuela Nacional de Agricultura.

Ferreira, Brancolina and João Gabriel L.C. Teixeira. 1988. "Constitutinte e reforma agrária: embates de classe." *Ciências Sociais Hoje*. São Paulo: Vértice, ANPOCS. 99–134.

Figueiredo, Argelina Maria Cheibub. 1987. "Political Coalitions in Brasil, 1961–1964: Democratic Alternatives to the Political Crisis." Ph.D. diss. University of Chicago.

Fioravanti, Eduardo. 1976. *Latifundio y Sindicalismo Agrario en el Perú*. Lima: Instituto de Estudios Peruanos.

Fiorina, Morris P. 1981. *Retrospective Voting in American National Elections*. Cambridge, MA: Harvard University Press.

Fitzgibbon, Russell, ed. 1948. *The Constitutions of the Americas*. Chicago: University of Chicago Press.

Flanz, Gisbert H., ed. 1971. *Constitutions of the Countries of the World*. Dobbs Ferry, NY: Oceana Publications.

Flores, Edmundo. 1963. *Land Reform and the Alliance for Progress*. Princeton: Center of International Studies.

Foxley, Alejandro. 1986. "The Neoconservative Economic Experiment in Chile." In *Military Rule in Chile*, ed. Arturo Valenzuela and J. Samuel Valenzuela. Baltimore, MD: The Johns Hopkins University Press.

Francis, Michael J. 1973. *The Allende Victory: An Analysis of 1970 Chilean Presidential Election*. Tucson, AZ: University of Arizona Press.

Frieden, Jeffry A. *Debt, Development, and Democracy: Modern Political Economy and Latin America, 1965–1985*. Princeton, NJ: Princeton University Press,

Fuenmayor, Juan Bautista. *Historia de la Venezuela Política Contempóranea 1899–1969*. Multiple volumes, vol. 5 (1979); vol. 6 (1980); vol. 7 (1981).

Gandrillas M., Guillermo. 1968. *Cartilla Cívica: El derecho a sufragio*. Santiago: Guillermo Echiburu L.

Geddes, Barbara. 1995. "The Politics of Economic Liberalization." *Latin American Research Review* 30 (2).

Geddes, Barbara. 1994. *Politician's Dilemma: Building State Capacity in Latin America*. Berkeley: University of California Press.

Geddes, Barbara. 1990. "How the Cases You Choose Affect the Answers You Get: Selection Bias in Comparative Politics." *Political Analysis* 2: 131–50.

Geddes, Barbara and Artur Ribeiro Neto. 1992. "Institutional Sources of Corruption in Brazil." *Third World Quarterly* 13 (4).

Germani, Gino. 1969. "Mass Immigration and Modernization in Argentina." In *Latin American Radicalism*, ed. Irving Louis Horowitz, Josué de Castro, and John Gerassi. New York: Random House.

Ghose, Ajit Kumar. 1983. *Agrarian Reform in Contemporary Developing Countries*. New York: St. Martin's Press.

Gil, Federico G. 1966. *The Political System of Chile*. Boston: Houghton Mifflin Company.

Gil, Federico G. and Charles J. Parrish. 1965. *The Chilean Presidential Election of September 4, 1964*. Washington, DC: ICSPS, Institute for the Comparative Study of Political Systems.

Gleijeses, Piero. 1992. "La Reforma Agraria de Arbenz." In *500 años de lucha por la tierra: estudios sobre propeidad rural y reforma agraria en Guatemala*, ed. Julio Castellanos, Cambranes, vol. 1. Guatemala: FLACSO.

Gomes da Silva, José. 1992. "Um novo estatuto da terra." *Democracia na Terra* 5 (May/June).

Gomes da Silva, José. 1989. *Buraco negro: a reforma agrária na Constitutinte de 1987–88*. Rio de Janeiro: Paz e Terra.

Gomes da Silva, José. 1988. "Reforma agraria na Constituição Federal de 1988: Uma avaliação crítica." *Reforma Agrária* 18 (2).

Gomes da Silva, José. 1987. *Caindo por terra: crises da reforma agrária na nova república*. São Paulo: Busca Vida.

Gómez, Alejandro, ed. 1982. *Rómulo Betancourt: contra la dictadura de Juan Vicente Gómez, 1928–1935*. Caracas, Venezuela: Ediciones Centauro.

Gorvin, Ian, ed. 1989. *Elections Since 1945: A Worldwide Reference Compendium*. Chicago and London: St. James Press.

Graziano da Silva, José. 1987. "Mas, qual Reforma Agrária?" *Reforma Agrária* 17 (1).

Graziano da Silva, José. 1987. *"Balanço e perspectivas: as possibilidades da reforma agrária em 1987 enquanto opção de política social."* mimeo. São Luis (MA): Anais da SOBER.

Graziano da Silva, José. 1986. "O PNRA da Nova República: a reforma agrária sob o controle do latifúndio." Campinas: UNICAMP. Typescript.

Griffen, Keith. 1976. *Land Concentration and Rural Poverty*. London: MacMillan Press.

Grindle, Merilee. 1986. *State and Countryside: Development Policy and Agrarian Politics in Latin America*. Baltimore: Johns Hopkins University.

Grofman, Bernard and Arend Lijphart, eds. 1986. *Electoral Laws and Their Political Consequences*. New York: Agathon.

Guevara, Pedro. 1989. *Concertación y Conflicto: el pacto social y el fracso de las respuestas consensuales a la crisis del sistema político venezolano*. Caracas: Universidad Central de Venezuela.

Haggerty, Richard A., ed. 1991. *Dominican Republic and Haiti: Country Studies*. Area Handbook Studies, U.S. Government, Secretary of the Army.

Hagopian, Frances. 1996. *Traditional Politics and Regime Change in Brazil*. New York: Cambridge University Press.

Hagopian, Frances. 1993. "After Regime Change: Authoritarian Legacies, Political Representation, and the Democratic Future of South America." *World Politics* 45 (April): 464–500.

Hagopian, Frances. 1992. "The Compromised Consolidation: The Political Class in the Brazilian Transition." In *Issues in Democratic Consolidation: The New South American Democracies in Comparative Perspective*, ed. Scott Mainwaring, Guillermo O'Donnell, and J. Samuel Valenzuela. Notre Dame: University of Notre Dame Press.

Hagopian, Frances. 1990. "'Democracy by Undemocratic Means'? Elites, Political Pacts, and Regime Transition in Brazil." *Comparative Political Studies* 23 (2): 147–70.

Hall, Linda B. 1981. *Álvaro Obregón: Power and Revolution in Mexico, 1911–1920*. College Station: Texas A&M University Press.

Handelman, Howard. 1980. *Ecuadorian Agrarian Reform: The Politics of Limited Change*. Hanover, NH: American Universities Field Staff Reports.

Handelman, Howard. 1975. *Struggle in the Andes: Peasant Political Mobilization in Peru*. Austin: University of Texas Press.

Haney, Emil B. and Wava G. Haney. 1989. "The Agrarian Transition in Highland Ecuador." In *Searching for Agrarian Reform*, ed. William Thiesenhusen. Boston: Unwin Hyman.

Hanratty, Dennis M., ed. 1991. *Ecuador: A Country Study*. Washington, DC: Department of the Army.

Hansis, Randall G. 1971. "Álvaro Obregón, the Mexican Revolution, and the Politics of Consolidation, 1920–1924." Ph.D. diss., University of New Mexico.

Hartlyn, Jonathan. 1989. "Colombia: The Politics of Violence and Accommodation." In *Democracy in Developing Countries: Latin America*, ed. Larry Jay Diamond, Juan J. Linz, and Seymour Martin Lipset, vol. 4. Boulder, CO: Lynne Rienner Publishers.

Hartlyn, Jonathan. 1988. *The Politics of Coalition Rule in Colombia*. Cambridge: University of Cambridge Press.

Havens, A. Eugene, William L. Flinn, and Susana Lastarría-Cornhill. 1980. "Agrarian Reform and the National Front: A Class Analysis." In *Politics of Compromise: Coalition Government in Colombia*, ed. Albert R. Berry, Ronald G. Hellman, and Mauricio Solaún. New Brunswick, NJ: Transaction Books.

Hayami, Yujiro. 1991. "Land Reform." In *Politics & Policy Making in Developing Countries*, ed. Gerald Meier. San Francisco: ICS Press.

Hayami, Yujiro, Maria Agnes R. Quisumbing, and Lourdes S. Adriano. 1990. *Toward an Alternative Land Reform Paradigm*. Manila: Ateneo de Manila University Press.

Hellinger, Daniel C. 1991. *Venezuela: Tarnished Democracy*. Boulder: Westview Press.

Herman, Donald. 1980. *Christian Democracy in Venezuela*. Chapel Hill: The University of North Carolina Press.

Hewitt, Cynthia N. 1969. "Brazil: The Peasant Movement of Pernambuco, 1961–1964." In *Latin American Peasant Movements*, ed. Henry A. Landsberger. Ithaca: Cornell University Press.

Hillman, Richard S. 1994. *Democracy for the Privileged: Crisis and Transition in Venezuela*. Boulder & London: Lynne Rienner.

Hirschman, Albert O. 1963. *Journeys Toward Progress*. New York: The Twentieth Century Fund.

Hirschman, Albert O. 1961. *Latin American Issues: Essays and Comments*. New York: Twentieth Century Fund.

Horton, Alan W. 1980. "Agrarian Reform and the International Consensus." *American Universities Field Staff Reports* 45. Hanover, NH: American Universities.

Hudson, Rex A. and Sandra W. Meditz, eds. 1992. *Uruguay: A Country Study*. Washington, DC: Department of the Army.

Huntington, Samuel P. 1968. *Political Order in Changing Societies*. New Haven and London: Yale University Press.

IBASE. 1984. *Os Donos da Terra e a luta pela Reforma Agrária*. Rio de Janeiro: Codecri.

IBGE (*Instituto Brasileiro de Geografia e Estatística*). 1989, 1992, 1993. *Anuário estatístico*. Rio de Janeiro.

IBGE. 1990. *Censo demográfico 1980*, vol. 1 (Brasil), Tomo 4, No. 1. Rio de Janeiro.

IBGE. 1988a. *Perfil dos eleitores: Pesquisa Nacional por Amostra de Domicílios 1988*. Rio de Janeiro: IBGE.

IBGE. 1988b. *Pesquisa Nacional*. Rio de Janeiro.

IBGE. 1985. *Censo agropecuario*. Rio de Janeiro.

ICSPS. 1968. *Venezuela Election Factbook*. Washington, DC: ICSPS (December 1).

ICSPS. 1965. *Methods of Electing National Executives and National Legislatures in South America*. Washington, DC: ICSPS.

ICSPS. 1962. *Brazil Election Factbook*. Washington, DC: ICSPS (October 7).

INCRA (Instituto Nacional de Colonização e Reforma Agrária). 1987. *Evolução da estrutura agrária do Brasil*. Brasília: INCRA, Diretoria de Cadastro e Informática (March).

Inter-American Development Bank. 1986. *Economic and Social Progress in Latin America, 1986 Report*. Washington, DC: Inter-American Development Bank.

Jemio Ergueta, Angel. 1973. *La Reforma Agraria en Bolivia*. La Paz: CEDAL.

Karl, Terry Lynn. 1990. "Dilemmas of Democratization in Latin Ameria." *Comparative Politics* 23 (1): 1–21.

Karl, Terry Lynn. 1986. "Petroleum and Political Pacts: The Transition to Democracy in Venezuela." In *Transitions from Authoritarian Rule: Latin America*, 2nd ed., ed. Guillermo O'Donnell, Philippe C. Schmitter, and Laurence Whitehead. Baltimore, MD: The Johns Hopkins University Press, 196–219.

Kaufman, Robert R. 1972. *The Politics of Land Reform in Chile, 1950–1970*. Cambridge, Massachusetts: Harvard University Press.

Kaufman, Robert R. 1967. *The Chilean Political Right and Agrarian Reform: Resistance and Moderation*. Washington, DC: Institute for the Comparative Study of Political Systems.

Kay, Cristóbal. 2001. "Reflections on Rural Violence in Latin America." *Third World Quarterly* 22 (5): 741–75.

Kay, Cristóbal. 1983. "The Agrarian Reform in Peru: An Assessment." In *Agrarian Reform in Contemporary Developing Countries*, ed. Ajit Kumar Ghose. New York: St. Martin's Press.

Kay, Cristóbal. 1982. "Achievements and Contradictions of the Peruvian Agrarian Reform." *The Journal of Development Studies* 18 (2).

Kay, Cristóbal. 1981. "Political Economy, Class Alliances, and Agrarian Change in Chile." *The Journal of Peasant Studies* 8 (4).

Kay, Cristóbal and Patricio Silva, eds. 1992. *Development and Social Change in the Chilean Countryside: From the Pre-Land Reform Period to the Democratic Transition.* Amsterdam, The Netherlands: CEDLA (Centre for Latin American Research and Documentation).

Keck, Margaret E. 1992. *The Workers' Party and Democratization in Brazil.* New Haven and London: Yale University Press.

King, Russell. 1977. *Land Reform: A World Survey.* London: G. Bell and Sons.

Kinzo, Maria D'Alva Gil. 1980. *Representação Política e Sistema Eleitoral no Brasil.* São Paulo: Símbolo.

Kline, Harvey F. 1983. *Colombia: Portrait of Unity and Diversity.* Boulder, CO: Westview Press.

Kornblith, Miriam. 1991. "The Politics of Constitution-making: Constitutions and Democracy in Venezuela." *The Journal of Latin American Studies* 23 (February): 61–89.

Korovkin, Tanya. 1997. "Indigenous Peasant Struggles and the Capitalist Modernization of Agriculture: Chimborazo, 1964–1991." *Latin American Perspectives* 24 (May): 25–50.

Lamounier, Bolivar. 1989. *Partidos e Utopias: o Brasil no limiar dos anos 90.* São Paulo: Edições Loyola.

Lamounier, Bolivar and Judith Muszynski. 1989. "*O processo eleitoral brasileiro, da velha à Nova República.*" Idesp series, texto no. 34, São Paulo.

Lamounier, Bolivar and Rachel Meneguello. 1986. *Partidos políticos e consolidação democrática: o caso brasileiro.* São Paulo, editora brasiliense.

Landsberger, Henry A., ed. 1969. *Latin American Peasant Movements.* Ithaca: Cornell University Press.

Laranjeira, Raymundo. 1983. *Colonização e Reforma Agrária no Brasil.* Rio de Janeiro: Civilização Brasiliera.

Lastarria-Cornhiel, Susana. 1989. "Agrarian Reforms of the 1960s and 1970s in Peru." In *Searching for Agrarian Reform*, ed. William Thiesenhusen. Boston: Unwin Hyman.

Leal, Victor Nunes. 1977. *Coronelismo: The Municipality and Representative Government in Brazil.* Translated by June Henjrey. Cambridge, New York: Cambridge University Press.

Lehmann, David, ed. 1974. *Agrarian Reform & Agrarian Reformism: Studies of Peru, Chile, China and India.* London: Faber and Faber.

Lehmann, David. 1971. "Political Incorporation Versus Political Stability." *Journal of Development Studies* 7 (4).

Levine, Daniel H. 1989. "Venezuela: The Nature, Sources, and Prospects of Democracy." In *Democracy in Developing Countries: Latin America*, ed. Larry Jay Diamond, Juan J. Linz, and Seymour Martin Lipset, vol. 4. Boulder, CO: Lynne Rienner Publishers.

Levine, Daniel H. 1978. "Venezuela since 1958: The Consolidation of Democratic Politics." In *The Breakdown of Democratic Regimes: Latin America*, ed. Juan J. Linz and Alfred Stepan. Baltimore, MD: The Johns Hopkins University Press.

Levine, Daniel H. 1973. *Conflict and Political Change in Venezuela*. Princeton: Princeton University Press.

Levinson, Jerome and Juan de Onís. 1970. *The Alliance That Lost Its Way: A Critical Report on the Alliance for Progress*. Chicago: Quadrangle Books.

Lijphart, Arend. 1984. *Democracies*. New Haven: Yale University Press.

Lima Júnior, Olavo Brasil de. 1993. "O Mercado Político e o Sistema Partidário no Brasil: 1945 a 1990." Presented at the XVII Encontro Anual da ANPOCS, Caxambu, Brazil, October 22–26.

Lima Júnior, Olavo Brasil de, ed. 1991. *Sistema eleitoral brasileiro: teoria e prática*. Rio de Janeiro: Rio Fundo Editora and IUPERJ.

Linz, Juan J. and Alfred Stepan, eds. 1978. *The Breakdown of Democratic Regimes: Latin America*. Baltimore, MD: The Johns Hopkins University Press.

Lipton, Michael. 1993. "Land Reform as Commenced Business: The Evidence Against Stopping." *World Development* 21 (4): 641–57.

Lipton, Michael. 1974. "Towards a Theory of Land Reform." In *Agrarian Reform & Agrarian Reformism: Studies of Peru, Chile, China and India*, ed. David Lehmann. London: Faber and Faber.

Loehr, William, David Price, and Satish Raichur. 1976. *A Comparison of U.S. and Multilateral Aid Recipients in Latin America, 1957–1971*. International Studies Series number 02-040, vol. 4. Beverly Hills: Sage Publications.

López Pintor, Rafael. 1969. *Algunos Aspectos de la Participación Política en Chile*. Santiago, Chile: Publicaciones INSORA.

Love, Joseph. 1970. "Political Participation in Brazil, 1881–1969." *Luso-Brazilian Review* 7 (December): 3–24.

Love, Joseph. 1966. "Brazilian Crisis." *Studies on the Left* 6 (4): 94–104.

Loveman, Brian. 1979. "Political Participation and Rural Labor in Chile." In *Political Participation in Latin America Volume II*, ed. Mitchell A. Seligson and John A. Booth. New York and London: Holmes & Meier.

Loveman, Brian. 1976a. *Struggle in the Countryside: Politics and Rural Labor in Chile, 1919–1973*. Bloomington: Indiana University Press.

Loveman, Brian. 1976b. "The Transformation of the Chilean Countryside." In *Chile: Politics and Society*, ed. J. Samuel Valenzuela and Arturo Valenzuela. New Jersey: Transaction Books.

Lowenthal, Abraham, ed. 1991. *Exporting Democracy: The United States and Latin America*. Baltimore: Johns Hopkins University Press.

Mainwaring, Scott. 1993. "Brazilian Party Underdevelopment in Comparative Perspective." *Political Science Quarterly* 107 (4): 677–702.

Mainwaring, Scott. 1991. "Politicians, Parties, and Electoral Systems: Brazil in Comparative Perspective." *Comparative Politics* 24 (1): 21–43.

Mainwaring, Scott. 1989. "Grassroots Popular Movements and the Struggle for Democracy: Nova Iguaçu." In *Democratizing Brazil: Problems of Transition and Consolidation*, ed. Alfred Stepan. Oxford: Oxford University Press.

Mainwaring, Scott and Timothy R. Scully. 1995. *Building Democratic Institutions: Party Systems in Latin America*. Stanford: Stanford University Press.

Marini, R.M. 1972. "La Reforma Agraria en América Latina." In *Transición al Socialismo y Experiencia Chilena*, ed. CESO-CEREN. Santiago: Prensa Latinoamericana.

Martínez-Lara, Javier. 1994. *Building Democracy in Brazil: The Politics of Constitutional Change, 1985–1993*. Ph.D. diss. Oxford University.

Martins, José de Souza. 1984. *A militarização da questão agrária no Brasil*. Petrópolis: Editora Vozes.

Martins, José de Souza. 1981. *Os camponeses e a política no Brasil*. Petrópolis, Brasil: Editora Vozes.

Martins Rodrigues, Leôncio. 1987. *Quem é Quem na Constituinte: Uma Análise Sócio-Política dos Partidos e Deputados*. São Paulo, Oesp-Maltese.

Martz, John D. 1997. *The Politics of Clientelism: Democracy & the State in Colombia*. New Brunswick and London: Transaction.

Martz, John D. 1992. "Party Elites and Leadership in Colombia and Venezuela." *Journal of Latin American Studies* 24 (1): 87–122.

Martz, John D. 1967. "Costa Rican Electoral Trends, 1953–1966." *Western Political Quarterly* 20 (4): 888–909.

Martz, John D. 1966. *Acción Democrática: Evolution of a Modern Political Party in Venezuela*. Princeton, New Jersey: Princeton University Press.

Martz, John D. and Enrique Baloyra. 1976. *The Venezuelan Election of 1973*. Chapel Hill: The University of North Carolina Press.

Mayhew, David R. 1974. *Congress: The Electoral Connection*. New Haven and London: Yale University Press.

McClintock, Cynthia. 1984. "Why Peasants Rebel: The Case of Peru's Sendero Luminoso." *World Politics* 37 (1).

McClintock, Cynthia. 1981. *Peasant Cooperatives and Political Change in Peru*. Princeton, NJ: Princeton University Press.

McDonald, Ronald H. and J. Mark Ruhl. 1989. *Party Politics and Elections in Latin America*. Boulder: Westview Press.

Medeiros, Leonilde Sérvolo de. 1989. *História dos movimentos sociais no campo*. Rio do Janeiro: FASE.

Meditz, Sandra W. and Dennis M. Hanratty, ed. 1987. *Panama: A Country Study*. Washington, DC: Department of the Army.

Meier, Gerald, ed. 1991. *Politics & Policy Making in Developing Countries*. San Francisco: ICS Press.

Melville, Thomas and Marjorie Melville. 1971. *Guatemala: The Politics of Land Ownership*. New York: The Free Press.

Menéndez-Carrión, Amparo and Fernando Bustamante. 1995. "Purposes and Methods of Intraregional Comparison." In *Latin America in Comparative*

Perspective: New Approaches to Methods and Analysis, ed. Peter H. Smith. Boulder: Westview Press, 59–80.

Meyer, Carrie. 1989. *Land Reform in Latin America: The Dominican Case*. New York: Praeger, 1989.

Mitchell, Brian R. 1993. *International Historical Statistics: The Americas 1750–1988*. New York: Stockton Press.

Moisés, José Alvaro. 1993. "Elections, Political Parties and Political Culture in Brazil: Changes and Continuities." *Journal of Latin American Studies* 25: 573–611.

Molina Vega, José E. 1987. "La personalización del sufragio en Venezuela." In *Venezuela: un sistema político en crisis*, ed. Alfredo Ramos Jiménez. Mérida, Venezuela: Kappa Editores, 77–108.

Molina, José Enrique. 1989. *La participación electoral en Venezuela*. Cuadernos de CAPEL no. 31. Cosa Rica: CAPEL (Centro de Asesoria y Promoción Electoral, Instituto Interamericano de Derechos Humanos).

Montgomery, John D., ed. 1984. *International Dimensions of Land Reform*. Boulder, CO: Westview Press.

Morães, Clodomir. 1970. "Peasant Leagues in Brazil." In *Agrarian Problems & Peasant Movements in Latin America*, ed. Rodolfo Stavenhagen. Garden City, NY: Anchor Books, 453–501.

Muller, Edward N., and Mitchell A. Seligson. 1987. "Insurgency and Inequality." *American Political Science Review* 81 (June): 425–51.

Muñoz, Heraldo. 1991. "Chile: The Limits of 'Success.'" In *Exporting Democracy: The United States and Latin America*, ed. Abraham Lowenthal. Baltimore: Johns Hopkins University Press, 161–74.

Myers, David J. 1973. *Democratic Campaigning in Venezuela: Caldera's Victory*. Caracas: Editorial natura.

Nelson, Harold, ed. 1983. *Costa Rica: A Country Study*. Washington, DC: Department of the Army.

Neuse, Steven M. 1978. "Voting in Chile: The Feminine Response." In Booth and Seligson, eds., vol. 1, 129–44.

Niemi, Richard G. and Herbert F. Weisberg. 1993. *Controversies in Voting Behavior*. (3rd ed.). Washington, DC: CQ Press.

Niess, Frank. 1990. *A Hemisphere to Itself: A History of US–Latin American Relations*. London and Atlantic Highlands, New Jersey: Zed Books.

Nohlen, Dieter, ed. 1993. *Enciclopedia Electoral Latinoamericana y del Caribe*. San José, Costa Rica: Instituto Interamericano de Derechos Humanos.

Nyrop, Richard F., ed. 1983a. *Brazil: A Country Study*. Area Handbook Studies, U.S. Government, Secretary of the Army.

Nyrop, Richard F., ed. 1983b. *Guatemala: A Country Study*. Area Handbook Studies, U.S. Government, Secretary of the Army.

Ochoa, Enrique. 1987. "The Rapid Expansion of Voter Participation in Latin America: Presidential Elections, 1845–1986." In James Wilkie and David Lorey, eds., *Statistical Abstract of Latin America*. Los Angeles: UCLA Latin American Center.

O'Donnell, Guillermo, Philippe C. Schmitter, and Laurence Whitehead, eds. 1986. *Transitions from Authoritarian Rule: Latin America* (2nd ed.). Baltimore, MD: The Johns Hopkins University Press.

Olson, Mancur. 1965. *The Logic of Collective Action*. Cambridge: Harvard University Press, 1965.

Osterling, Jorge P. 1989. *Democracy in Colombia: Clientelist Politics and Guerrilla Warfare*. New Brunswick, NJ: Transaction Publishers.

Paiva, Maria Arair Pinto. 1985. *Direito político do sufrágio no Brasil (1822–1982)*. Brasília: Thesaurus Editora.

Palhares Moreira Reis, Antonio Carlos. 1985. *As duras eleições nordestinas*. Pernambuco: Editora ASA Pernambuco.

Parrish, Charles J., Arpad J. von Lazar, and Jorge Tapia Videla. 1967. *The Chilean Congressional Election of March 7, 1965*. Washington, DC: Institute for the Comparative Study of Political Systems, Election Analysis Series no. 4.

Patch, Richard W. 1960. "Bolivia: U.S. Assistance in a Revolutionary Setting." In Adams (1960).

Payne, James. 1968. *Patterns of Conflict in Colombia*. New Haven: Yale University Press.

Pearse, Andrew. 1970. "Agrarian Change Trends in Latin America." In *Agrarian Problems & Peasant Movements in Latin America*, ed. Rodolfo Stavenhagen. Garden City, NY: Anchor Books, 11–40.

Peeler, John A. 1985. *Latin American Democracies: Colombia, Costa Rica, Venezuela*. Chapel Hill: University of North Carolina Press.

Petras, James. 1976. "Nationalization, Socioeconomic Change, and Popular Participation." In *Chile: Politics and Society*, ed. J. Samuel Valenzuela and Arturo Valenzuela. New Jersey: Transaction Books, 172–200.

Powell, G. Bingham, Jr. 1980. "Voting Turnout in Thirty Democracies." In Richard Rose, ed., *Electoral Participation*. Beverly Hills: Sage.

Powell, John. 1971. *Political Mobilization of the Venezuelan Peasant*. Cambridge, Massachusetts: Harvard University Press.

Powell, John D. 1969. "Venezuela: The Peasant Union Movement." In *Latin American Peasant Movements*, ed. Henry A. Landsberger. Ithaca: Cornell University Press.

Powelson, John D. 1984. "International Public and Private Agencies." In *International Dimensions of Land Reform*, ed. John D. Montgomery. Boulder, CO: Westview Press, 89–113.

Prosterman, Roy L. and Jeffrey M. Riedinger. 1987. *Land Reform and Democratic Development*. Baltimore: The Johns Hopkins University Press.

Prosterman, Roy. L., Mary N. Temple, Timothy M. Hamstad, eds. 1990. *Agrarian Reform and Grassroots Development: Ten Case Studies*. Boulder and London: Lynne Rienner.

Prothro, James W. and Patricio E. Chaparro. 1976. "Public Opinion and the Movement of Chilean Government to the Left, 1952–72." In *Chile: Politics and*

Society, ed. J. Samuel Valenzuela and Arturo Valenzuela. New Jersey: Transaction Books.

Quezada Lagos, Fernando. 1984. *La elección presidencial de 1970*. Santiago, Chile.

Rae, Douglas W. 1967. *The Political Consequences of Electoral Laws*. New Haven and London: Yale University Press.

Ramos Jiménez, Alfredo, ed. 1987. *Venezuela: un sistema político en crisis*. Mérida, Venezuela: Kappa Editores.

Reis, Elisa P. 1989. "Brasil: cem anos de questão agrária." *dados—Revista de Ciências Sociais*. *Rio de Janeiro* 32 (3): 281–301.

Rego, Rubem Murilo Leão. 1992. "Dilemas da questáo agrária brasileira: tem futro a reforma agrária?" *Revista latinoamerica*, ano 13, (48), October–December, Rome, Italy: 63–74.

Remmer, Karen L. 1984. *Party Competition in Argentina and Chile: Political Recruitment and Public Policy, 1890–1930*. Lincoln: University of Nebraska Press.

Reynolds, Lloyd G. 1996. "Some Sources of Income Inequality in Latin America." *Journal of Interamerican Studies and World Affairs* 38 (2/3).

Rezazadeh, Reza and Joseph Mac McKenzie. 1978. *Political Parties in Colombia*. Ann Arbor, Michigan: University Microfilms International.

Rodrigues, José Honório. 1965. *Conciliação e reforma no Brasil: um desafio histórico-político*. Rio de Janeiro: Civilização Brasileira.

Rokkan, Stein et al. 1970. *Citizens, Elections, Parties*. New York: David McKay.

Romero, Aníbal. 1997. "Rearranging the Deck Chairs on the Titanic: The Agony of Democracy in Venezuela." *Latin American Research Review* 32 (1): 7–36.

Rowles, James P. 1985. *Law and Agrarian Reform in Costa Rica*. Boulder: Westview Press.

Ruddle, Kenneth and Kathleen Barrows, eds. 1974. *Statistical Abstract of Latin America*. Los Angeles: UCLA Latin American Publications.

Ruddle, Kenneth and Philip Gillette, eds. 1972. *Latin American Political Statistics: Supplement to the Statistical Abstract of Latin America*. Los Angeles: UCLA Latin American Center.

Rudolph, James D., ed. 1985. *Argentina: A Country Study*. Area Handbook Studies, U.S. Government, Secretary of the Army.

Rueschemeyer, Dietrich and Peter B. Evans. 1985. "The State and Economic Transformation: Toward an Analysis of the Conditions Underlying Effective Intervention." In *Bringing the State Back In*, ed. Peter B. Evans, Dietrich Rueschemeyer, and Theda Skocpol. Cambridge: Cambridge University Press.

Russett, Bruce M. 1964. "Inequality and Instability, The Relation of Land Tenure to Politics." *World Politics* 14 (April).

Sánchez-Albornoz, Nicolás. 1989. "Population." In *Latin America: Economy and Society, 1870–1930*, ed. Leslie Bethell. Cambridge: Cambridge University Press.

Sanders, Thomas G. 1980. "Food Policy, Decision-Making in Colombia." *American Universities Staff Reports* no. 50, Hanover: American Universities.

Sarles, Margaret J. 1982. "Maintaining Political Control Through Parties: The Brazilian Strategy." *Comparative Politics* 15 (October): 41–71.

Schlesinger, Stephen and Stephen Kinzer. 1999. *Bitter Fruit: The Story of the American Coup in Guatemala.* Expanded ed. Boston, MA: Harvard University, David Rockefeller Center for Latin American Studies.

Scott, Robert E., ed. 1973. *Latin American Modernization Problems: Case Studies in the Crises of Change.* Urbana: University of Illinois Press.

Seligmann, Linda J. 1995. *Between Reform & Revolution: Political Struggles in the Peruvian Andes, 1969–1991.* Stanford: Stanford University Press.

Seligson, Mitchell A. 1980. *Peasants of Costa Rica and the Development of Agrarian Capitalism.* Madison: University of Wisconsin Press.

Serxner, Stanley. 1959. *Acción Democrática of Venezuela: Its Origin and Development.* Monograph Series. Gainesville: University of Florida Press.

Silva, Patricio. 1992. "The State, Politics, and Peasant Unions." In *Development and Social Change in the Chilean Countryside: From the Pre-Land Reform Period to the Democratic Transition,* ed. Cristóbal Kay and Patricio Silva. Amsterdam, The Netherlands: CEDLA (Centre for Latin American Research and Documentation).

Silva Herzog, Jesús. 1959. *El agrarismo mexicano y la reforma agraria: Exposición y crítica.* Mexico: Fondo de Cultura Económica.

Skidmore, Thomas. 1989. "Brazil's Slow Road to Democratization: 1974–1985." In *Democratizing Brazil: Problems of Transition and Consolidation,* ed. Alfred Stepan. Oxford: Oxford University Press.

Skidmore, Thomas. 1988. *The Politics of Military Rule in Brazil, 1964–85.* New York: Oxford University Press.

Skidmore, Thomas. 1967. *Politics in Brazil, 1930–1964: An Experiment in Democracy.* New York and Oxford: Oxford University Press.

Smith, Peter H., ed. 1995. *Latin America in Comparative Perspective: New Approaches to Methods and Analysis.* Boulder: Westview Press.

Smith, T. Lynn, ed. 1965. *Agrarian Reform in Latin America.* New York: Alfred A. Knopf.

Smith, Tony. 1991. "The Alliance for Progress: The 1960s." In *Exporting Democracy: The United States and Latin America,* ed. Abraham Lowenthal. Baltimore: Johns Hopkins University Press.

Soriano, Joaquim and Elizabeth Freitas. "O impasse na reforma agrária." In Vânia Lomônaco Bastos and Tânia Moreira da Costa. *Caderno CEAC/UnB,* ano 1, No. 2.

Souza, Maria do Carmo Cmpello de. 1976. *Estado e Partidos Políticos no Brasil (1930–1964).* São Paulo: Editora Alfa-Omega.

Stallings, Barbara. 1978. *Class Conflict and Economic Development in Chile, 1958–1973.* Stanford: Stanford University Press.

Stavenhagen, Rodolfo. 1970. *Agrarian Problems & Peasant Movements in Latin America.* Garden City, NY: Anchor Books.

Stepan, Alfred, ed. 1989. *Democratizing Brazil: Problems of Transition and Consolidation.* Oxford: Oxford University Press.

Stepan, Alfred. 1971. *The Military in Politics: Changing Patterns in Brazil*. Princeton and London: Princeton University Press, 1971.

Stevens, Robert D. and Cathy L. Jabara. 1988. *Agricultural Development Principles: Economic Theory and Empirical Evidence*. Baltimore and London: Johns Hopkins University Press.

Stoller, Richard. 1995. "Alfonso López Pumarejo and Liberal Radicalism in 1930s Colombia." *Journal of Latin American Studies* 27: 367–97.

Suárez Figueroa, Naudy, ed. 1977. *Programas Políticas Venezolanas de la Primera Mitad del Siglo XX*, 2 vols. Caracas: Universidad Católica Andrés Bello.

Swift, Jeannine. 1971. *Agrarian Reform in Chile*. Lexington, MA: DC Heath and Company.

Taagepera, Rein and Mathew Soberg Shugart. 1989. *Seats and Votes: The Effects and Determinants of Electoral Systems*. New Haven: Yale University Press.

Tai, Hung-Chao. 1974. *Land Reform and Politics: A Comparative Analysis*. Berkeley: University of California Press.

Tavares, Ricardo. 1989. *Reforma e contra-reforma agrária na transição política—Brasil 1979–1988*. Rio de Janeiro: IUPERJ.

Tannenbaum, Frank. 1968. *Mexico: The Struggle for Peace and Bread*. New York: Alfred A. Knopf.

Taylor, Lewis and Michael C. Hudson. 1972. *Handbook of Political and Social Indicators* (2nd ed.). New Haven: Yale University Press.

Teixeira, Caio Hilton de Freitas and Marcelino Tavares de Araújo. 1992. *A reforma agrária—antes e depois da Constituição de 1988*. Brasilia: Assessoria legislativa, Câmara dos Deputados (May), Typescript.

Thiesenhusen, William C., ed. 1989. *Searching for Agrarian Reform in Latin America*. Boston: Unwin Hyman.

Thiesenhusen, William C. 1984. "The Illusory Goal of Equity in Latin American Agrarian Reform." In *International Dimensions of Land Reform*, ed. John D. Montgomery. Boulder, CO: Westview Press.

Thiesenhusen, William C. and Jolyne Melmed-Sanjak. 1990. "Brazil's Agrarian Structure: Changes from 1970 Through 1980." *World Development* 18 (3): 393–415.

Thompson, John. "The Third Congressional District Election of March 23." *Hispanic American Report* 11 (3): 160–5.

Torres Dujisin, Isabel. 1989. *Historia de los cambios del sistema electoral en Chile, a partir de la constitución de 1925*, Chile: Facultad Latina Americana de Ciencias Sociales.

Tullis, F. Lamond and W. Ladd Hollist, ed. 1987. *Pursuing Food Security: Strategies and Obstacles in Africa, Asia, Latin America, and the Middle East*. Boulder, CO: Lynne Rienner.

Tullis, F. Lamond and W. Ladd Hollist, ed. 1986. *Food, the State, and International Political Economy*. Lincoln: University of Nebraska Press.

United Nations. 1985. *La Pobreza en América Latina: Dimensiones y Políticas*. Santiago, Chile: United Nations.

U.S. President. 1962. *Public Papers of the Presidents of the United States: John F. Kennedy, January 20 to December 31, 1961*. Washington: United States Government Printing Office.

Urzúa Valenzuela, Germán. 1992. *Historia Política de Chile y su Evolución Electoral (Desde 1810 a 1992)*. Santiago: Editorial Jurídica de Chile.

Valenzuela, Arturo. 1978. *The Breakdown of Democratic Regimes: Chile*. Baltimore and London: The Johns Hopkins University Press.

Valenzuela, Arturo. 1977. *Political Brokers in Chile: Local Government in a Centralized Polity*. Durham: Duke University Press.

Valenzuela, J. Samuel. 1985. *Democratización Via Reforma: La expansión del sufragio en Chile*. Buenos Aires: Ediciones del IDES.

Valenzuela, J. Samuel. 1976. "The Chilean Labor Movement: The Institutionalization of Conflict." In *Chile: Politics and Society*, ed. J. Samuel Valenzuela and Arturo Valenzuela. New Jersey: Transaction Books.

Valenzuela, J. Samuel and Arturo Valenzuela, eds. 1986. *Military Rule in Chile: Dictatorship and Oppositions*. Baltimore, MD: The Johns Hopkins University Press.

Valenzuela, J. Samuel and Arturo Valenzuela, eds. 1976. *Chile: Politics and Society*. New Brunswick, New Jersey: Transaction Books.

Vanhanen, Tatu. 1975. *Political and Social Structures: American Countries 1850–1973*. Tampere, Finland: University of Tampere.

Veiga, José Eli da. 1990. *A reforma que virou suco: uma introdução ao dilema agrário do Brasil*. Rio de Janeiro: Petrópolis.

Venezuela. 1992. Dirección General de Estadística y Censos Nacionales. *Anuario Estadístico de Venezuela*.

Venezuela. 1985. Gobierno del Estado Miranda. *Ecos de una Campaña: Programa Político y Discursos del Candidato Popular Rómulo Gallegos*. Caracas: Comisión Centenario del Natalicio de Rómulo Gallegos.

Venezuela. 1966. Comisión para Reglamentar la Ley de Reforma Agraria. *Reforma Agraria: Jurisprudencia y Doctrina en Materia de Reforma Agraria*. Caracas: Ministerio de Agricultura y Cría.

Venezuela. 1964. Instituto Agrario Nacional. *Reforma Agraria en Venezuela: una Revolución Dentro de la Ley*. Caracas: Instituto Agrario Nacional.

Venezuela. 1960a. *Ley de Reforma Agraria (Copia de la Gaceta Oficial N°. 610 Extraordinaria, del 5 de marzo de 1.960)*. Caracas: Tip la Torre.

Venezuela. 1960b. *La Ley de Reforma Agraria en las Cámaras Legislativas*, 2 vols. Caracas: Publicaciones de las Secciones de Información y Prensa e Imprenta del Congreso Nacional.

Verba, Sidney, Norman Nie, and Jae-On Kim. 1978. *Participation and Political Equality*. Cambridge: Cambridge University Press.

Warriner, Doreen. 1969. *Land Reform in Principle and Practice*. Clarendon Press: Oxford).

Welch, Cliff. 1995. "Rivalry and Unification: Mobilising Rural Workers in São Paulo on the Eve of the Brazilian *Golpe* of 1964." *Journal of Latin American Studies* 27: 161–87.

Wesson, Robert and David Fleischer. 1983. *Brazil in Transition.* New York: Praeger.

Weyland, Kurt. "Social Movements and the State: The Politics of Health Reform in Brazil." *World Development* 23 (10): 1699–712.

Wilde, Alexander. 1978. "Conversations among Gentlemen: Oligarchical Democracy in Colombia." In *The Breakdown of Democratic Regimes: Latin America,* ed. Juan J. Linz and Alfred Stepan. Baltimore, MD: The Johns Hopkins University Press.

Wilkie, James W. 1974. *Measuring Land Reform.* Los Angeles, CA: UCLA Latin American Center.

Wilkie, James W. and Albert L. Michaels, eds. 1969. *Revolution in Mexico: Years of Upheaval, 1910–1940.* Tucson: The University of Arizona Press.

Wilkie, James W., Enrique C. Ochoa, and David E. Lorey, eds. 1990. *Statistical Abstract of Latin America,* vol. 28. Los Angeles: UCLA Latin American Publications.

Womack, John Jr. 1969. *Emiliano Zapata and the Mexican Revolution.* New York: Alfred A. Knopf.

World Bank. 1980. *World Development Report, 1980.* Washington, DC: The World Bank.

Yashar, Deborah J. 1997. *Demanding Democracy: Reform and Reaction in Costa Rica and Guatemala, 1870s–1950s.* Stanford: Stanford University Press.

Young, Christopher. 1992. "The Strategy of Political Liberalization: A Comparative View of Gorbachev's Reforms." *World Politics* 45 (1): 47–65.

Zaldívar, Ramón. 1974. "Agrarian Reform and Military Reformism in Peru." In *Agrarian Reform & Agrarian Reformism: Studies of Peru, Chile, China and India,* ed. David Lehmann. London: Faber and Faber.

Zamosc, Leon. 1994. "Agrarian Protest and the Indian Movement in the Ecuadorian Highlands." *Latin American Research Review* 29 (3).

Zamosc, Leon. 1990. "Peasant Struggles and Agrarian Reform: The Ecuadorian Sierra and the Colombian Atlantic Coast in Comparative Perspective." *Latin American Issues* (8).

Index

206 • Index

National Front, *Frente Nacional*
(Colombia), 42, 166n. 10
National Liberation Party, PLN (Costa
Rica), 45, 168n. 24
National Party, *Partido Nacional*, PN
(Chile), 58, 64 (table), 65 (table),
73, 75, 77, 80, 169n. 7, 172n. 51
National Society of Agriculture, SNA
(Brazil), 145
National Society of Agriculture (Chile),
71, 79, 171n. 35, 171n. 43
Neves, Tancredo, 49, 132, 134, 178n.
28, 178n. 29, 179n. 47
Nicaragua, 14, 24
null, *see* ballot

Obregón, Álvaro, 10, 14, 37–9
OCB, *Organização das Cooperativas do
Brasil*, 134–5
Operation Pan America, 29–30

PADENA, *Partido Democrático
Nacional*, National Democratic
Party (Chile), 65 (table), 77, 162,
172n. 51
Paiva, Maria Arair Pinto, 126, 128, 130,
178n. 18
PAL, *Partido Agrario Laborista*,
Agrarian Labor Party (Chile), 58,
64 (table), 162
Panama, 35
assistance, international,
30–3, 35
beneficiaries of reform, 13–14 (table),
34 (table), 35
illiteracy, 25 (table)
land concentration/distribution,
26–8
suffrage, 13–14 (table), 34 (table),
35, 163–4 (table)
voting, mandatory, 13–14 (table),
163–4 (table)
workforce, 26–7

Paraguay, 24
participation, *see* proportional
representation, suffrage, voting
party
identification, 15, 123, 124–6,
136, 139, 150–1, 152–3,
157–9
discipline, 16–18, 57, 85, 90–1,
117–18, 119, 124–5,
158–9
inchoate, 2, 16–19, 20, 22, 35, 48–9,
119–20, 123–5, 142, 152–3,
157–9
institutionalized, 2, 12, 16–21, 35,
40, 43, 51–2, 90, 117–18,
152–3, 157–9
list, 16, 44, 76, 90–1, 106, 107, 124,
158, 175n. 43
multiple, 5–6
party strength, *see* party,
institutionalized
party weakness, *see* party, inchoate
Pastoral Land Commission, *Commisão
Pastoral da Terra*, CPT (Brazil),
121, 134
Patriotic Military Union, *Unión
Patriótica Militar*, UPM
(Venezuela), 93–4
patronage, *see* clientelism
Paulinelli, Alysson, 145, 147 (table)
Paz Estenssoro, Víctor, 10, 36, 167n. 11
PCB, *Partido Comunista Brasileiro*,
Brazilian Communist Party, 134,
138 (table), 141, 142, 143, 147,
151 (table), 161, 180n. 50
PCCh, *Partido Comunista de Chile*,
Communist Party of Chile, 58–60,
61, 63, 69, 77, 78, 80, 82, 162,
169n. 6, 169n. 8, 172n. 51
PCdoB, *Partido Comunista do Brasil*,
Communist Party of Brazil, 134,
138, 141–3, 147, 151 (table), 161,
180n. 50